ONE SIGNAL
PUBLISHERS

ATRIA

A RETURN TO COMMON SENSE

HOW TO FIX AMERICA BEFORE WE REALLY BLOW IT

LEIGH McGOWAN

The Creator of *PoliticsGirl*

ONE SIGNAL PUBLISHERS

ATRIA

New York • London • Toronto • Sydney • New Delhi

ONE SIGNAL PUBLISHERS

ATRIA

An Imprint of Simon & Schuster, LLC
1230 Avenue of the Americas
New York, NY 10020

First One Signal Publishers/Atria Books hardcover edition September 2024

ONE SIGNAL PUBLISHERS / ATRIA BOOKS and colophon are trademarks of Simon & Schuster, LLC

Simon & Schuster: Celebrating 100 Years of Publishing in 2024

For information about special discounts for bulk purchases, please contact Simon & Schuster Special Sales at 1-866-506-1949 or business@simonandschuster.com.

The Simon & Schuster Speakers Bureau can bring authors to your live event. For more information or to book an event, contact the Simon & Schuster Speakers Bureau at 1-866-248-3049 or visit our website at www.simonspeakers.com.

Interior design by Dana Sloan

Manufactured in the United States of America

1   3   5   7   9   10   8   6   4   2

Library of Congress Control Number: 2024011851

ISBN 978-1-6680-6643-0
ISBN 978-1-6680-6645-4 (ebook)

To my chosen country
I believe in you

CONTENTS

★ A RETURN TO COMMON SENSE ★

INTRODUCTION

★ ★ ★

Common sense is seeing things as they are; and doing things as they ought to be.

—Harriet Beecher Stowe

When I proposed this book to my publisher, I was deeply inspired by Thomas Paine's *Common Sense*, a book published in 1776, right before the American Revolution, that took colonial America by storm. At the time, we were a nation on the brink, not sure if we should stay part of the British Empire or venture out on our own. We were waffling with the very idea of independence until Thomas Paine came along and said, "We should do this."

In modern terms, *Common Sense* went viral, selling an estimated half million copies that would circulate throughout the thirteen colonies and shift the course of a nation. Thomas Jefferson's biographer Joseph Ellis would write that Paine's ideas "swept through the colonies like a firestorm, destroying any final vestige of loyalty to the British crown," but unlike other Founding Fathers, who were well-educated landed gentry, Thomas Paine came from humble beginnings, and wrote for regular people in regular language. He was able to bridge the gap between highbrow and lowbrow when he urged the colonists to embrace their "common sense" and consider how the country should be run. Looking back, it's clear the Declaration of Independence was, in many ways, a response to the popularity of Paine's call to arms.

A lot has changed since 1776, but the parallels between Paine's time and ours have become too obvious to ignore. You don't have to be a genius to know something's gone wrong in the Land of the Free and the Home of the Brave. Far too many Americans look around these days and feel disappointed and disillusioned. Most of us are still trying to act as if the American experience is working for us, but deep down we know it's not. Even if you're someone living the absolute pinnacle of the American Dream, you can't look around at the rest of us and think, *Yep, this is it. It's working.* I mean sure, it's working for you, Mark Zuckerberg, but you're also building a five-thousand-square-foot underground bunker in Hawaii so . . . something's up.

The truth is American progress has slowed to a crawl because for years our government has been in a forty-car pileup with very little getting through. The fact that the Biden administration was able to pass an infrastructure bill in 2021 was amazing. America hadn't done any real maintenance on the country in more than fifty years, and why not? Infrastructure should be a no-brainer. Everybody likes clean drinking water and bridges that don't fall into rivers. How is it that we call ourselves a first world country, but our trains and airports look like we still live in the 1960s, our roads are a mess, and a fair amount of people in "the richest country in the world" can't afford a place to live?

It's hard to make changes when the powers that be don't want it because the status quo suits them. Over time we've allowed a handful of people—many of whom are in it for themselves—to make all our decisions. We're now at a place where one party, in a two-party system, seems ready to abandon the American experiment of democracy and rule of law, and go all-in on power for power's sake, and far too many people either don't know, or don't care, it's a real possibility.

It is time for us to decide who we are. Are we a nation of freedom and opportunity where anyone from anywhere can make it if they just work hard enough? Or are we a slaver nation that built its wealth on the backs of others and continues to use humanity as a tool in a rich man's game? Are we a nation of immigrants, or a white, Christian nation where anyone who doesn't fit into a specific box is marginalized? Are we the country we sell to the world—a shining city on a hill, a beacon of democracy, and a land of innovation—or are we a corrupt and violent nation that tries to overturn elections and favors owners over creators? Ultimately, are we a nation who can learn from our mistakes, or simply a country doomed to repeat them?

Once again, America finds itself at a tipping point where it could go one of two ways. Once again, our leaders need the inspiration and courage to pick the harder, but more rewarding path. And once again, it will come down to the will of the people to determine our fate. If we choose to continue down this path of division and inequality, with hatred and misinformation impeding our progress, we'll end up right back where we started, under some form of top-down rule. However, if we choose to address our flawed but inspired democracy now, I believe we can rebuild this nation on a stronger foundation than we began on. It's my belief, as Paine argued all those years ago, that there's only one right path, and if we fail to choose it, we'll lose the opportunity to choose again. This time the choice isn't between subjugation or independence, but democracy and plutocracy. We either continue to favor the wealthy and influential, while we strip citizens of their rights and shore up minority rule, or we get serious about living up to the ideals we've sold to the world.

As we know, the first step to fixing a problem is to admit you have a problem. Acknowledging America's not living up to its potential doesn't mean it's unable to live up to its potential, but it does mean we can't be so distracted by what screenwriter Aaron Sorkin would call our "star-spangled awesomeness" that we're unable to collectively demand better. We deserve more than we've been given, better than what we've allowed, and our children certainly don't deserve this chaos we're handing them.

I'm not going to pretend to be a historian. I'm not an economist or a political scientist. What I am is an American citizen. An immigrant who chose to be a part of this nation and would unapologetically call herself a patriot. I love this country, but when you love something, you can't allow it to be its worst; you have to push it to be its best, and you can't give up simply because it's hard. I think any reasonable person can see that what we're doing in America isn't working. That we're a a divided nation, a time bomb of resentment and frustration, and as Jesus himself said, a kingdom divided against itself cannot stand.

I've been inspired by this country since I was a child. America was everything I thought a country should be. The hero of every story. The optimistic, eternal superstar out there fighting for the little guy, just punching Nazis. A land of opportunity where you could move up the social and financial ladder through sheer tenacity and hard work. The only thing holding you back in America was lack of will. That's how the country became the bold innovator of the airplane, the internet, and the personal computer. This was the country that put a man on the moon. I thought America was the greatest country in the world . . . and I was Canadian.

America, the story of America, the values of America—like freedom, liberty, and the pursuit of happiness—make up a very important and beautiful brochure. A brochure for a place most of us want to live. The place I personally *chose* to live. The problem is that place doesn't actually exist. We have all the raw materials but have yet to put them together in a way that truly stands for our values. In the grand scheme of things, America is a young nation. We're not children but we're not grown. We're basically teenagers with a ridiculous amount of money and power and no one to tell us no. We're 2013 Justin Bieber and we're melting down.

The truth is, we built this nation on noble goals but a shaky foundation, and it's coming back to haunt us. This doesn't mean we don't have great potential. The Constitution of the United States is a genuinely amazing document, especially when you remember that the Framers knew it wasn't finished—that between the Bill of Rights and the other amendments, the country was a work in progress. But we've kicked the can down the road long enough. We deal with this now or lose the opportunity to deal with it again.

As Thomas Paine wrote in 1776, "The cause of America is, in great measure, the cause of all mankind." What we're dealing with isn't just local problems, problems that will remain within our borders. What we choose to do here will become everyone's problem. Not because Americans are so much more important than citizens of other countries, but because America itself has become so big, so essential, so powerful that the decisions we make at home have no choice but to reverberate around the world. We've essentially become "too big to fail."

I want you to consider a world where America abandons democracy. The fact that we have political leaders tolerating the suggestion that a former president might want to be a dictator should scare the hell out of everyone, and for those who say, "Well, if America goes wrong, I'll just move," where on earth do you think you're safe from the world's biggest military run by a dictator who answers to no one? How soon until that version of America turns its eyes on a place like Canada and says, "Hmmm, here's an unprotected border with all these lovely natural resources and a limited ability to fight back . . ."

Who rallies the allied forces of liberal, Western values if America is hanging with the autocrats? Who does something when a nation invades another and commits genocide or mass murder for its own power and glory? Who defends the defenseless? If America's the bad guy, how long do the good guys stand a chance?

How long does the planet last if it's being run by people who refuse to believe what most of the world's scientists are screaming at us to believe? America is the world's biggest polluter after China. If we don't lead by example no one else will. The richest people on the planet are trying to figure out a way to live in space, but the rest of us are stuck here.

The fact is, the American system is primed to implode and every bad actor across the globe is hoping to capitalize on it. We have a short but important window to choose the direction in which we want to go. To pick leaders who won't take a blowtorch to the powder keg we've become, simply to rule over the ashes. Leaders who believe in the American experiment and will fight for the American people. Will they be perfect? No. Are any of us? No. We're all a work in progress. Just like we need our country to be.

★   ★   ★

Anyone who knows me will tell you I've been going on about this for years. How government works. What's going wrong. What's going right. What could be better. I understand it can feel boring or complicated. Believe me, I've watched my friends' eyes glaze over when I start talking about this stuff. People don't want to think about it, they don't want to *have* to think about it, but unfortunately that many people not caring about how the country works, not wanting to talk about politics, not quite getting around to voting, that's what brought us to where we are, and where we are is *not* good. We, the people, are supposed to be in charge of our government, we're the ones our elected officials are supposed to answer to—and we've let them go unchecked for too long.

I moved to America in my early twenties. The tragedy of 9/11 unfolded outside my apartment window. It was New York's response to that crisis, America's response, that convinced me this was the country I needed to be a part of. I cried when I became a citizen. I was so proud to be part of this scrappy, upstart nation. A nation that defied an empire for its independence and built its government around the ideas of freedom and the rights of man.

Looking around America today, I understand why people feel disillusioned. There's a reason people don't like America. Why for years American backpackers have found they're treated better abroad if they sew Canadian flags on their backpacks. It's because

Americans are known to be arrogant and self-important. We're loud and rich and say things like "We're number one!" Imagine the richest, best-looking kid in school going around telling everyone he's number one. Reminding everyone of his money and power. Eye. Roll. It's no wonder other nations have such a love-hate relationship with America. It's also no wonder that Americans, with the expansion of the internet and the success of things like TikTok, now see how people in other countries live and are recognizing that maybe we don't have it so great after all. That maybe we've been sold a bill of goods. While we were busy flag-waving and winning Olympic gold medals, other countries were offering universal health care, free college, and affordable childcare.

I've felt that way myself. I know I could go back to Canada, but I believe we need people here who want to fix things, and I'm one of those people. So, if it takes a little immigrant like me to remind you that what you have here is wonderful, or at least could be wonderful, then I'm doing my part. I wasn't born here, so like any outsider I have a different perspective. I'm part of your society but not of it, and I'm telling you, you're in danger of losing everything that makes this country special if you don't stand up and fight for it.

In April 1776 John Adams wrote that "Common Sense, like a ray of revelation, has come in seasonably to clear our doubts, and to fix our choice." It was a persuasive and popular piece of writing that forced the Founders' hands, because when enough people ask for the same thing, it becomes impossible to ignore. That's my goal. To get enough people asking for the same thing that we force the hand of the people in charge to look up from how it's always been and set a course for how it could be.

We *have* to fix America. We have to inspire our friends and family to *want* to fix it. We have to understand enough so we can explain why it *needs* to be fixed, and it's going to be a big job. Think of America like a hoarder's house that needs to be cleaned out. At first, it's paralyzing, and I understand the instinct to just live with the mess because it's too much work, or burn the whole place to the ground because you can't imagine it ever being what you want it to be, but neither option is possible. We talk a big game, but most of us aren't going anywhere and we don't have the luxury of time to start again. This is it. We work until it's a place we can all be proud of. There's no quick fix for America and being a brat about how you wish it was easier or different isn't going to help. This is going to be a one-step-at-a-time kind of deal. So, let's stop complaining and roll up our sleeves.

At the end of the day, I believe in the American experiment, and I'm convinced we can fix what's broken. I understand we stand at a terrifying precipice, but it's one of great opportunity. I want nothing less than for America to be the country it says it is.

★ ★ ★

So, thank you for caring enough to pick up this book. Please know this passionate and mouthy immigrant stands on the shoulders of those who came before to tell you this nation is wonderful, but it needs help. I write this book with hope. I want people to share the information they learn in these pages at their dining room tables, in their classrooms, and yes, where I live, on social media. I want readers to come away from this with a common language in which to speak about change, and a clear understanding of where we sit in history, because you can't know where you're going unless you know where you've been.

Thomas Paine writes in *Common Sense*, "In the following pages I offer nothing more than simple facts, plain arguments, and common sense." Like Paine, I want to speak plainly to a nation at a crossroads. To say, We're broken, here's why, and here's what I think we should do about it. I want to get back to common sense—not the specific writings of a man I admire, but perhaps few others know—but actual common sense, the way of thinking and being.

I want nothing more than for you to come to this book with an open mind. To leave your preconceptions at the door and simply sit with the ideas presented. To decide not how you're expected to feel, or how people might want you to feel, but what—when things are laid out in front of you—you truly believe is right.

And if all else fails, just return to your common sense.

AMERICA 101: THE US GOVERNMENT

Before we go any further into the book, I think it's important to remind ourselves how we got here in the first place, because it's hard to know how to fix something if you don't understand how it works. If you already know how American government functions, who's in charge of what, how our laws are made and elections work, then go ahead and skip this section. However, if you don't know the basics as well as you'd like, don't beat yourself up. The lack of knowledge and apathy most people feel toward government and politics is by design. What have we been told not to talk about our whole lives? Politics and religion. And what are the two things that have caused the most problems in the history of the world? Politics and religion. Most schools barely teach American civics at this point, so we have no idea how the system is supposed to work. Combined with our lack of broadcasting laws, which allows people to lie to us for profit, and the fact that our Supreme Court has opened the door to unlimited money in politics, inundating us with disingenuous and deceptive information till we can't tell truth from fiction, and it's no wonder the American people are confused, ripe for manipulation, and largely checked out.

Overall, the citizens of this nation are uninformed, overworked, and underpaid, and every two years we're trotted out to vote for positions and issues we don't really understand or have the time or resources to figure out, and who does that serve? It serves the people in charge and moneyed interests who put them there. So, who does it feel like the government ends up representing? The people in charge and the moneyed interests who put them there. So, it's reasonable when people look at the government and think, *Why should I bother? They don't care about me. Why should I care about them?*

I need you to understand that you should care about them because whether we're paying attention or not, what happens in government directly affects us. Politics touches almost every aspect of what we do, or might want to do, in modern society. It's the steering wheel for the direction the country is going. Our government decides everything from the seemingly innocuous, like how fast we can drive, to the life-changing, like if we have autonomy over our own bodies. Checking out of politics doesn't mean politics doesn't affect you; it means you can't affect *it*. That's how most people in government like it and, if we're being honest, that's kind of how our government was set up.

Welcome to America 101.

★ ★ ★

Let's start with the idea that the government of a country is an organization that does many things. It defends the country from outside enemies, keeps order within its borders, and provides its people with services. In return, the people typically pay taxes to the government for doing its job and obey the laws the government has set up to keep the peace and uphold the social order.

Every government has institutions and ways of organizing things to accomplish these tasks. America, like many other countries, has a constitution, or a document that spells out the rules that govern the country. Most modern countries have some type of document that does this. Most also have some version of three branches of government—the leader, the group that creates the laws, and the group that upholds the laws. In America's case, our three branches are the Executive, the Legislative ,and the Judicial. Our states have a similar three-branch system, but this book will focus primarily on the federal government.

The three branches were set up by our "Framers," a word often used interchangeably with our "Founding Fathers," but who more specifically came up with how our country would work. The Founding Fathers signed the Declaration of Independence, declaring America independent from the British Empire, then fought a war to make it true. The Framers set up the country using the Constitution *after* we'd won the war. Many of them were the same people, famous names like George Washington, John Adams, Alexander Hamilton, John Jay, Benjamin Franklin, and James Madison, but some are different, so we refer to them with different names if we're being specific.

★ ★ ★

THE CONSTITUTION

The Framers wrote and signed the Constitution after the War of Independence to establish how our new government would work. Article 1 lays out that our laws will be created by Congress; it explains how Congress works, what powers Congress has, what it can and cannot do, and who can be a member. It also talks about money, taxes, and specifies what individual states cannot do. Article 2 is all about the president. Article 3 is about the Judiciary. Article 4 sets out the rules for the states. Article 5 explains how to amend the Constitution. Article 6 says the Constitution is the supreme law of the land and government officers must take an oath to both abide by and uphold it, while also laying out that no religious tests can ever be required to qualify for any office or public trust, and Article 7 basically says, "Yay, we did it," and as soon as two-thirds of the state conventions agree to it (so nine states of the original thirteen), it'll go into effect. So, although the Constitution was signed in 1787, it wasn't officially the law of the land until 1789, and the Bill of Rights, which includes many of the things you're used to hearing about—like freedom of speech and the right to bear arms—wasn't ratified until 1791.

★ ★ ★

The US Constitution established a political system called federalism, which is the division and sharing of powers between the national and state governments. The states have their own power and autonomy (states' rights), but according to Article VI of the Constitution, when the laws of the federal government directly conflict with those of a state government, federal law will supersede state law. This is called the Supremacy Clause.

I should note that most historians who aren't selling you American mythology will tell you the Constitution barely made it. The Framers had to make a series of concessions to the delegates of the original colonies to get the Constitution out of the starting gate, including allowing the practice of slavery to continue. Many delegates also refused to sign the Constitution because they were concerned the document gave the federal government too much power, and wanted assurances that there would be more rights than they were seeing. So, the Framers deliberately left things adjustable. There are only seven articles in the Constitution, and one of them is devoted solely to updating it. The Framers never intended for our laws to be fixed. They saw the Constitution as a "living document" that would change over time. This is not to say they made it a simple process—amendments typically require a two-thirds majority in both the House and the Senate, followed by ratification in the legislatures of three-quarters of the states—but they did make it *possible*. Since 1789 the Constitution has been amended twenty-seven times. Of those twenty-seven amendments, the first ten are collectively known as the Bill of Rights.

The original Constitution was ratified by only three votes, and the decisions the Framers made were so fraught that people gave formal names to the concessions that were made—the Great Compromise, the Three-Fifths Compromise—to get the whole thing over the finish line. In fact, many of the problems we're dealing with today can be directly tied to the trade-offs that were made to move forward: namely to allow the South to keep slavery, to grant smaller states equal power in the US Senate, to count Black Americans as three-fifths of a person for the purpose of congressional representation, and to use something called the Electoral College to elect the president. Filmmaker Matthew Cooke notes that these agreements were less of a compromise and more of a "détente" between the Southern and Northern states. It wasn't so much an agreement as a pause in disagreement, to keep the union together with the sense that they should probably reconvene and renegotiate later.

Despite the fact the Constitution is brilliant and remains

relevant to this day, we should be careful about romanticizing or idealizing the American origin story. The compromises made during the negotiations would ultimately lead to the Civil War, the necessity of the Thirteenth Amendment to abolish slavery, the civil rights movement and the ongoing battle for racial justice in America, and the unfair advantage certain states wield in our government that, over time, has solidified the power of the minority over the majority. While we might be able to logically understand that these compromises may have seemed like the only way to arrive at the result of a *United* States of America, we have to accept the fact that if you build a country on those kinds of trade-offs, it leads to a rot in the foundation that will eventually need to be addressed.

So, despite how much the Framers got right, we should acknowledge we are a modern nation working with an antiquated text that was ultimately a stopgap. A set of ideals and rules created by white men for white men in a country that now has a thousand creeds and colors. So, it's not unreasonable to think that almost 240 years later, we might want to consider some updates to our national terms and conditions.

★ ★ ★

The US Government

The Framers of the Constitution intended the three branches of government to have separate but equal power, to allow each branch to act as a check on the others. This structure of government was created in response to previously having been ruled by a king, whose unchecked power the Framers believed was corrosive and not in the people's best interest. The Framers were adamant that the power of the government never be concentrated into too few hands. It was an ingenious plan and, sadly, something the modern American government is struggling to manage.

As mentioned, the federal government is made up of three branches:

1. The legislative branch, called Congress, which makes and passes our laws, controls the country's budget and money, and is the only branch with the power to declare war.
2. The executive branch, which includes the president and their cabinet—all the departmental secretaries, like the secretary of state, secretary of transportation, education, interior, etc.—the vice president, all the federal agencies, and the Department of Justice, which is not part of the judicial branch, as most people think.
3. The judicial branch, which is our entire federal court system, including the appellate courts and the Supreme Court.

THE LEGISLATIVE BRANCH

America was built in opposition to hereditary rule. In contradiction to a monarchy, which is why anyone saying "I alone can fix it" should feel deeply un-American to you. According to our founding documents, our citizens have the right to self-governance and self-determination. If the country was working correctly, we should be choosing our representatives and then replacing them when they no longer serve the common good.

Congress itself is divided into two parts: the House of Representatives and the Senate.

The House of Representatives has 435 members. States are given House seats, or districts, based on population. The bigger the state's population, the more congresspeople that state will have. State populations are determined by the national census taken every ten years.

House members are elected to two-year terms. To be a member of the House of Representatives you must be twenty-five years old, a citizen for at least seven years, and, when elected, a resident of the state you wish to represent. The House also has six nonvoting members representing the District of Columbia (Washington, DC), the Commonwealth of Puerto Rico, and four other US territories: American Samoa, Guam, the US Virgin Islands, and the Commonwealth of the Northern Mariana Islands. Congresspeople win by a popular vote in their district. Majority rules.

The Senate has 100 senators, two from each of the fifty states, elected to six-year terms. To be a member of the Senate, you must be thirty years old, a citizen for at least nine years, and, at the time of the election, must reside in the state you wish to represent. Senators win by a popular vote in their state. Majority rules.

State governments have their own version of the two deliberative bodies, usually called the State House of Representatives and the State Senate, although some go by different titles like State Assembly, House of Delegates, or General Assembly.

Whether state or federal, the party that wins the most

seats in an election is considered the majority party and is responsible for their respective body. The top job in the House of Representatives is the speaker of the House, who is elected by a majority vote in the House typically at the beginning of a new Congress after the general election. Not only does the speaker of the House get more power (and a bump in salary), but the position also puts them in the presidential line of succession. So, if something happened to both the president and the vice president, the speaker would become president of the United States.

It's a big deal to be the majority party, particularly in the House, because unlike the Senate, the House always passes bills by simple majority, so the majority party has a lot of opportunity, provided it works and votes together, to get plenty of legislation (laws) passed. Now, that legislation might go on to die in the Senate, but we'll get to that later. The point is, having the House majority is significant—you get to set the rules in the House, and are responsible for budgets and impeachments. The majority party also decides which bills come to the floor for a vote, and when those votes will happen.

In the Senate the majority leader is simply called the Senate majority leader, there's no special name, but the majority leader does get to decide, as the speaker does, which bills come to the floor for a vote. The Senate is responsible for approving federal judges, including Supreme Court justices, after the president has nominated them, and approving the president's cabinet, top military officers, foreign diplomats, and treaties.

Congressmembers don't have term limits, or a set period of time in which they're allowed to do the job before they have to leave. House members and senators can stay in their jobs indefinitely if they continue to win their elections. It doesn't matter how many years they've been there—you can stay in office if you're an accused criminal, if you're sick, if you don't do your job, or even if your beliefs are in complete opposition to the positions you claimed to hold when you were elected.

Congressional members only leave office if they fail to get reelected, resign, die, or if the Senate or House takes direct action to expel them with a two-thirds vote.

Recall elections—or elections where voters have the power to remove an elected official before their term is over—only exist at the state level, and even then, only in nineteen states. The power to recall your representative was adopted to make sure elected officials would act in the interest of their constituents rather than in their own interest or that of their political party. The states that allow recalls are: Alaska, Arizona, California, Colorado, Georgia, Idaho, Illinois, Kansas, Louisiana, Michigan, Minnesota, Montana, Nevada, New Jersey, North Dakota, Oregon, Rhode Island, Washington, and Wisconsin. Which explains why the state representative in North Carolina and the mayor of Dallas, who both flipped parties in 2023 after deceiving their voters to get elected, weren't recalled. Neither state has that option.

Over the years recall elections have successfully removed all types of officials—judges, mayors, governors. While not often used—and sadly a tactic often abused by parties seeking to get rid of political rivals when voters aren't paying attention—for the most part the idea of a recall can be a great way to hold elected representatives accountable to the people.

THE EXECUTIVE BRANCH

The executive branch of the federal government is run by the president, who is elected to a four-year term for no more than two terms and is considered the head of state and the commander in chief of the armed forces. The only requirements to be president are that you must be thirty-five years old, a natural-born citizen, and a resident of the United States for at least fourteen years. The executive branch is responsible for implementing and enforcing the laws that Congress writes and passes.

The executive branch of the government is responsible for such a vast array of things—from overseeing deals with foreign countries, to managing our nation's defense, to the success of our economy—that no one person could ever do it on their own. Which is why it's essential when we choose our president, we choose a leader who's a good manager. Who can hire the right people and delegate. The president might make the final decisions, or act in consultation before decisions are made, but we have entire departments to accomplish these responsibilities. What we're hiring when we elect a president is a visionary with serious administration skills.

The people who see and work most closely with the president day-to-day are in the Executive Office of the President (EOP) and are overseen by the White House chief of staff. The EOP is responsible for everything ranging from communicating the president's messages to our trade interests abroad.

While a Senate confirmation is required for some of the advisory positions, the president usually gets to hire who they want for this office. The roles the American public are probably most familiar with in the EOP are the White House press secretary and the White House communications team. It's the press secretary you see doing most of the daily briefings for the media keeping the American people informed of the president's activities and agenda. A less well-known position in the EOP would be the National Security Council, which advises the president on foreign policy, intelligence, and national security; or the Office of Scheduling and Advance, which is responsible for preparing locations ahead of any kind of presidential visit.

FUN FACT: *While the senior advisors in the EOP work in the West Wing, the office wing of the White House, as opposed to the East Wing, which holds the offices of the first lady and her staff, or the central Executive Residence in the center where the first family actually lives, the EOP has grown so much since it was created by Franklin D. Roosevelt in 1939 that the majority of the staff now work in the Eisenhower Executive Office Building, which is part of the White House compound, but not in the White House itself.*

The president's closest advisors, after the chief of staff, are the people appointed to head the various executive departments, or what's called the cabinet. The cabinet, under the leadership of the president, is responsible for all aspects of the federal government from the health and safety of the people to transportation and foreign affairs. This also includes protecting our natural resources, including our water and air, national forests and parks.

When the country was created, there were four cabinet positions: secretary of the treasury, secretary of state, secretary of war, and attorney general. President Washington developed the cabinet system by asking the heads of the three executive departments, plus the attorney general, to meet with him on a regular basis. In the meetings they would report on the work of their departments and discuss the issues they believed were the most important to the country.

As the country grew, so did the cabinet. At the time of publication, there are fifteen executive departments each led by an appointed member of the president's cabinet. The departments are as follows: agriculture, commerce, defense, education, energy, health and human services, homeland security, housing and urban development, interior, justice, labor, state, transportation, treasury, and veterans affairs. The cabinet secretaries are joined by other executive agencies—whose heads are also appointed by the president, with the "advice, consent and confirmation" of the Senate—such as the Central Intelligence Agency (CIA) and the Environmental Protection Agency (EPA)—both of which are not part of the cabinet, but are given cabinet rank under the authority of the president—plus the vice president and chief of staff.

The Department of Justice (DOJ) is part of the executive branch, and insulated from politics, but can't be considered completely independent, so long as the president is empowered to hire and fire Justice Department appointees.

After Watergate, Congress considered legislation to make

the Justice Department completely independent to be able to address the worst abuses of the Nixon era, but instead it passed a reform bill called the Ethics in Government Act of 1978, which sadly expired in 1999 after both parties had been embarrassed by independent counsel investigations (Iran-Contra/Clinton-Lewinsky) and both wanted to avoid future scrutiny. Attorney General Janet Reno authorized the appointment of the Office of Special Council that same year, in order to have at least some part of the Justice Department where presidential influence was limited. It's clearly an imperfect system, and, in the wrong hands, one could argue the president can wield far too much influence over our nation's justice.

The Department of Justice is overseen by the nation's top lawyer, the attorney general, who represents the United States in lawsuits, advises the president and heads of federal departments on legal matters, and whose mission is to "uphold the rule of law, keep our country safe, and to protect civil rights." The department oversees more than forty separate organizations and over 115,000 employees, including, among others, all US Attorneys, the Drug Enforcement Administration (DEA), the Federal Bureau of Investigation (FBI), the Bureau of Prisons, the US Marshals, INTERPOL, the Bureau of Alcohol, Tobacco, Firearms and Explosives (ATF), and separate civil rights and antitrust divisions. These departments are all autonomous agencies, separate from the rest of the executive branch, who answer to their own superiors. The FBI, for example, answers to the attorney general and the director of national intelligence, not the president, even though the director of the FBI is appointed by the president and confirmed by the Senate.

The president is also responsible for appointing the heads of more than fifty independent federal commissions, the heads of several federal agencies, federal judges, ambassadors, and other federal officers. Many of the roles the president appoints last longer than the president's term. The Federal Trade Commission (FTC), for example, is run by five commissioners who are appointed by the president and confirmed by the Senate. Each commissioner serves a seven-year term, and their terms are staggered.

Other independent organizations for which the president has the opportunity to appoint leaders are the commissioners of the Federal Communications Commission (FCC), who actually answer to Congress, the administrator of the National Aeronautics and Space Administration (NASA), which is an independent civilian space agency that takes its agenda from the president, the National Transportation Safety Board (NTSB), and the Securities and Exchange Commission (SEC).

The vice president of the United States must be ready to take over should something happen to the president. Much like an understudy in a play, the vice president must know exactly how to step into the role should there be a crisis. Therefore the VP must be just as up-to-date and prepared as the president but has far less power and authority. I think it's fair to say the vice president of the United States is a fundamentally weird job. We've had VPs who primarily served as the top advisor to the president, above the chief of staff, but we've also had chiefs of staff who wielded more power than the VP. Ultimately, it's a thankless role. You can't steal focus from the president and you have to defer to their administration and be a team player, but you also must distinguish yourself if you want to be considered for the top post when your boss is done. The Constitution lays out the specifics of the job, but ultimately, the vice president serves at the president's command. The VP is, however, president of the Senate, and from 1789 to the 1950s that was the vice president's main job. Today, the VP typically only goes to the Senate on special occasions, like when they are needed to break a tie or to count the electoral ballots cast in the presidential election. Contemporary vice presidents have taken on specific issues like health care, immigration, or education, while others have been experts in things like international affairs. It ultimately depends on the president, and what the president needs from their VP. In 1793, when John Adams was George Washington's vice president, he wrote to his wife, Abigail, saying, "My country has in its wisdom contrived for me the most insignificant office that ever the invention of man contrived or his imagination conceived." I'd be surprised if most vice presidents didn't agree on some level with Adams's assessment.

FUN FACT: *When our country started, voters didn't cast separate votes for president and vice president. Whoever got the most votes became president and the runner-up became vice president. As I'm sure you can imagine, that wasn't such a great idea because political rivals don't often work that well together. Who wants to play second fiddle to the guy you just lost to, especially if you don't like their ideas? Can you imagine Hillary Clinton being Donald Trump's VP? So, after four elections, Congress passed the Twelfth*

Amendment, specifying that electors would cast separate votes for president and vice president moving forward.

THE JUDICIAL BRANCH

In 1789 the Framers were concerned the country would splinter. That, based on the country's size, each state would eventually end up deferring to its own laws and customs—so they were committed to the necessity of a federal court system, particularly a Supreme Court, to uphold the articles of the Constitution and hold the country together under one set of overarching rules.

The judicial branch includes the entire federal court system with the Supreme Court at the top. All federal-level judges and justices are appointed by the sitting (which means: current) president and confirmed by the Senate. The courts can't just weigh in on laws. They can only rule on cases that come before them, and you can only bring a case to the court if you have what's called "standing"—as in, you can prove you have the right to stand before the court. Cases brought before the federal judiciary typically start at the district court level. Then, if the ruling (decision) is not satisfactory to either party, the case goes on to an appellate court. Finally, if either party don't agree to *that* ruling, it can end up before the Supreme Court. The Supreme Court is the last place someone can appeal a decision, and its decisions are final. There is no higher authority in the American judicial system than the US Supreme Court. Which is why it matters so much who sits on the bench.

Judges and justices serve no fixed term, so they are in the job until they retire, die, or are impeached by the House and convicted by the Senate. But since only fifteen federal judges have ever been impeached in the history of our country, and only eight of them were actually convicted and removed, if you are confirmed as a federal judge, it's pretty much a "you get the job, you keep the job" kind of thing. That's why we call federal judgeships "lifetime appointments."

LAWS

So, we've talked about the three branches of government, but how do we get our laws? Well, if you're old like me, we used to have a TV show called *Schoolhouse Rock!* that taught children American civics. On that show there was a great song sung by Jack Sheldon called "I'm Just a Bill," which explained the whole process in a fun animated short. So, while I may not be as cute as an animated bill, here goes . . .

A bill to create a law can be introduced in either chamber of Congress—the House or the Senate. It can be written by anyone, but only a sitting member of Congress can introduce legislation. However, according to the White House, "Some important bills are traditionally introduced at the request of the president, such as the annual federal budget."

Once a bill is introduced, it's assigned to a committee. Each committee oversees a specific policy area, and the subcommittees get even more precise. For example, the House Committee on Ways and Means includes subcommittees on Social Security, work and welfare, trade, taxes, health, and government oversight.

The committees are not set in stone and often change in number or form depending on congressional leadership. Currently there are 17 Senate committees, with 70 subcommittees, and 26 House committees, with 104 subcommittees.

So once a bill is directed to the appropriate subcommittee, the members will research and discuss, then accept, amend, or reject the proposed bill. If a subcommittee agrees to move the bill forward, it goes to the full committee, where it repeats the process. Throughout this phase the committee and subcommittees can call hearings to invite experts, advocates, and opponents to testify before them on the merits or flaws of the bill. Congress has what's called subpoena power, which it can use to force people to testify if they're refusing to do it voluntarily.

Until recently congressional subpoena power really meant something. If Congress told you to show up and testify, you either did or were held in contempt, but since the early 2020s this power has been challenged numerous times, mostly by congressional members themselves when they were called to be witnesses before committees. This has opened a door to others rejecting congressional subpoenas, which, as I'm sure you can imagine, is problematic for the efficient and successful functioning of our government.

If the full committee votes to approve a bill, the Senate majority leader or speaker of the House decides when to bring that bill to the full Senate or House floor for consideration (to ultimately vote on it). When the bill comes up—*if* it comes up, because majority leaders are not actually *compelled* to bring bills to the floor—each chamber has a different protocol. The

House has a very rigid debate process. Each member who wants to speak is given a specific amount of time, and the number and kinds of amendments they can suggest are usually quite limited. This is why you might see House members doing little speeches on C-SPAN or saying things like "reclaiming my time" or "I yield the rest of my time to . . ." Much like in congressional hearings, House members only get a certain amount of time to make their point, and they don't want to lose a second of it.

The Senate has fewer members, and because it's always been considered the more serious deliberative body (whether it deserves that credit or not), its debate on bills is less limited. Senators can even talk about things that have nothing to do with the bill under consideration. This behavior is typically seen when senators want to filibuster a bill, or talk so much that it delays the vote, and by extension, the bill's passage. (We'll talk about the filibuster more later in the book.)

If the bill passes in one of the chambers of Congress, it goes to the other chamber to go through the exact same process again: subcommittee, committee research, discussion, potential hearings, amendments, floor vote. Once both bodies have voted to accept the bill, and they've worked out any differences between the two versions, they vote on the final bill and, if that passes, they present the bill to the president.

It's now the president's job to consider the bill. Realistically, the president knows the bill is coming. This isn't news to them. In many cases, they've been in talks with members of their party, or small bipartisan congressional groups, throughout the process. If the president approves the bill, it gets signed into law. If the president doesn't approve the bill, they use what's called a presidential veto. If vetoed, the bill is dead unless Congress can override the veto by getting two-thirds of both chambers to vote to do so. If they can swing that, then the bill becomes law despite the president's veto.

If the president just doesn't sign the bill, and Congress is in session, the bill becomes law automatically after ten days. If the president doesn't sign the bill and Congress isn't in session, the bill dies. This is what's called a pocket veto, and a pocket veto can't be overridden by Congress like a regular veto. This doesn't happen very often, but it's good to know.

At the end of the day, there are a lot of steps before a bill can become a law, and the president can only sign legislation if it shows up on their desk. The president *does* have the right to sign something called an executive order (EO), but that's not the same as a congressionally passed law as it can be overturned for any number of reasons, most simply by the next president as soon as the current one leaves office. While the president oversees the day-to-day management of the country, Congress is the branch responsible for addressing the people's needs with new and updated legislation. So if you find yourself upset with something you feel is not being addressed, whether that's the price of eggs, low wages, the skyrocketing price of housing, or even our defense budget, the only people who can really address that are Congress. The state legislatures can make lots of changes and have gross amounts of power to affect your life, but we're talking about the federal government here. There are only 535 people in the entire country who can make federal laws. Which is why we should take each and every one of the people we give this power to extremely seriously.

ELECTIONS

America is a representative democracy, which means people vote for representatives to work in government and vote on our behalf. Election Day in America is the first Tuesday following the first Monday in November. I know that sounds arbitrary, but it's actually quite clever, as it avoids our elections ever falling on a weekend or the first day of the month. Every US citizen, eighteen years and older, is allowed to vote, but you can't just vote in America; first you must register to vote.

At our founding only certain people got to vote so, despite the fact we're finally at a point in our nation's history where every citizen over eighteen is *allowed* to vote (some felons, people in conservatorship, or those with mental incapacities are excluded), we still have a pretty lame tradition of making it harder than it should be to cast a ballot. Over the years this has primarily been due to racism, classism, and sexism, but most recently it's been spearheaded by party politics.

Elections happen every two years, in even-numbered years. They are all considered general elections (meaning everyone gets to vote), but they're either presidential elections, which happen every four years, or midterm elections, which happen between the presidential elections. The entire US House of Representatives is on the ballot in every election because their term is only two years long. The congressmembers on the ballot are then joined by whatever senators' six-year terms are up, along with state representatives—state senator, state house members, state attorney general, etc.—any local representatives like council or school board members, mayors, sheriffs, and finally, any state or local propositions, measures, or ballot initiatives. Propositions, measures, and ballot initiatives are when voters get to weigh in on specific legislation or laws directly. Some states even allow the voters to propose the ballot initiatives themselves, and that's when you really see democracy in action, because the people have chosen what they want to vote on, and the government is responsible to honor the voters' decision. Voter-proposed ballot initiatives are extremely cool, and one of those things I believe all states should have.

America also has what are called off-year elections, meaning elections held in odd-numbered years, or on a date other than the first Tuesday after the first Monday in November, as well as special elections, meaning elections that are off the typical cycle or are held because of special circumstances. Five states hold off-year state elections for governor and other statewide offices—Kentucky, Louisiana, Mississippi, New Jersey, and Virginia—the rest of the states hold elections at the regular time, or what are called "on-cycle" elections. Special elections usually happen when someone dies or has to leave office before their term is over, or there's a referendum on some issue. We have special elections for pretty much every office except the president, vice president, and most US Senate seats.* If the president leaves office early, they're

---

*Four states require the seats be filled *only* by special election. Nine states allow the governor to appoint a replacement, but generally require a stand-alone special election sooner than the next general election, and thirty-seven states allow the governor to choose a senator who will hold the seat until the next regularly scheduled general election.

replaced by the vice president. If the vice president leaves office early, the president nominates a new VP, who must be confirmed by majority vote in the House and Senate. If a senator dies or leaves office before their term is over, their state's governor appoints someone to do the job until the next scheduled election or appoints someone until a special election has been completed. Special elections can also happen for a state constitutional change, or something the state legislature decides can't wait until the next general election, but typically elections happen every two years, say it with me . . . on the first Tuesday after the first Monday in November.

If a candidate for an election is *new*, rather than what's called an *incumbent* (meaning they already have the job and are running for reelection), then that candidate might have gone through a primary election before the general. Primary elections happen when there's more than one candidate from the same party who wants the job. Before they can run against an opposition candidate, they must run against candidates from their own party.

A primary election can happen in three ways: open, closed, semi-closed/mixed. Open primaries are open to all registered voters, no matter which party they're registered with, and include independent voters, who aren't registered with any party, as well as people changing party affiliation. A closed primary limits participation to registered members of that party, and a semi-closed, or mixed, primary, allows independent or unaffiliated voters to take part in the primary election of the party they choose, while voters who have already picked a side can only take part in their own party's primary. Once a candidate wins the primary, they will run against the opposition candidate in the general election.*

I feel like this is a good place to remind people that if you want your voice to be heard, you have to register to vote, and if you want to vote in a primary, then you might want to consider affiliating yourself with either the Democratic, Republican, or Independent party. There are lots of wonderful websites like vote.org and organizations like Field Team 6 that will help you register. You can do it at the DMV, many government offices, or with your state secretary of state. You can also go directly to the official government website, vote.gov, to register, find voter registration deadlines, check to make sure you haven't been purged from the voter rolls, register after you've moved, choose or change your party affiliation, or get a voter registration card if your state has specific requirements for voter ID. The site will also give you information on absentee voting, Election Day voting, and the election process itself.

Since the 1850s America has functioned primarily as a two-party system, the Republicans and the Democrats. Despite people's objections to what they often feel as being forced to choose between the "lesser of two evils," this is just how the system is set up, particularly at the federal level. We do have other parties, like the Green Party, the Libertarian Party, and the Constitution Party, as well as independents who are not affiliated with any party but typically caucus (aka hang out and vote) with one of the two major

---

* California, Washington, and Nebraska use "top-two primary systems," which means the two candidates who get the most votes in the primary election advance to the general, regardless of party affiliation. So theoretically you could have a general election with a Democrat vs. a Democrat or a Republican vs. a Republican.

parties. You could theoretically create your own party in America if you wanted, but you would need a certain number of signatures to get on the ballot, and often without the backing of one of the two major parties, or hundreds of millions of dollars, that's difficult to swing. Not impossible, but certainly not easy.

Before we move on, I'd like to address a common talking point that "America isn't a democracy, it's a republic," because I don't think this statement means what people think it does and it sets us up to fight one another when we don't have to. Yes, America is a republic, but more specifically America is a constitutional republic, and a constitutional republic is a form of democracy.

Republic comes from the Latin *res publica*, which means "public affair." It's a form of government in which the country is considered a "public matter" and not the "private concern" or "property" of the rulers. The primary positions of power in a republic can be attained through democracy (rule by the people), an oligarchy (rule by the select few), or a mix of the two. Now, we could discuss how much oligarchy is sneaking into American politics and public life, or how one party seems to be leaning hard toward autocracy, but in the context of US constitutional law, the definition of republic refers to a form of government in which elected individuals represent the citizens and exercise their power according to the rule of law under the Constitution. So, in other words, a democracy. A government *theoretically* set up to represent the will of the people, rather than the will of the rulers, and we use our Constitution as a type of instruction manual that lays out the parameters in which we function.

THE SIX AMERICAN PRINCIPLES

★ ★ ★

I believe it's in America's best interest to try something new. To know where we came from and use that to build a better, stronger foundation for our nation to rest on. If we truly want to be a land of freedom and opportunity where everyone has a shot at a good life, then we have to find the courage to step out of our comfort zones and off our team benches to agree that the ideals of America are worth saving. We fought a revolutionary war for the idea of self-governance and the pursuit of happiness. We can't just give up on it now.

So, how do we build this better, stronger nation? What are the fundamental building blocks we can all agree make America, America? What do we, the citizens of this nation, believe are the bedrocks of the United States? Drawing on our founding documents, and important moments in our country's history, I propose the Six American Principles. Six things that we, the people, no matter our politics, persuasion, or background, can agree on. Six ideals we can use as guideposts to not only find our way out of the mess we're currently in, but to set a course for a future of which we can actually be proud. If we start here, we start strong.

1. America is a land of freedom.

2. Everyone should have the opportunity to rise.

3. Every citizen should have a vote, and that vote should count.

4. Representatives should represent the people
   who voted for them.

5. The law applies to all of us.

6. Government should be a force for good.

★ ★ ★

AMERICA IS A LAND OF FREEDOM

Freedom is the fundamental principle on which America was built. The word *freedom* polls higher than any other word in this country. It even polls higher than the word *America*. It doesn't matter your political persuasion, everything in the United States comes back to the central idea of freedom. Our anthem is about the land of the free. We have Lady Liberty on our shore, the shining beacon of freedom and opportunity. When Americans say "my rights" they mean "my freedom"—what we're allowed to do, allowed to have, allowed to say. There is a popular meme Europeans like to share to tease Americans that's just an extreme close-up of a serious-looking bald eagle that reads, "I'm sorry, I can't hear you over the sound of my freedom." This idea of freedom is integral to the American national identity, but I worry many of us have forgotten what it actually means.

America is not unique. There are lots of countries in the world with "freedom." In fact on the 2023 Human Freedom Index, America doesn't even crack the top 10, so we need to ask ourselves, when we say "freedom," what are we actually talking about? What did freedom mean to the Founding Fathers of the Southern colonies? The men who wouldn't sign the Constitution without the inclusion of chattel slavery. What was freedom to President Andrew Jackson, who ran the brutal Indian Removal Campaign so white settlers could continue their western expansion? What did freedom mean to the men who passed the Fifteenth Amendment after the Civil War, protecting the voting rights of every American citizen "no matter their party, faith, color, or district" but left out gender? Was freedom on the mind of those who opposed Reparations with Black Codes and white violence, or when Jim Crow laws took over the South and segregated everything from bathrooms to schools, adding endless obstacles to make sure the people who were now free to vote couldn't?

America's history is packed with oppression. Every step forward expanding our freedom has been hard-won, which is why it means so much to us, and why we shouldn't be cavalier when people try to take it away. Early Americans gambled the future of our nation on the dream of liberty. They risked it all for the chance to make their own rules, establish their own government, and create a nation of the people, by the people, for the people. The Declaration of Independence, the document we sent to the King of England telling him we no longer wanted to be part of his empire, laid it out, "We hold these truths to be self-evident, that all men are created equal, that they are endowed by their Creator with certain unalienable Rights, that among these are Life, Liberty and the pursuit of Happiness." Or in common speak, we believe this to be true without question, that everyone is created equal. That we are born with certain rights that cannot be taken from us, and among those are our right to life, to freedom, and to the ability to seek that which makes us happy.

Now of course, we'd be fools to pretend this idea of liberty was originally offered to everyone. It would be a disservice to the history of our country, and to the memory of the people who fought for the expansion of rights, not to acknowledge that at our inception, liberty and justice were only for *some*. The only people who could vote in our original elections were white male landowners, over twenty-one, but over the centuries we have expanded the rights and freedoms of the American people with action and deliberation—with blood, sweat, and tears. Very little in this nation's history was simply given to us. Every step forward has been a fight. From the day we declared our independence, to the day you are reading this book, we have been a nation of people asking for more. A nation of people looking around and saying, "Nope, we could do better."

The Founding Fathers might have been a bunch of white guys who mostly owned slaves and didn't think much about women, but they were forward thinkers. Enlightened men who knew they were creating the documents of a nation within the confines of their time. The Framers deliberately left things open so they'd be able to evolve. They understood the freedoms originally offered to a small group would eventually, over the course of time, be expanded. Which is why it matters that after two centuries of progress, our freedoms are once again under attack.

James Madison, who wrote so much of the Constitution he's known as the "Father of the Constitution," also wrote nineteen additions that would act as an addendum to the original Constitution and called them "the great rights of mankind." Ten of the nineteen would end up being ratified as constitutional amendments and are now collectively known as the Bill of Rights. If the original Constitution is the country's operating manual, the Bill of Rights, and the amendments that came after, are often what people think of when they talk about American "freedoms."

Freedom of speech is in the First Amendment of the Constitution, and is the one Americans often base their national identity on. "I'm an American. I have freedom of speech." The problem is, most people think freedom of speech means you're allowed to say whatever you want to say, whenever you want to say it, and no one can do anything about it. What people forget is that the Constitution was written to shape the power of the government, not necessarily the behavior of the citizens. We built this country on the idea of independence—that we are our own nation, our own people—but we transposed that national identity onto the individual. The idea of freedom of speech is so integral to the American sense of self, but we're often a little fuzzy on the details of the actual amendment.

In its entirety, the First Amendment says: "Congress shall make no law respecting an establishment of religion, or prohibiting the free speech thereof; or abridging the freedom of speech, or of the press; or the right of the people peaceably to assemble, and to petition the Government for a redress of grievances." So, let's break down what that means.

Under the First Amendment, the government can't tell you what to say. It can't stop you from criticizing it. No one can lock you up for your political beliefs, your political speech, or your peaceful political actions. No one can drag you away, throw you in jail, or execute you for treason for criticizing the government like they do in other countries. You can even make a list of things you believe are wrong and publish them. This freedom to openly express your anger and disappointment with the very seat of power is a wonderful addition to the Constitution. The point of the amendment is that the weight of the federal government cannot, and will not, be used against its people for the things they say.

Americans take for granted how this isn't the case everywhere else. We talk endlessly about the *importance* of freedom of speech, but I'm not sure we truly realize what an important freedom it is, because it's how we make *change*. It's how we're able to stand up and say, "This isn't right." How we can get elected on our ideas. How we can speak our truth in government about government.

Freedom of speech is essential to everything we hold dear, but many have reduced it to the ability to act like a jerk without liability. Which is why when neo-Nazis were being de-platformed on the original Twitter people got upset. They argued that removing them was against freedom of speech. Except an agreement between a private company and its users has nothing to do with the government. The government gives you the constitutional right to say whatever hateful garbage you want—that's why we have neo-Nazis marching in American cities without federal officers stepping in—freedom of speech protects you from the *government*, not the repercussions of your speech from private companies or public groups. You can't just scream at a comedian in a comedy club or yell your opinions in a crowded lecture hall without being removed. Americans are offered freedom from *tyranny*, not freedom from *accountability*.

You can't threaten to murder someone or deliberately incite a riot and call it free speech. To be clear, those are actually considered "true threats," and the Supreme Court has ruled the government is allowed to prosecute someone who intentionally threatens another person with death or bodily harm. The Supreme Court has also ruled that the First Amendment doesn't protect you from inciting violence or causing a harmful situation, like yelling "Fire!" in a crowded theater. Freedom of speech means the government can't come after you for the things you say. It doesn't shield you from slander, libel, false or misleading speech, or intellectual property violations, and it doesn't mean you can't be fired for using the N-word at work.

The First Amendment is such an essential addition to the Constitution that we should give props to those holdout delegates who refused to sign the document until a bill of rights was included. Just as we should feel concerned that current state leaders are now writing laws to roll those essential rights back—like making protesting illegal, allowing people to hit protestors with their car, or banning journalists they don't like from press conferences. Many of us were concerned when President Donald Trump started talking about jailing his political opponents ("Lock her up!"), or when he asked General Mark Milley if they could "just shoot [the protesters]" in the summer of 2020. General Milley had to remind the president that the people had a constitutional right to peacefully gather and protest. It doesn't matter how you feel about President Trump; any government official believing they have the authority to violate the people's First Amendment right to peacefully protest, or who use their power in direct opposition to the people's fundamental freedoms, should feel alarming.

★ ★ ★

Freedom of the press was included in the First Amendment for a reason. While the three branches of government are meant to act as a check on one another, the press keeps tabs on all three. That's why it's often called the Fourth Estate. This group can research what the government is doing and report back to the public. The public can then understand the positions, actions, and behaviors of their government, and vote or act accordingly. The United States is an enormous country. We couldn't possibly keep up, or know if our representatives were corrupt or deceitful, without a dedicated group of people whose job it was to report on what was happening. I realize we might have forgotten this important fact in the golden age of infotainment, but the press has an obligation to hold those in power accountable. It's an essential element of American freedom to expose those who are corrupt or lawless to public scrutiny.

It was freedom of the press that allowed Ida B. Wells to document the lynching and mistreatment of Black people in the South, that allowed Ida Tarbell to publish a nineteen-part series revealing oil tycoon and billionaire John D. Rockefeller's illegal monopolistic practices, and the First Amendment was how journalists Bob Woodward and Carl Bernstein were able to break the Watergate scandal that would have led to Nixon's impeachment had he not chosen to resign.

Ida Tarbell's work on Rockefeller led to new antitrust laws that would help move the country out of the great wealth disparity of the Gilded Age, in the early part of the twentieth century, and change the course of the nation by stopping giant corporations from consolidating nearly unlimited power—laws that would be severely rolled back during the Reagan administration of the 1980s. Forty years ago there were fifty companies in charge of most American media. Today, 90 percent of the media in the United States is controlled by six corporations. Along with removing antitrust laws to encourage competition, the Reagan administration also got rid of the Fairness Doctrine, a policy created in 1949 requiring anyone who held a broadcast license "to present fair and balanced coverage of controversial issues to promote 'a basic standard of fairness' in broadcasting." During this time, licensees were "obliged not only to cover fairly the views of others, but also to refrain from expressing their own views to ensure that broadcasters did not use their stations simply as advocates of a single perspective," and without that regulation in place, the way our country took in information went completely off the rails.

There's a popular saying about journalism that goes, "If someone says it's raining and another person says it's dry, it's not your job to quote them both. Your job is to look out the window and find out which one is true." Unfortunately, without the Fairness Doctrine the truth part wasn't as necessary anymore, and America became inundated with polarized media, particularly right-wing radio, with hosts like Rush Limbaugh, which laid the framework for future right-wing news channels like Fox News and Newsmax.

Almost overnight we created a media environment where people only had to hear one side of the story, and often that side was skewed to activate people to vote or behave in certain ways. Instead of giving people facts, it gave people spin, and within that spin our nation began to erode. I'm sure you've noticed how difficult it is to discuss or debate an issue if you come to the table from two completely different *realities*. Add to that the twenty-four-hour news cycle and the increasing reach of cable television—which doesn't require the same broadcast license as network television, so it doesn't have to follow the same rules—and we had a crisis waiting to happen.

There are differences between companies like NBC, who must apply for broadcasting licenses from the Federal Communications Commission (FCC), and private cable companies like Fox News, who do not. You can see how the different sets of regulations affect broadcast vs. cable media in court. Years ago, Fox News's Tucker Carlson was in a defamation trial at the same time NBC was in a defamation trial. Broadcast network NBC had to pay a huge settlement after it turned out something it reported wasn't the full story. Fox News, on the other hand, won its case because the judge ruled "no reasonable person would think Tucker was telling the truth." The problem is, many clearly do.

The loss of the Fairness Doctrine and rise of cable media and the internet, in combination with the shrinking number of companies who own all media, has made freedom of the press very muddy. Today, the American public is forced to walk a fine line between information and propaganda, and it's far too easy to become confused. Which is why 30 percent of the electorate—the people who vote in America—still believe, despite all evidence and court cases to the contrary, that President Joe Biden did not legally win the 2020 election. This is categorically false, but if members of the media don't have to *say* that, then where does that leave us?

Modern politicians are also taking major liberties with freedom of the press—passing laws to limit press access, blocking public disclosure, referring to them as the "enemy of the people" or discrediting them by calling them "fake news." Much of this behavior is not only unconstitutional, but should place politicians engaging in it squarely in the spotlight. What is it they're trying to hide?

We need freedom of the press to hold those in power accountable, and we should, at the very least, be requiring new legislation prohibiting the known dissemination of false or misleading information. Despite how people *feel*, truth still exists. We may not like it, but it's real. If this country could pass an amendment making booze illegal (Eighteenth Amendment), surely we could pass an amendment that makes public deception illegal.

★ ★ ★

After the initial changes to the Constitution with the Bill of Rights, and the two amendments that came after, America went sixty-one years without any formal additions to the Constitution, but we also had a civil war, and coming out of that war it was obvious we needed new amendments to address some of the things we had missed the first time around. This is how we got the Thirteenth, Fourteenth, and Fifteenth Amendments, and how American "freedom" took on a whole new meaning.

According to the National Museum of African American History & Culture in Washington, DC, although Abraham Lincoln had always been personally against slavery—believing it was unjust and placed too much power in the hands of wealthy men—he wasn't sure if Black people should become American citizens. Lincoln began the Civil War believing former slaves should be sent out of the country after they were free, because how could they ever live alongside those who had enslaved them? Over time his views changed, in part credited to his relationship with

Frederick Douglass, the escaped slave who became one of the most important leaders in the African American civil rights movement. By the end of his life Lincoln was speaking in favor not just of citizenship, but of African American voting rights. He was shot by John Wilkes Booth before the final ratification of his greatest legacy, the Thirteenth Amendment (1865)—the outlawing of chattel slavery and involuntary servitude in the United States.

AMERICA 101: JUNETEENTH

I think it's important not to pass over this essential moment in the expansion of our nation's freedom without mentioning June 19, or what's called Juneteenth. Juneteenth marks the day in June 1865 when Union soldiers arrived in Galveston, Texas, to enforce the emancipation of the last slaves, because the white people there simply weren't doing it. The fact is, not everyone in America celebrates Independence Day on the fourth of July, because on July 4, 1776, Black Americans were still enslaved. So modern-day Black Americans might enjoy a BBQ on July 4, but many of them will understandably never see that day as symbolizing their own independence or liberty. Juneteenth is therefore a commemorative holiday celebrating the day in 1865 when Union soldiers arrived in the last town in the South to tell them enslaved people were free. Over the years, Juneteenth has been called Freedom Day, Emancipation Day, Black Fourth of July, and the Second Independence Day, and despite the fact that Juneteenth has only been a national holiday in America since 2021, the day has been sacred to many Black communities for more than 150 years. And while slavery might have been abolished in 1865, the fight for civil rights in America continues to this day, so Juneteenth gives us the opportunity to reflect on our past and consider the true legacy of freedom in America.

While the Thirteenth Amendment did stop chattel slavery, and theoretically give Black Americans the right to freedom, it was the enforcement of those rights that was problematic. Reconstruction, the period after the Civil War when America tried to figure out how to integrate the newly freed African Americans into society, was a turbulent time in our nation's history as Lincoln's replacement, President Andrew Johnson, was a strong proponent of states' rights and didn't believe the federal government should have a say in how they were run. This left the Southern states largely in the hands of the ruling class—traditionally white plantation owners and former Confederates—and following the passage of the Thirteenth Amendment, state legislatures in the South passed a whole series of restrictive rules called the Black Codes to control the behavior and freedoms of the formally enslaved. This effectively kept many newly freed African Americans dependent on their former owners, forced into specific trades, and fined or jailed for random infractions, all while limiting what they could do, what they could own, and where they could live. To add insult to injury, Black Codes were enforced by all-white police forces and state militia often made up of Confederate veterans, and President Johnson took the land that had been given to the freed slaves and returned it to their former owners.

AMERICA 101: JIM CROW LAWS

To be clear: When people talk about the Jim Crow South, they're not talking about a person but referring to a persona. Jim Crow was a character created by a white actor, Thomas D. Rice, in 1830 for a popular theatrical form called minstrel shows that reached their peak popularity between 1850 and 1870. The character of Jim Crow was played by a white man in blackface mocking African Americans as basically slow-witted buffoons who were there to jump around and act a fool for a white audience. It was a demeaning caricature that helped white people rationalize the way Black people were treated, as it played into the idea that Black people were innately inferior, which helped justify any laws created to deliberately keep the African American population down. These laws were then referred to as "Jim Crow" laws.

Post-Restoration Black Codes made way for Jim Crow laws that continued to hold back Black Americans for generations. If you want to learn about Black American history and understand why people talk about things like reparations and systemic racism and teach courses like critical race theory in law school, you can't stop at slavery. You have to recognize what came after and realize how slow the progress to "liberty and justice for all" has really been in this country. While slavery might have come to an end after the Civil War, there were still lots of people who fought tooth and nail against the freedom of African Americans. We see their legacy to this day in the sentiments of those people still arguing that America is a white nation. Despite the fact that every decade since the end of slavery has found Black Americans, on the whole, more educated, with more wealth, and more status, we've never properly dealt with racism, or the perpetuation of violence against Black people, in this country. America couldn't even get a federal anti-lynching law passed until the Biden administration in 2022, and as everyone from Emmett Till to George Floyd shows us, we still have a long way to go if we want to truly call ourselves the land of the free.

AMERICA 101: THE EXCEPTION CLAUSE

While the Thirteenth Amendment ended chattel slavery by banning the exploitation of someone's labor against their will, and theoretically giving Black Americans their right to freedom, it was also the beginning of using our prison population as near slave labor. The Thirteenth Amendment includes what's called the Exception Clause, which allows workers in prisons to be exploited, underpaid, and excluded from workplace safety protections. The Exception Clause ended up encouraging the criminalization and re-enslavement of Black people after the Civil War to keep them working for free, and despite the fact all prisoners fall under the clause, over time it's had a disproportionate effect on Black Americans.

When we brag about "American freedom," we should probably keep in mind that America also has the highest prison population in the world, with just 4.23 percent of the world's population but 20 percent of the world's prisoners, and we use that population as a lucrative industry of cheap labor that often gets rented out. In fact, the University of Chicago reported that nearly two-thirds (65 percent) of incarcerated people working in America today—roughly 800,000 inmates—have no choice but to work for little to no pay. The same study informs us that incarcerated workers produce at least $2 billion in goods, and at least $9 billion in prison maintenance to subsidize the cost of the industry. It's an incredibly lucrative business to own a prison in America, and the more prisoners you have, the more money you make. So, when we crow about American freedom, we might also want to consider getting serious about American prison reform.

The Fourteenth Amendment (1868) offered, among other things, birthright citizenship to everyone born in the United States, as well as due process under the law (the Constitution gave due process under federal law, but this was specifically for the states). It gave Black men the right to vote through their citizenship, punishing states with decreased representation in

Congress should they not be allowed to vote, and it ended the Three-Fifths Compromise, with every Black American now being counted as a whole person to determine House representation. The Fourteenth Amendment did not, however, affect "non-taxed Native Americans" (which at the time were 92 percent of the Indigenous community), each of whom still counted as zero percent of a person. This would go on to affect Native Americans' ability to become citizens, which wasn't granted to them until the Indian Citizenship Act of 1924. So, while Indigenous people were 100 percent America's First People, they were the last to gain American citizenship and share in our rights.

Unsurprisingly, the Fourteenth Amendment wasn't a strong enough deterrent to those who wanted to disenfranchise Black voters, so Congress had to explicitly add the Fifteenth Amendment (1870) to stop citizens from being barred from voting because of their race, and we would still need the Voting Rights Act of 1965 to make it stick.

Reading American history, it's difficult not to see how incredibly unjust many of America's laws and societal behaviors have been over the years. It's hard not to be discouraged at just how dead set certain groups of Americans have been about denying freedoms to those they deem lesser. Which, to be clear, wasn't just Black Americans, but also immigrants, the working class, the LGBTQIA+ community, and women.

From the founding of the United States, women had been almost completely excluded from American politics. After the Civil

War, however, women believed their time had come, but while the country seemed prepared to extend voting rights to Black men, it wasn't ready to extend them to women. Many women abolitionists put their dream of universal suffrage (voting for everyone) aside to make sure newly freed Black men were given the same right to vote as white men, but other women in the movement were outraged.

A heated argument about whether it was the Black man's or white woman's turn to vote went back and forth until Black women stood up and expressed their unique perspective, which was that in neither of those scenarios were they included. The idea being, we keep talking about Black men getting the right to vote because of slavery, but if we don't include women, then Black women will be left out, and how is that fair if the standard to meet is having been enslaved?

The debate ultimately split the women's movement into two distinct groups. One group focused on a constitutional amendment for women's suffrage, while also working on other political issues like divorce laws and temperance (moderation of, or abstinence from, alcohol), while the other worked primarily for women's suffrage at the state level, but mostly stayed out of other political issues. Historians believe the split within the women's movement was both inevitable and probably one of the reasons it took so long for women to finally get the vote. While the amendment to let women vote was introduced to Congress in 1878, and would be reintroduced every year after that, it wouldn't pass until forty-one years later, in 1919, becoming the law of the land through ratification as the Nineteenth Amendment in 1920.

This dance between marginalized groups in America has been

going on since the beginning. We founded America with rights and freedoms for one specific group, and somehow ended up pitting those left out against each other, instead of having them unite in their demands to be included. It's a shame we were forced to choose between Black men's and women's votes. Why didn't the Fifteenth Amendment just include universal suffrage? It's because those in power are not always inclined to share that power unless their hand is forced. Which is why it should concern us that our modern-day Supreme Court is actively rolling back those enforcements—like gutting the Voting Rights Act to once again make it easier to suppress Black votes, or reversing *Roe v. Wade* to control women's bodies, or passing laws to deny the LGBTQIA+ community equal protection under the law. People fought and died for equality and freedom in America—so watching our modern court system limit people's rights is deeply distressing but should also be extraordinarily activating.

★ ★ ★

Along with freedom of speech, freedom to protest, and freedom of the press, the First Amendment is also the amendment that addressed religion. We take this right for granted, but it's one we absolutely count on and cannot undersell. The original Constitution says "no religious test shall ever be required as a qualification to any office or public trust," and the Framers followed that up with the First Amendment, claiming there shall be "no law representing an establishment of religion or prohibiting the free exercise thereof."

The first part, "no law representing an establishment of religion," is called the Establishment Clause, and the second part, "no law prohibiting the free exercise thereof," is called the Free Exercise Clause. The Establishment Clause prohibits the government from establishing an official religion, and the Free Exercise Clause protects a citizen's right to practice religion as they please so long as it doesn't interfere with "public morals," infringe on a "compelling" government interest, or break the law. So, I'm sorry to say, no human sacrifices or public orgies. Whenever the Free Exercise Clause comes into question, it's the courts that ultimately decide what does and doesn't fit within the law.

AMERICA 101: SEPARATION OF CHURCH AND STATE

To be clear, the Framers didn't include the religious stipulations in the founding documents because they were a bunch of atheists, but because they were mostly men of faith. The Framers included the statements because they believed in what Thomas Jefferson referred to as the "separation between church and state." This wasn't so much to protect the state from the church—you're free to speak your religious values from any place in government, and Congress has been opening each day's proceedings with a prayer since 1789—but so the government couldn't interfere in religion. The Founders were adamant that government and religion should not mix, which is one of the reasons the federal government has never taxed religious institutions. Today, "establishment of religion" is often determined under a three-part test laid out in the 1971

Supreme Court case *Lemon v. Kurtzman*. Under the "Lemon test" the government can assist religious institutions only if:

- The primary purpose of the assistance is secular;
- The assistance neither promotes, nor inhibits, religion; and
- There is no "excessive entanglement" between church and state.

So, you might ask, if our government was created to represent all the people of the United States, no matter their faith, or lack thereof, why then is "God" on our money? Good question—and I think a pretty striking error that should be addressed.

Putting "In God We Trust" on our money was originally proposed by a minister during the Civil War as something for people to hold on to in troubling times. The secretary of the treasury put the motto on the two-cent coin in 1864, Congress authorized it to be printed on all silver and gold coins in 1865, and it has appeared on all coins since 1938.

In 1954, during the height of the Cold War, "under God" was added to the Pledge of Allegiance—which had been used for fifty years without mention of a deity—as a way to place ourselves in opposition to the atheist Soviet Union. In 1956 America declared "In God We Trust" our new *national* motto for the same reason, and in 1957 the Treasury started printing the motto on our paper currency. "In God We Trust" is now on all US currency, along with many government buildings, and was adopted as the official motto of the state of Florida in 2006.

Theoretically, having "God" on American money breaches the Establishment Clause by specifically promoting one God (monotheism) over many Gods (polytheism), or no God (atheism), but more than that, it's also far less unifying than our original motto, "E pluribus unum," which means "out of many, one." While most people polled say they don't really care that "God" is on American money because they think it's just patriotic or ceremonial, I think it's important to acknowledge it's not. Adding "God" to our money was suggested by a minister, extended in opposition to atheism, and is, in itself, the opposite of patriotic as the Constitution is very clear that the government should not endorse any religion or belief.

FUN FACT: *Most presidents, while being given the oath of office—as laid out in the Constitution—have used the Bible. Not because the Constitution specifies that they use a Bible, but because our first president, George Washington, used a Bible and most of the other presidents just followed suit. However, John Quincy Adams used a book of law, and President Theodore Roosevelt didn't use anything.*

Having religious slogans on state-sponsored institutions like money, schools, courts, and government buildings is the opposite of separation. A religious person shouldn't want the church and state combined any more than an atheist, because it blurs the lines.

God is not supposed to have a part in our government, just as the government is not supposed to play a part in how you worship your god. There are many who argue we need religion back in our lives, but if you require the government to impose it, then it's no longer about faith but control, which is, of course, the antithesis of freedom.

Which is why it should concern Americans that a particular sect of the Christian religion has turned into a radical ideology and appropriated one of our country's major political parties. It should worry us that the speaker of the House refers to himself as the "new Moses," chosen by God, and flies the flag of the far-right New Apostolic Reformation—a group dedicated to turning America into a religious state—outside his office. It should concern us that sitting representatives are not just talking about their faith, but claiming to speak on *behalf* of God and know what God wants for America. What God has anointed, and who God wants to be president.

Conservative think tanks like the Heritage Foundation, who have actively been advising Republican presidents since Ronald Reagan, are funded by some of the biggest right-wing billionaires, and are closely aligned with the religious Right and Evangelical movements, who have been the primary voting base for the Republican Party since the late 1970s. Now, the Heritage Foundation, in combination with the Federalist Society, the far-right legal group responsible for the conservative supermajority on the Supreme Court, along with more than a hundred other far-right groups, have formed an organization called Project 2025, which revolves around a list of policy proposals titled *Mandate for Leadership: The Conservative Promise*. Project 2025 lays out the plan for the next Republican president, which includes dismantling the federal government as we know it, and fundamentally demolishing the checks and balances of the coequal branches of government as laid out in the Constitution, to more effectively implement Christian biblical-based ideologies, reforming everything from education, to voting, to immigration.

Project 2025 includes consolidating the power of the federal government around the executive branch, replacing career civil servants with party loyalists, defunding the Department of Justice, and having the president assume control of our system of law. It plans to dismantle the FBI and the Department of Homeland Security, eliminate the Department of Education and Commerce, and drastically limit the Department of Health and Human Services. Project 2025, which is supported by every major conservative group in America from Moms for Liberty to Turning Point USA, also plans to roll back civil rights and freedom of the press, while providing extended protections for "traditional beliefs" about marriage, gender, and sexuality. The new Republican administration is also expected to enact policies that respect religious exercise in the workplace, provided that religion is "biblically based." Project 2025 is the long-term plan for all major right-wing donors, politicians, and thought leaders for 2025 and beyond. The group has been clear they're training an "army" for a long-term, far-right, Christian-based agenda.

So, if we don't want to see a reimagining of the federal government using religious doctrine, antithetical to the founding principles of our nation, it shouldn't matter our voting preference, religious affiliation, or personal beliefs. It's essential we recognize Project 2025 for the threat it is. America was predicated on a Constitution, a secular body of laws that derives its power from the will of the people. If we pivot to reestablish our government based on religious doctrine, from a *specific sect* of Christianity, then we can kiss American freedoms goodbye.

The best way to think about what's happening in America right now, and to unemotionally consider if something is in line with our Constitution, and therefore our fundamental American rights, is ask yourself if the actions being taken by the government are *giving* freedom, or taking it *away*. What rights the government has, or what values America is supposed to stand for, can become confusing when they align with what you personally want. For example, you might think the idea of a Christian nation sounds wonderful, but if you want to know if it's in line with America's founding principles, you need to flip what's happening and see if you still agree. What if the American government told you the country would now be set up around the doctrine of the Quran and we would all be abiding by the tenets of Islam? My guess is many people who would feel incredibly comfortable setting up the government around the Christian faith would feel equally uncomfortable with the suggestion of using another religious doctrine.

Look at the entire "tradwife" (traditional wife) movement, or the "return to family values" resurgence that's happening in America today. Now if it was just about freedom—freedom of religion, freedom of speech, freedom of expression—then anyone should be able to stay home or go to work as they choose, and their choice should be supported by both the government and society. However, if you find yourself wanting to tell women they *have* to stay home—like the country more or less did before the 1970s, when women had little to no access to their own money, couldn't have bank accounts or credit cards, or apply for a mortgage without their husband's permission—flip it. What if the government was telling women they *had* to go to work? That they couldn't stay home with their children? I think people would immediately recognize that was wrong, a clearly anti-American infringement on women's rights and freedoms. Which is how you know the government telling you what to do in your own home, with your own life, and with your own children, is not in line with American values, no matter how much the idea itself might appeal to you. At the end of the day just getting what you want does not equal "freedom."

It's the same with the abortion issue. You might have tremendously strong feelings about the medical procedure called abortion, and that's your right. Say what you want to say about it, feel how you want to feel, sway people to your way of thinking and behaving with your passion and arguments, but in a land of freedom one of the most fundamental freedoms is the right to your own body. Your body belongs to you, and you alone. You can't touch another person's body without their permission. You can't use another person's body without their consent. All our laws are set up to acknowledge this fundamental truth. Despite the fact it happens so frequently, rape is illegal, assault is illegal, pedophilia is illegal. You can't desecrate a corpse. A hospital can't even take organs from a dead body to save someone else without the express consent from the deceased before they died. Everybody has bodily autonomy. So then why would our government make a different set of rules for people who are pregnant?

Forget everything you feel about the abortion issue. The question on the table is: Do you believe the American government has the authority to force a citizen to use an organ in their own body against their will? You might never need an abortion, but would you support the government forcing people to give up a kidney? Should the government be able to force citizens to give up a part of their liver, or donate blood? What if it was going to help someone live? No, right? That would be government overreach and against our personal freedom. Why then would we give our government the power to force women to use their uterus against their will? Even if you believe it would save a life?

I believe the problem is that this argument should never have been about abortion. It should always have been about autonomy. This is one of those places where I believe we require a new constitutional amendment. An amendment that formally establishes that your body belongs to you. That no one gets to decide what you do with it. If you want a tattoo, get one. If you want top surgery, that's your choice. If you want a hysterectomy, have it. If you are dying of a terminal disease and want to end your life peacefully on your own terms, that is your decision. The American government has no right to tell you what you can and cannot do with your own body. And if you decide you want to have an abortion, that should also be your choice. We need to acknowledge the government has no place in any of those decisions. If you still feel conflicted, then let's try that same thought experiment where you take the original premise and flip it.

If you feel confident the government has the right to tell someone they can't have an abortion and they must have a baby, how would you feel if the government was telling people they had to have an abortion and they couldn't have a baby? This isn't unprecedented. The Chinese government told its people exactly that in 1980 when it implemented its one-child policy. Concerned with overpopulation, the Chinese government subjected millions of women to forced contraception, forced sterilization, and forced abortions for thirty-five years. This was a government-mandated law. Possible, of course, because China has a Communist government with top-down authoritarianism that dictates what its people can do, and shouldn't be possible in a liberal democracy like ours, but if our government has decided it can tell us we *must* have children, then how different is it from telling us we *can't*?

It never works out when governments intrude on human freedoms like reproduction. China's one-child policy has caused it endless problems. It now has way too many adult men and not enough women. For years, the one-child policy, in combination with the Chinese culture of favoring a boy to carry on the family name, led to girl children being aborted or murdered after they were born. The adult men born at this time, particularly in small villages, now have no one to marry, no one to procreate with, and China is experiencing an epidemic of loneliness and low birth rates. The government came in, meddled with reproduction, and made an absolute mess of its culture.

How different is that from what's occurring in America right now? Republican states are currently taking control of women's reproductive rights for the flip side of the original Chinese problem—they feel we don't have enough people. The American Right wants to control women's reproduction because it's concerned there won't be enough workers, soldiers, and taxpayers in the next generation. Now, of course, there's a solution to our declining population at our borders, but that same group believes that's the wrong "type" of population growth. Which is why sitting Supreme Court justice Samuel Alito included a footnote in the

2022 *Dobbs* decision, the case that reversed *Roe v. Wade* and the federal right to a safe and legal abortion, that America's "domestic supply of infants" has become virtually nonexistent, and Supreme Court justice Amy Coney Barrett suggested that "safe haven laws," which allow women to drop off babies anonymously in certain places after birth, would take care of the problem of women being forced to be parents against their will. But what about being pregnant against your will? Because that feels like the first problem we have to solve.

We could talk about how forcing women to have babies pushes them back into the home, the place where the conservatives writing these laws would prefer they would stay. We could talk about the economic ramifications of forcing families to have children they can't afford, how abortion is truly an economic issue. We could talk for days about how America's adoption and foster care system is overcrowded and underfunded, which forces government agencies to leave children with people who aren't appropriate guardians. I could cite the growing homeless population, and how many of them are young adults who simply aged out of foster care, and point out that this already broken system will only be exacerbated by adding more children who weren't wanted to it. I could horrify you with the reality of not being able to cross state lines without being forced to take a pregnancy test, or rapists getting parental rights, literally getting to choose the mother of their children against the will of the woman, but the bottom line is, in a land of freedom, the government should not be able to force women to give birth. It's antithetical to the founding principles of this nation.

★ ★ ★

It is also antithetical in a land that calls itself free to tell people who they can love, who they can sleep with, or who they can marry. Which is why we should be concerned that America is once again putting the rights and freedoms of the LGBTQIA+ community on the line. Rights that have been actively fought for since World War II. The LGBTQIA+ community—which includes lesbian, gay, bisexual, transgender, queer, intersex, and asexual individuals, along with anyone who sees themselves reflected under this umbrella but doesn't fit into any of the aforementioned categories—is a terrific example of that old expression about power that says, "Equal rights for others does not mean fewer rights for you. It's not pie." By expanding its group to include more, rather than narrowing its group to include fewer, the LGBTQIA+ community has expanded their collective power. It's one of the reasons conservatives are targeting the transgender community. If you can break apart a coalition, you limit the power of the entire group. You only have to look at the women's rights movement to see that internal struggle has always been an effective way to weaken the collective and limit its combined influence.

As I write this, the LGBTQIA+ community theoretically shares the same rights as every other citizen in America, its marriage rights are even federally protected by both the 2015 Supreme Court decision in *Obergefell v. Hodges* and President Joe Biden's 2022 Respect for Marriage Act, but now state governments and federal courts are calling those rights into question. Conservative states have also begun to pass an increasing number of "religious liberty" laws allowing businesses to deny services to the LGBTQIA+ community due to its "religious beliefs," as well as limiting access to things like gender-affirming care, passing bathroom laws, and writing what feels like endless legislation targeting transgender youth and, in some states, their parents.

We have to understand that giving the government the authority to limit certain people's rights is a threat to everybody's rights. If you're confused about a certain law, ask yourself, Does this government action *expand* on an established right or freedom, or does it *limit* it? If it's taking freedom away, then you should see it in opposition to the fundamental identity of this country and the foundational rights of our Constitution.

The thing about American freedoms, as they're laid out in the Constitution, is that they aren't based on our personal desires, but established on the rights the Framers believed were bestowed on us by the very nature of our existence. I could argue that the Second Amendment—the right to bear arms—and the Eighteenth Amendment—the Prohibition amendment—were both based on personal desires, which is why neither of them really worked. The Eighteenth Amendment was reversed by the Twenty-first Amendment because it was a poorly thought out change based on a group of individuals' personal "feels" rather than the population's inherent rights, and the Second Amendment, as Warren Burger, former chief justice of the Supreme Court, pointed out, has been deliberately misinterpreted and is "the subject of one of the greatest pieces of fraud," and he repeated fraud, "on the American public by special interest groups that I have ever seen in my lifetime" because it continues to cater to individual desires rather than the collective population's innate rights. How free are we if we can't go to school, a movie theater, a parade, or a concert without worrying about being shot? Easy access to advanced weaponry that allows distressed individuals to mass murder their fellow citizens is not what the Framers had in mind when they wrote, "A well regulated Militia, being necessary to the security of a free State, the right of the people to keep and bear Arms, shall not be infringed," and defending it like it is has arguably made Americans less free, and the rest of the world look at us like we're insane. If you ask me, it's well past time to throw an amendment at that amendment.

★ ★ ★

When we talk about freedom, we have to remember all the things we take for granted. Not just things like freedom of speech, or freedom of the press, or the right to own firearms—which, as mentioned, I believe needs adjusting—but our right to a fair trial, and to vote in free and fair elections. Our daily lives are free because we have the luxury of not living in a war zone. We might disagree with our government's policies, but the system itself, the institution of American government, has our back. I'm talking about the kind of freedom that includes everything from not worrying about taking a painkiller because you know our government has approved what's gone into it, to the government implementing policies to stop food-borne illness or help its citizens survive a pandemic. Our modern society is free from diseases like smallpox and polio because our government paid for safe, healthy vaccines. Which is why the people who undermine these incredibly important programs and advances are doing the country such a disservice. They're literally messing with our collective freedom.

At the end of the day, I consider freedom the "American way," the ideal on which our society was built, and when I think of American freedom, I often consider the series of paintings by American artist Norman Rockwell in 1943 called the *Four Freedoms*, titled individually: *Freedom of Speech*, *Freedom of Worship*, *Freedom from Want*, and *Freedom from Fear*.

If you've never seen these paintings, I highly recommend you look them up. I went to the Rockwell Museum in Upstate New York when I was a kid, and I was so moved by the works I still remember them to this day. In fact, when the *Four Freedoms* toured the country after America joined World War II, they raised more than $130 million in war bonds. People donated a lot of money, right after a depression, to see that reflection of patriotism and American values.

Freedom of Speech shows a man bearing a strong resemblance to a young Abraham Lincoln standing in a local town hall sharing his thoughts. Others from the community look on, some with doubt, some in agreement, but everyone is listening, and the man—who seems not powerful or rich, but an everyman—is safe to speak and use his voice to talk about his government. He is a citizen respected by his country.

Freedom of Worship gives us a close-up of different faces in profile. There are men, women, Black, brown, young, old. Most are praying, but one appears to simply be contemplating. It is a multicultural, religiously diverse image. Of the four paintings, this is the only one with text, and it reads in block letters across the top: "Each according to the dictates of his own conscience." This is the freedom of religion America should stand for. A nation where we are united as one people, free to worship or not worship, as we see fit. If 1943 America got this, I'm not sure how it became complicated in 2024.

Freedom from Want is probably the most well-known of the four pieces. Even if you're not familiar with Norman Rockwell, there's a solid chance you've seen this image. It's a painting of a classic American Thanksgiving. It's framed almost like a close-up photograph with someone looking cheekily at the painter from the bottom right-hand corner of the canvas. It's a natural and authentic image, but the purpose of the painting is to show plenty. Well, maybe not plenty, but enough. The room isn't fancy, but the table is nicely set. The clothes are dressy, but not formal. It's an image of joy, of family, of togetherness and connection. A full table that will soon provide full bellies. These are people whose needs are met so they have the freedom to focus on each other.

I feel like this particular painting is a solid analogy of what we should all be striving for in America. Salaries that are respectful enough that we can feed and clothe our families. Housing that's affordable enough to give our people a place to live. American citizens should expect to be clean, happy, healthy people. Yes, it's a particularly white painting, both metaphorically and literally—I remember reading that Rockwell had used something like seventy shades of white for this image—not just for the people at the table, but the ice water in the clear glass on the white linen tablecloth—but, taken metaphorically, this is the kind of freedom we should all be fighting for. Freedom *from* want. We shouldn't need to hug a flag or wear stars and stripes to prove we love this country. We should be fighting for the kind of life this country stands for and continuing to work for everyone's best shot at that kind of happiness.

Freedom from Fear is the last painting in the series and perhaps the timeliest because I don't believe people feel safe in America anymore. Fear and anger seem to have become our default, and those kinds of emotions strip us of our freedom. *Freedom from Fear* was created during the heart of World War II, the biggest war the world had ever seen. The image is of two children sleeping peacefully in their bed while their mother tucks them in and their father looks on. The father is holding a newspaper with a terrifying headline about the war overseas, but the painting is one of security. That is how American citizens should feel in this country. That things can be chaotic, and the world can rage, but we are safe here at home. Americans should be free to put their heads down at night knowing responsible people are looking out for us. We should seek a government that cares for us like the parents in this painting—solid, calm, trustworthy—understanding of the trials of the world, but protective of the people in their charge. A government who provides its people a safe place to build a life of worth and dignity. Leadership that believes we all deserve to live without fear, or persecution, or want.

This is the kind of freedom all Americans should be demanding.

★ ★ ★

The Framers might have been men of the past and products of their time, but they had vision. They knew things would change and we should change with them. As I said, there are only seven articles in the Constitution, and one is completely devoted to amending it. The supreme law of the land was designed to grow as our country did. To literally be, as people like to call it, "a living document."

Thomas Jefferson once proposed revising the Constitution every nineteen years to write a new one. He wrote:

> *I am not an advocate for frequent changes in laws and constitutions, but laws and institutions must go hand in hand with the progress of the human mind. As that becomes more developed, more enlightened, as new discoveries are made . . . and manners and opinions change . . . institutions must advance also to keep pace with the times. We might as well require a man to wear still the coat which fitted him when a boy as a civilized society to remain ever under the regimen of their barbarous ancestors.*

Consider that the men who wrote the Constitution didn't know about airplanes, let alone nuclear weapons, computers, or AI, but they created a system that would allow for future generations to update our rights as need be. The Constitution isn't locked, it's simply the framework we were given on which to build a nation. The Founders made compromises from the beginning to get the Union together, but they punted the ball of "liberty and justice for all" to a later date. Throughout history, each generation has picked up that ball and run with it. Which is why modern Americans should hesitate when someone, particularly a Supreme Court justice whose job it is to interpret the Constitution, calls themselves a "textualist" or an "originalist" and attempts to gaslight us into thinking we're supposed to be living under the scope of the law as it was written in the late 1700s, because (a) the Constitution was already a compromise, and (b) the men who wrote it were very clear that things should change.

Which is also why we should be concerned that we haven't had a new constitutional amendment since 1971. Sure, we got the Twenty-seventh Amendment in 1992, but it was really an amendment from 1789 about congressional pay raises, so it had nothing to do with what we'd learned as a country or evolving with the times. The last amendment that really mattered was ratified in 1971 when Congress passed the Twenty-sixth Amendment to lower the voting age from twenty-one to eighteen. Most people think the move to make this change started during the Vietnam War when "Old enough to fight, old enough to vote" was used in every youth/antiwar movement across the country, but the amendment was actually introduced during World War II, after the government lowered the draft age from twenty-one to eighteen. Jennings Randolph, a Democrat from West Virginia, introduced the amendment eleven times between 1942 and 1971, never changing any of the wording but always speaking of the great faith he had in the young, because they possessed "a great social conscience" and were "perplexed by the injustices in the world and anxious to rectify those ills."

This is exactly what Jefferson was talking about when he proposed updating the Constitution every two decades. The goal was to honor the people who came *after*, those who would live in a different world, with different needs, and require different rules. If we were supposed to be living under the same rules of 1776, slavery would still be legal and women wouldn't have the vote, and while I recognize that idea would thrill some people, it's not at all in line with what the Founders imagined, nor is it in line with what the majority of 336 million Americans would want.

Freedoms are only as strong as the society in which they are placed. America started with freedoms for few, and moved to freedom for some, but the closer we got to freedom for *all* the less we progressed. We allowed ourselves to stagnate, we stopped evolving, and now, if certain people get their way, we'll begin to move backward. As Jefferson said, it's as if we're being jammed back into clothes that no longer fit us, and that type of constriction is a prison that has no place in a land of freedom. We evolve or we die.

★ ★ ★

EVERYONE SHOULD HAVE THE OPPORTUNITY TO RISE

The concept of the American Dream is still one of the most uniquely American ideals. The United States has always sold itself as the land of opportunity. A country where anyone from anywhere could make it if they just worked hard enough. That the only things holding us back were our own will and lack of tenacity. We're all supposed to have the opportunity to be Thomas Edisons in the making. Where you can start poor but you don't have to stay that way. That if you bring your gifts and your grit, you too can change the world. As Edison himself said, "Opportunity is missed by most people because it is dressed in overalls and looks like work."

It's not that Edison was wrong. If you want to make it in this world, hard work is essential. If you also happen to be exceptionally talented? Even better. Beyoncé Knowles and her mother, Tina, are the American Dream. Taylor Swift is the American Dream. Steve Jobs, Viola Davis, Barack and Michelle Obama are the American Dream. It doesn't matter who you are or where you started,

America is supposed to be a country of upward mobility, freedom, and equality. We don't have a formal caste system like India, or an established class system like Great Britain. In America, where you were born in the pecking order isn't *supposed* to determine your destiny.

And yet it often does, doesn't it? The truth of the matter is the American Dream has become a fantasy for most of us. Many people are barely getting by. The majority are struggling to make ends meet. Life, liberty, and the pursuit of happiness? That's not the reality for most Americans, certainly not for most Americans under fifty. It's more like we've been set up to pay bills until we die. Or sometimes, die because we can't pay bills.

Forget our "unalienable right to life"; in America you get the life you can afford. This is the dark side of capitalism and the unfortunate reality of a for-profit healthcare system. The cold, hard truth is that our system is broken, or more specifically, it's broken for regular Americans (the system is working beautifully for the ultra-rich and corporations). I was at a drugstore recently and the line to see the pharmacist was about ten people. As I waited in line, I looked around. Half the shelves were understocked. There weren't enough employees. The paint was peeling off the walls and the carpet had water stains. This was a major store in a major city center, and all I could think was, *These companies make billions of dollars a year. Where is the money going?* Looking at the bare shelves and the number of people in front of me, it certainly wasn't going to the customer experience, the store, or the employees. Look, if you build a successful company in America, you should reap the rewards, but looking around this pharmacy, I wasn't seeing success, just profit. The money being made was clearly not going back into the business, it was going to the shareholders, the CEO, and the people who get bonuses no matter what product they bring to market. In today's America, a "successful business" is measured by profit, and when you're in the business of keeping people healthy or alive, that becomes a pretty troubling trade-off.

As I waited, I listened to people negotiating the price of their drugs. "I brought a coupon," "I'm on a grant program," "Last month it didn't cost this much," and I thought, *What are we doing here, America?* Most of these drugs are pennies on the dollar in other countries. The same drugs that cost Europeans two dollars, Americans are paying two hundred for, and European governments are paying for health care. Meanwhile American citizens are being nickel-and-dimed just to stay alive while the companies rake it in.

We're not taking care of our people in America. Some days I'm not even sure we're considering them. Government-funded or "universal" healthcare systems are in over seventy countries around the world and offer health care to more than 90 percent of their citizens. Along with providing health care, universal healthcare systems are also government regulated, which ensures the care is high-quality and affordable so as not to inflict financial hardships on its citizens. In most cases healthcare through universal programs is free, or very low cost, regardless of the patient's income.

Now, every country implements their universal healthcare system differently. The UK has completely free health care provided through public facilities owned by the government. Germany has a government fund that pays for coverage for private doctors and hospitals. Lots of countries have a blended public/private system to maximize both access and what the system can do. South Korea, whose healthcare system is often considered one of the best in the developed world, has universal health care that covers up to 60 percent of all medical expenses, and South Koreans supplement this with private insurance to cover the remaining costs. Brazil provides free health care to everyone—from citizens to tourists to refugees. All the major Western nations have some form of universal health care—Australia, Germany, France, Canada, New Zealand, Italy, Spain, and the UK—but it's also in Romania, Russia, Kuwait, Costa Rica, Albania, Algeria, the Czech Republic, Cuba, and the Seychelles—yet it somehow remains off the table in the United States. Why? Short answer: profit and racism.

According to the 1619 Project, when President Truman asked Congress to expand America's hospitals as part of a larger health-care plan in 1945, the Southern segregationists—voting as a bloc—only agreed to vote for the expansion if the act gave the states control of the funds and allowed the states to segregate the resulting facilities created by those funds. So, the federal government paid to build new hospitals, but certain states made sure those hospitals weren't for everybody. Black doctors were already barred from joining the American Medical Association, most medical schools excluded Black students, most hospitals and health clinics segregated Black patients, and now America had a new federal healthcare policy designed to exclude Black Americans.

In response to being left out, Black communities did what they've been doing since America's inception and created their own systems to fill in the blanks: Building national community healthcare movements and raising funds for Black health facilities. Educating their communities on things like nutrition, sanitation, and disease prevention. Since they weren't allowed membership in the AMA, Black doctors and nurses established their own professional institution called the National Medical Association, which by the 1950s started pushing for a federal healthcare system for all Americans.

According to the 1619 Project, this fight for national health care put the Black-run National Medical Association in direct conflict with the white-run American Medical Association, which opposed any nationalized health plan and had previously defeated two national healthcare proposals in the 1930s and '40s, calling them "socialist and un-American" and warning people about "government intervention in the doctor-patient relationship." The AMA would use all the same smears in the mid-1960s when Medicare was introduced, and the National Medical Association would counter those smears with the idea that health care was a basic human right.

So, America never passed a universal healthcare bill or acknowledged, as our peer nations did, that health care was a basic human right, because there were people in our government who simply couldn't get their heads around giving health care to everyone because that "everyone" would include Black people. In fact, when you look at it, it's amazing how many things we don't have in this country because some white lawmaker, or donor, didn't want Black people to have it. When people say racism hurts us all, this is what they're talking about.

Today, health care has become such a profitable industry that big corporations and donors don't want universal health care because it would eat into their profits. There are absolutely ways to do universal health care in this country, but it'll take the collective will of the people to demand it, and the right set of lawmakers to make it happen. Historically, even when we try to do the right thing in this country, we can always count on someone to do the opposite. While the Affordable Care Act has brought health insurance to nearly twenty million previously uninsured Americans since 2010, ensuring many more couldn't be thrown off their health insurance based on preexisting conditions or age, and prohibiting lifetime caps that punished people who got sick young or had complicated, expensive diseases, several states (most of them part of the former Confederacy) have refused to participate whenever they can. These are the states that rejected the federal money from the ACA Medicaid expansion, or attempted to tie access to the program to work requirements that were extremely difficult to meet, especially if you were sick or disabled, and the results of these actions have been striking. According to the National Bureau of Economic Research, states that took the federal dollars and expanded Medicaid with the ACA saw an exponential drop in disease-related deaths, while the states that didn't take the money now sit at the bottom of the country's health expectancy.

I believe at this point in our country's history you could make a strong argument that many states have lost the privilege to care for their citizens using "states' rights," since time and again they've failed to do so. We clearly require a federal universal healthcare program that, if we were being smart, would take the best of all the working programs around the world and implement them for ourselves. It's not like America has to start from scratch. There are seventy-plus options to choose from, and many of them include a private insurance industry, so we wouldn't have to destroy anyone's capitalistic dreams. The Affordable Care Act has already given the states the discretion to build their own programs off its basic structure. States are allowed to create programs that lower premiums, offer subsidies, and reduce the cost of coverage. A few states even offer plans to compete with private companies. Today there are ten states that have an uninsured rate below 5 percent. That's not quite universal coverage, but it's close. Canada has universal health care, but if you want to see a doctor faster or get more personalized service you can pay extra, which is very similar to what we do in America with public vs. private education. The point is there are options for this country that we really should insist on if we truly want the opportunity to rise. Some states are making moves to care for the health of their citizens, while others are doing the opposite, and if you happen to live in a state that keeps rejecting federal help for health insurance, you need to ask why, because the answer is often the same as it was in the past. They'd rather no one have health care than *those people* have health care.

The whole thing is a reminder that Americans have to pay attention not just to what's happening in the federal government but also to what's happening at the state level. Members of the federal government fought hard for the Affordable Care Act under President Obama, to make it illegal to deny people insurance for things beyond their control or because they were hospitalized longer than insurance companies wanted to pay. They worked hard under President Biden to negotiate lower drug prices for seniors, and to change the law so you couldn't be forced into bankruptcy for medical debt. We complain that "all politicians are the same," but frankly that's just not true, and that kind of blanket statement leaves no room for nuance and only serves to let them *all* off the hook. If no one expects *anything* from politicians, then politicians don't have to *do* anything, and we need them doing things.

To be clear, the states denying Medicaid expansion and federal money for ACA programs are the same states denying abortions and attempting to get rid of contraception. Health care is just another way to control people. It's hard to start your own business if you can't leave your job because that's where you get your health insurance. You're stuck with an abusive spouse if you're sick and depend on their health insurance to keep you alive. Being unable to plan when you expand your family, that limits your opportunities. Frankly, we're holding the American people back with one solvable problem. Trapping our citizens by limiting their healthcare choices is antithetical to the American Dream. It's hardly a meritocracy if every time you try to rise, your need for health care grabs you by the ankle and pulls you back down.

This idea of being in charge of your own destiny—of your path not being set—is supposed to be a fundamental American principle, and yet it often feels as if we're given the illusion of choice, but within a structure where we actually have very little control. Think about education. We're told an education is the first step to a successful life. But what if you miss that first step? What if you can't afford it? What if that step was deliberately kept from you? Like the school in your neigborhood was underfunded. Do you lose your opportunity to rise? Yes, often you do, and that's by design.

There's a reason groups like the Taliban and the Iranian government withhold education from those they want to keep down. There's a reason children in Africa have been known to walk ten miles to school each day, or people who can afford it pay extraordinary amounts for private education. It's because education matters. Education has always been a game changer, an equalizer, a springboard to opportunity. Education opens doors that would otherwise be closed. There has always been a direct correlation between education and wealth in the United States. In the early days, even basic education was reserved for the children of the rich, and college was basically a finishing school for the American elite. Over time, our culture changed and education became something that was recommended, and eventually required, for all American children. But, since knowledge is power, education continues to remain a source of controversy. A struggle between progressive and conservative values. Do we really want an educated populace, or is it better if just some of the population is educated?

Education inspires curiosity and critical thinking. It expands opportunity and choice, but it's also been known to lead to the questioning of authority. Once you understand how something works, it's far easier to take it apart or build something new. Having your population thinking about how something *could* be doesn't always appeal to the people in charge of how things already are.

Most of the big changes that happened in the history of our country's education were caused by federal laws—laws that forced the game to change using the Supremacy Clause, meaning that federal law superseded the state law. Knowing the country's history, it's probably not surprising to hear that Massachusetts was the first state in the nation to make school mandatory in 1852, followed by New York. The South didn't have widespread public school for anyone until after the Civil War, with Mississippi being the last state in the Union to adopt mandatory education in 1918. (That sixty-six-year head start is one of the reasons Massachusetts has the best public schools in the nation today, and Mississippi is consistently in the bottom five, but it's also about the prioritization of education and the prioritization of who gets that education.)

In the years following the Civil War, Black Americans rightfully wanted to be included in public education. They saw white children going to school and wanted the same opportunity for their children, but when they asked to be included, the Supreme Court chose instead to uphold segregation in a case called *Plessy v. Ferguson* (1896). The *Plessy* ruling was actually about segregation in public transportation, but the decision ended up affecting everything from trains to public schools when the American ideal of "all men are created equal" was interpreted by the courts into what would become "separate but equal." After this ruling, racial segregation would go on to affect everything from housing to restaurants, bathrooms to water fountains. Classrooms were now segregated by law, instead of just by custom. For historical clarity, while segregation wasn't mandated in the North the same way it was in the Jim Crow South, Northern states were far from perfect and had their own forms of state-sponsored segregation. Racism was alive and well in Northern states based on your neighborhood, personal biases, and financial disparities. So, although the North didn't have formal segregation like the South, it doesn't get a free pass for being "antiracist."

Segregation and racism separated Black and white Americans in elementary and high schools until a lawyer named Thurgood Marshall, the man who would go on to become our first Black Supreme Court justice, argued the *Brown v. Board of Education* case in 1954. Marshall's argument was that racially segregated public schools violated the Equal Protection Clause of the Fourteenth

Amendment ratified after the Civil War. The court unanimously agreed, overturning *Plessy v. Ferguson*, and ruling against "separate but equal" because "*separate* was inherently *unequal*." The *Brown* decision would go on to lay the groundwork for integration across the country, the civil rights movement, and of course, giant blowback from people who felt giving people rights they already had was, in some way, unfair to them.

Segregation wasn't just for younger students; it also played a huge part in higher education. Free compulsory education in America only applied to primary and secondary students. Until the mid-1900s, college had been something reserved for wealthy people with time on their hands. George Washington didn't go to college; neither did Andrew Jackson, or Grover Cleveland, or Harry Truman. Abraham Lincoln was famously self-taught. This is to say, college wasn't always the precursor to success that it's been made out to be today. However, at the end of World War II the federal government passed the Servicemen's Readjustment Act of 1944, more commonly known as the G.I. Bill, offering millions of returning servicemen federal aid to purchase homes and businesses but also to pursue a higher education instead of simply entering the workforce, and college enrollment took off. In 1947, at peak enrollment, veterans made up 49 percent of college admissions, and by the time the G.I. Bill ended in 1956, 7.8 million World War II veterans—nearly half of the 16 million men who had served—had participated in government-funded free education or vocational training, and the percentage of Americans with bachelor's or advanced degrees went from 4.6 percent to 25 percent.

To this day, many people join the military because it still

pays for your education. There are lots of people with limited opportunities or means who willingly put their life on the line to pay for the very thing they think will get them a better life. However, while the G.I. Bill might have been written in race-neutral language, most universities at the time were not race-neutral. So, it didn't matter that the federal government would have paid tuition for Black veterans, Black veterans weren't being admitted to colleges that excluded nonwhite students. So while white veterans were getting a higher education and moving up the social ladder, Black veterans were mostly prevented from enjoying the same benefits they'd earned from their service. Millions of people were given unprecedented access to the next rung on the social and financial ladder based on their time in the war, while one group was mostly left out. This had the effect of limiting what careers Black Americans entered, and the amount they could earn in a lifetime, which ultimately had a long-term effect on American society.

The shared responsibility for educating our children is arguably one of the greatest achievements of a successful community. It gives our children a safe place to go during the day. It allows parents the time to work. It teaches a common set of facts and knowledge to the population so individuals can best interact with one another and the world around them, and ultimately it creates an educated workforce with the potential for upward mobility. I often think of the author John Green's statement about government-funded education where he said,

Public education does not exist for the benefit of students or the benefit of their parents. It exists for the benefit of the social

order. We have discovered as a species that it's useful to have an educated population. Which is why I like to pay taxes for schools, even though I don't personally have a kid in school: It's because I don't like living in a country with a bunch of stupid people.

There are some, however, who see this kind of democratized upward mobility as a financial burden, and it's typically the very wealthiest. Lower taxes and complacent workers are their priorities, and getting rid of public school would accomplish both. In fact, a large amount of the financial backing for the current "school choice" groups we're seeing around America, and the lobbying behind alternatives to public schools like voucher programs and charter schools, comes from the very people who don't personally use the public school system. Who can afford to have their children educated in the very best private schools and aren't interested in the shared community responsibility of quality public education. Over the last century, America's free public school system has created one of the most widely educated populations in the history of the modern world, yet there's an entire collection of powerful people who believe the federal government has no business in education.

It's this group, the group who *doesn't* require public school, who are using their money and influence to convince people who *do* require public school that the public education system is broken, corrupt, or "indoctrinating" their children in order to erode it from within. At the state level, we now see people demanding to exert power over education: what can be taught, what can be said, who can use what bathroom or play for what team, even what books can be read. The same parents who champion "school choice" and often believe they're looking out for their children's well-being are often helping sabotage the very system that provides their children the best opportunity to rise.

So when you hear about things like "vouchers" that might help you get into a paid charter or religious school, understand that most of these ideas are directly influenced by the group who would prefer public education not exist. You're not allowed to actively discriminate in public schools, but private, charter, and religious schools don't have those same requirements. It's difficult to get all the things you don't agree with—like say, the existence of gay people, or truthful Black history—out of public school without banging up against federal civil rights. It's far easier to undermine and defund public schools until the people who need them lose faith in the system, at which point you can swoop in and offer an alternative. Not an alternative to everyone mind you, just an alternative to those *you* want to teach, to learn the things *you* want them to know. There is an entire group of powerful Americans funding the conservative right wing who would prefer we return to a time when families were able to choose who their children went to school with, and the school system itself supported the status quo.

Now, once you do get an education, what do you do? You go to work, and what does the American Dream dictate we should do with the money we make from work? We should buy a house. Buying a house is a quintessential part of the American Dream. Which is why it was such a big deal in the 1940s and '50s when the government started subsidizing subdivisions in suburban neighborhoods, to make housing affordable for working-class families. This decision allowed a whole new group of people to get in on the idea of upward mobility. This is also when the American Dream started to be sold as a commodity.

Many Americans, and I should probably specify by saying many *white* Americans, think of the 1950s as a golden age. A time when one man's salary could afford a house, a new car, and a family of four. It was a time when you didn't need a college education to be a provider. It was a boom time for American industry, and the time of the "company man," where someone could work for the same corporation for their entire career and retire with benefits, a pension, and a gold watch. Those opportunities, however, were subsidized by the government with things like housing and affordable home loans.

The Federal Housing Administration subsidized builders to create affordable subdivisions, but Black Americans, if they could afford the house based on their salary, weren't allowed to buy in those neighborhoods. Even if they could find a house in a neighborhood that would take them, they had trouble getting mortgages based on a discriminatory practice called redlining. Redlining has come to mean racial discrimination of any kind in housing, but the phrase comes from government maps drawn during the mid-1930s where public and private housing officials designated certain neighborhoods "high risk," largely due to their racial demographics, and colored those areas in red. Those "red-lined" areas were then denied loans or government backing for loans. The system was set up to reduce lender risk, but in practice it just made it easier to discriminate against people of color and to limit home-buying opportunities and public investment to specific areas. So as the suburbs were built up and sold to white Americans, Black Americans were pushed into urban city centers. Though redlined maps were internal documents and never made public, the result was Black homeowners being left out of government-backed loans and insurance programs.

To add insult to injury, this was also the time the Federal Housing Administration recommended that highways might be a good way to separate African American neighborhoods from white ones. Again, this wasn't a formal law, simply a regulation from a government underwriting manual, but it had the practical effect of forcing even more segregation between Black and white communities. Do you ever wonder why you or your family didn't have more Black/white friends growing up? Why our communities are so segregated? It wasn't just a choice. It was public policy. Not to mention, states fund their public schools with property taxes. The cost of the homes around the schools directly affects the money the school has in its budget. By segregating our neighborhoods, America not only held back an entire racial group's opportunity to build wealth in homes, it gave it less money to run its schools. Which is one of the reasons why affirmative action, the act of actively going out into different communities to find standout students and to improve opportunities for African Americans—and later women, Native Americans, Latinos, and other minorities—was such an important program. The government was attempting to undo some of the damage it had done by offering opportunities to people who it had previously denied.

AMERICA 101: AFFIRMATIVE ACTION

If you've met America, I'm sure it won't surprise you to hear that less than ten years after affirmative action—defined as a set of policies and practices that seeks to benefit marginalized groups—was implemented the courts were hearing their first "reverse discrimination" case arguing that the entire program was unfair to white people. The Supreme Court would go on to hear many of these cases over the years, chipping away at affirmative action, until the current majority-conservative Supreme Court would rule to effectively eliminate the program for higher education in 2023. I should note that the same case that reversed affirmative action to make college acceptance more "fair" did not reverse legacy admissions. If affirmative action took minority status into account to diversify its student body, legacy admission takes the student's family into account, and prioritizes admissions to applicants whose family members have already attended the school. However, when you consider who was historically allowed to go to most of these schools and extrapolate to whom legacy admissions would most likely apply, you can see the Supreme Court's decision didn't really make things more "fair." If we want race-blind decisions in admissions then, to be impartial, we should also have privilege-blind decisions. Hopefully, someone is preparing that case.

By the time the federal government passed the Fair Housing Act in 1968, opening the suburbs to everyone, followed by the

Home Mortgage Disclosure Act of 1975, the damage was already done. The original homes, meant to be affordable to the working class, had now doubled in price. Black working-class families who could have afforded a home at the time they were offered to white families were now locked out of the market. Government policy had deeply limited the ability for certain members of our collective society to rise. African American families couldn't get homes in the suburbs when their white counterparts did, so they never gained the equity appreciation in those homes. While white working-class families were able to use that equity to send their children to college or pass wealth on to their heirs, giving them a leg up to move forward and do the same, those options weren't available to most Black Americans. Which is why today, while Black income is about 60 percent that of white income, Black wealth is still only around 4 percent of the country's total wealth, with white people controlling around 85 percent. That's a tremendous difference and it can be almost entirely attributed to federal policy that was implemented in the twentieth century—federal policy that put Black Americans working toward class mobility at a major disadvantage.

★ ★ ★

Being held back from the upward mobility of buying a home or going to college is something that many modern-day Americans understand, no matter their racial or ethnic background. You see generations before you owning property they could afford on one salary, while younger people drown in debt, and the idea of higher education or home ownership starts to feel further and further out of reach. It's not that people are working less than generations before, in fact statistics show younger generations are often working more hours with more education; it's simply that the housing market and cost of education have gone up so drastically that people can't keep up. Wages certainly haven't kept up. According to the Center for Economic and Policy Research, if the minimum wage rose with productivity growth today's workers would make more than $23 an hour. Currently the federal minimum wage is $7.25. Some cities and states have higher wages, but the federal minimum wage hasn't gone up in fifteen years. Which means American workers are creating more but able to afford less.

AMERICA 101: NATIONAL MINIMUM WAGE

The national minimum wage was established in 1938 and allowed workers at the bottom to share in the overall improvements in society's living standards. Until 1968, not only did the minimum wage keep pace with inflation, making sure minimum-wage earners could buy the same amount of goods and services through time while protecting them from price hikes, it rose with productivity growth, meaning workers who were able to produce more goods and services on average would be able to buy more goods and services through time. The rise in minimum wage was a side effect of the civil rights movement, where industries in general were becoming more fair. Since the late 1960s, however, there has been a downturn in how often the minimum wage has been increased, with proposals to raise it splitting along party lines—Democratic lawmakers argue increases are necessary to support working families, while Republicans argue higher wages affect business growth.

Many Americans today have trouble saving for retirement, go bankrupt paying for health care or trying to improve their opportunities through higher education. We struggle with the rising costs of living and the interest payments on the loans we took out to purchase the things we were told we need. We were taught what the American Dream should be, but America stopped paying people enough to afford it. Prices continued to rise, but the opportunities to keep up did not. We were offered credit to help keep pace (which, if we were using credit, we weren't actually doing), and now we have a huge amount of our population saddled with high-interest debt they can't get out from under. So, while most corporations and industries have done marvelously over the past forty years, regular Americans are often one paycheck away from bankruptcy.

The last time this country had this many people so close to poverty while a small group at the top enjoyed extraordinary wealth was the Gilded Age. From the end of Reconstruction in 1877 to the early 1900s was a time of rapid economic growth in America. Many industrialists in the North had become incredibly rich during the Civil War, and a lot of people in the West were becoming extremely wealthy because of land and gold. Agriculture, which had once dominated the economy—thanks in large part to the free labor of slaves—was now replaced by industry, and more people were moving to the cities. It was a fantastic time to be rich and a terrible time to be poor. The term "Gilded Age" was coined by American author Mark Twain and referred to the glittering surface that was laid on top of the widespread poverty, corruption, and labor exploitation that dominated the period.

Many of the problems America deals with today are rooted

in this time: wealth inequality, the distrust and villainization of immigrants, lack of housing, racism, political corruption, policy choices benefiting a favored group over the collective. Everything old is new again. People often say that America's original sin is slavery, but I've heard it said that America's original sin is greed. Greed for land, greed for money, greed for power. And slavery—and by extension the segregation and policies that followed slavery—was simply a by-product and manifestation of that greed.

The Gilded Age was also a time when many rich industrialists got into politics, and these new wealthy politicians started making decisions in their own best interest. By the 1870s many people in the Republican Party, which controlled the government post–Civil War and had used that power to protect formerly enslaved people with the Reconstruction amendments (Thirteenth, Fourteenth, and Fifteenth) and the Civil Rights Act of 1866, started to feel as if maybe they'd done enough for Black citizens and began to turn their attention away from reforming the Southern states and toward protecting their own wealth. When you hear about how the Republican and Democratic parties flipped ideologies, this is where that transition began.

The Gilded Age is known for being a period of unprecedented technological innovation, mass immigration, gross materialism, and blatant political corruption. The era (again, around 1870 to the early 1900s) was lorded over by a collection of entrepreneurs who were known as either "captains of industry" or "robber barons," depending on who you ask. These men, and they were all men, grew rich through monopolies of steel, oil, and railroads. I'm sure you've heard names like Rockefeller, Carnegie, Vanderbilt, Astor, and Morgan. In the Gilded Age, America moved from being an agrarian society of small producers to an urban society dominated by large corporations, something that still defines our nation to this day. This era birthed our country's obsession with the rich, and the rich's influence in politics.

If the pre–Civil War economy was mostly domestic and self-contained, this new economy, which was dependent on raw materials from other countries and sold goods on the global market, was far more international. Businesses grew exponentially, often consolidating to make monopolies, with an ever-shrinking group at the top succeeding while the rest of the country worked itself to the bone. The nation's biggest sectors at the beginning of the twentieth century were banking, manufacturing, mining, oil, railroads, sugar, steel, tobacco, liquor, textiles, and meatpacking. Thanks to the increasing number of factories and machinery, we could make more things and we could make them faster, and these growing industries required more workers, so this period saw a huge buildup in urban areas.

By 1900, about 40 percent of all Americans lived in cities, but many of them lived in abject squalor because the cities had been unprepared for such fast population growth. In New York nearly two-thirds of the population lived in tenement buildings and worked in unregulated factories or industries. Millions of people died during this time from poverty, accidents, and preventable disease.

Many of the great business tycoons of the Gilded Age became rich making backroom deals using their extensive political connections and used those connections to crush smaller businesses and competitors, or by ignoring the law completely in favor of profit—while paying off the right people to look the other way.

Early shipping tycoons also received huge amounts of money and land from the government to build railroads and ports and then used union busting, fraud, and violence to make sure they always got the best deal, with limited competition. It feels strikingly similar to today, with people like Elon Musk getting rich off government contracts for SpaceX or Tesla and then turning around to union bust his factories or advocate for top-down authoritarianism on Twitter (now X), the influential public square that his vast connections allowed him to buy.

The wealthy of the Gilded Age considered themselves American royalty and built themselves palaces to prove it: Biltmore in North Carolina; the Breakers, Rosecliff, and Belcourt Castle in Rhode Island; Whitehall in Florida; and Hempstead House in New York were all at one point private homes. There were a handful of ultra-rich who did try to do better by society than their peers. Men who still dominated their industries and squashed their competition, but also attempted to improve the lives of their employees, donated millions to charities and nonprofits, and built everything from libraries and hospitals to universities and public parks. These were men like Andrew Carnegie and Henry Frick, who probably deserve the "captain of industry" moniker far more than the others whose names still grace so much of our great nation.

Wealth inequality and the exploitation of workers became such a problem in the Gilded Age that something had to give. Although unions had existed for almost a hundred years, they really gained momentum during the Gilded Age as the number of dissatisfied workers grew. Starting with massive railroad strikes in the late 1870s, workers used strikes and boycotts to fight for higher wages and improved working conditions, while their bosses staged lockouts, wrote blacklists, and sent in replacement workers known to this day as scabs. The workers didn't always get what they wanted, but they learned, as did the owners, that there was strength in numbers and that organized labor had the potential to inflict major economic and political damage if used correctly.

The working class understood that no one would listen to them unless they banded together, but they often struggled to unify because of conflicts within their own groups. Immigration in America had drastically shifted during this time, and the majority of immigrants, who used to come from Britain, Canada, Germany, Ireland, and Scandinavia, were now coming from Hungary, Italy, Poland, and Russia. This altered the ethnic and religious population of the country, with the newcomers mostly being Catholic or Jewish, and most of them settling in the cities. This caused a lot of anti-immigration blowback and fights among the working class. Everyone wanted increased wages and better working conditions, but many were fixated on keeping women, immigrants, and Black people out of the workforce, so their messages became diluted. It's almost as if it doesn't matter what generation we're in, there's always going to be people from the old group telling people from the new group they don't belong while the rich exploit us and we fight among ourselves. This is one of the reasons the ultrarich love culture wars to this day. If we're busy fighting each other, we can't get it together to fight them.

While the unions were doing what they could to fight for workers' rights, the government of the time was so removed from the general public that they had very little idea what was really going on in their ever-expanding country.

AMERICA 101: WESTERN EXPANSION

The end of the nineteenth century was also the period when the western part of the country was truly settled. The discovery of gold, silver, and other precious minerals had prospectors and miners moving to places like California, Nevada, Colorado, Idaho, Montana, and South Dakota since the 1840s, but when the Transcontinental Railroad was completed in 1869, it was suddenly easier to transport people and goods over long distances, which led to the rapid settlement of the western United States. Between 1865 and 1890, Americans settled 430 million acres of the West, much to the devastation of the native population, which kept getting moved into smaller and smaller reservations to make room for the settlers. By 1893, the Census Bureau claimed the entire western frontier was now occupied.

Much of the increased awareness of the class divide of the Gilded Age can be credited to the press. Newspapers and magazines were mass produced by this point, and investigative journalism was born. In 1890 a reporter and photographer named Jacob Riis captured the disgusting and dangerous conditions of the tenements in New York in a book called *How the Other Half Lives*. The photographs and descriptions were so horrifying to people that they inspired New York politicians to pass legislation to improve housing conditions. In St. Louis in 1902 the journalist Lincoln Steffens published an article exposing how city officials were making deals with corrupt businessmen to maintain power and, as previously mentioned, Ida Tarbell published her nineteen-part series on the rise of Rockefeller, which eventually led to the breakup of his oil monopoly. In 1906 an exposé on the mistreatment of workers in the meatpacking industry was read by President Theodore Roosevelt, who was so shocked that he ordered an inspection of the entire industry that resulted in the Pure Food and Drug Act and the Meat Inspection Act of 1906.

Despite the mass corruption and the "you scratch my back, I'll scratch yours" mentality that dominated this period in American history, there were still members of the government pushing for reform. The Pendleton Civil Service Act of 1883 required government jobs be awarded to individuals based on merit and not political affiliation. From that point forward government employees would be chosen through competitive exams, not just nepotism. The Pendleton Act made it illegal to fire or demote government workers solely for political reasons. The Interstate Commerce Act of 1887 tried to end discrimination by railroad monopolies against smaller shippers. The act wasn't particularly effective, but it did lead to our first antitrust legislation, the Sherman Antitrust Act of 1890, which outlawed business monopolies. This act would be further expanded in 1914 with the Federal Trade Commission Act, which created the FTC to regulate business and ban "unfair methods of competition" and "deceptive acts or practices," and the Clayton Act, which expanded on the Sherman Act to include company mergers and acquisitions that may "substantially lessen competition" or end up with the same person being on the board of directors for competing companies. These are the laws the Reagan administration would go on to roll back in the 1980s, causing the reconsolidation of industries, an increased lack of competition, and the "greedflation" that defines modern-day America—where corporations just keep raising prices because they know we have nowhere else to go. So, we fixed it, then we broke it, and we need to fix it again.

AMERICA 101: REAGANOMICS

Under Ronald Reagan America was able to successfully compete and thrive in the global market, but we did so at the expense of the poor and middle class, and the American worker and consumer are paying for it now. Reagan's whole concept of "trickle-down economics," this idea that money given to the wealthy through tax cuts and market deregulation would eventually make its way down to the worker, has been completely debunked as of 2023. We were told that the economy would be like a tower of champagne glasses, where you pour champagne into the top glass and all the glasses underneath end up getting filled, when in reality, trickle-down economics was more like the top glass just kept getting bigger in order to take in more champagne, while the glasses underneath were left practically empty and cracking under the weight.

Since Reagan's presidency, the wealth gap between rich and poor has grown exponentially. Reagan often made speeches about how his policies were helping everyone rise, when in fact they were doing the opposite. From 1980 to 2016, income inequality in the United States rose by at least 20 percent, leaving us with the highest wealth gap of all the

G7 nations. This wealth disparity was only compounded by the pandemic, during which the ten richest men in the world doubled their fortunes while the incomes of 99 percent of the world's population fell. In the first two years of the pandemic 160 million people were forced into poverty, while ten people went from having $700 billion to $1.5 trillion.

According to OxFam International, "Extreme inequality is a form of economic violence, where policies and political decisions that perpetuate the wealth and power of a privileged few result in direct harm to the vast majority of ordinary people across the world and to the planet itself." I should note that the US and China—the world's two largest economies—are starting to consider policies that would reduce wealth inequality, including raising tax rates on the ultra-rich and passing laws against corporate monopolies, which could provide us with some hope, but realistically, only one of America's political parties is interested in such change. The other party, the party whose policies launched us down this path in the first place, is doubling down on tax cuts for the wealthy while planning to cut social programs for everyone else. That's not a partisan statement. It's just facts. Unless you are wildly wealthy or own a giant corporation, you're not getting a great deal in America right now. And, to be clear, the trickle-down system doesn't serve you even if you're sitting pretty in the glass at the top. At this rate, the society holding you up is going to collapse. A practical person would realize their best chance to stay on top would be to stabilize and strengthen the base below . . .

A lot of people imagine the "Great" in "Make America Great Again" refers to the Golden Age of the 1950s: the white-picket-fence lifestyle and the collective desire to return to a time where you knew your neighbors, they looked like you, and one salary could pay for everything. This is certainly what most voters think of when they talk about making America great again. What we need to understand is the people paying for the MAGA movement, and the political leaders beholden to them, aren't thinking of the Golden Age, they're thinking of the Gilded Age, and you only have to look around at the increasing wealth gap, the growing monopolies, the price gouging, the housing crisis, the increased child labor, the decreased regulations, and the disrupted unions to see the plan for what it is, and how few of us it will actually serve. It's why the ultra-rich continue to buy politicians and gobble up media companies, so there's no one left to call them out, or change the laws to stop them.

The American Dream has always been about the prospect of success, but it didn't always mean what it does now. The original American Dream wasn't about individual wealth. In fact, the entire concept of the American Dream was born in reaction to the Gilded Age. There was this sense that power acquired through wealth was fundamentally un-American because it was democratically and inherently unequal. We built the country in opposition to hereditary monarchy, why would we build a new aristocracy?

We could ask ourselves the same question today. As I said, corporate consolidation really started happening again in the mid-1980s when the US government almost abandoned antitrust enforcement. Now, two-thirds of American industries are concentrated in the hands of an increasingly smaller group, which gives them insane market power. Banks, broadband, pharmaceutical companies, airlines, Big Tech, consumer staples: the concentration of power in these industries means they don't really have to compete, and they can pass any cost increases on to their consumers and continue to post incredible profits. To be clear, what's happening in modern-day America isn't just *good* profits, it's *record-breaking* profits. In fact, corporate profits are the highest they've been in more than seventy years.

Now we have politicians telling us America can't afford to keep up with our social programs or fund the IRS because of our debt, when the signature piece of legislation from the Trump administration, the tax cut for the ultra-rich, added trillions of dollars to it. They argue we have to cut programs for the poor, eliminate Social Security, and phase out Medicare, when in truth we could afford all those things, they just don't want their donors to pay a cent more in taxes. The reality is, they don't *want* the IRS funded because then the IRS could do its job and go after the wealthiest tax cheats in America, the majority of whom also happen to fund their campaigns. We're at a place in this country where such a small group of people own such a large amount of the wealth and industry that experts are now referring to it as the "New Gilded Age."

It's time for a reset. We need to look at the economy and the nation as something that can be fixed. We know there are solutions if we put the right people in place to make them. Our country has been in this terrible position before, but we chose a government able to lead with courage and vision and we turned things around. We simply have to do that again.

When the stock market crashed in October 1929, launching the country into the Great Depression, it ended an era of great, if unbalanced, prosperity in America. Historians and economists don't entirely agree on the explanations for the crisis—some blame wealth inequality and unregulated and uninsured banks, others blame the country's agricultural slump as people moved from rural areas to cities, and some credit the international instability from the fallout of World War I. Whatever the causes, the Great Depression was the catalyst for a massive political shift in America. Herbert Hoover was the Republican president at the time, and despite the fact that he tried a number of different ideas to stimulate the economy, the impression was he wasn't going to use the government to intervene and help people, so the public blamed him for the Depression. This left a giant opening for the Democrats (now the party of the working class) to walk right through. Franklin Delano Roosevelt campaigned for president on the promise of government intervention for the prosperity of the American people and, in doing so, won the 1932 election in a landslide.

From the jump, Republicans opposed everything about FDR's plans. They didn't like his social programs, his "New Deal" politics, or the expansion of the federal government that would be necessary to accomplish all that was planned. In direct contradiction to the Gilded Age's philosophy of hands-off capitalism, the New Deal embraced the idea of a government-regulated economy, and suddenly the Republicans were the party talking about states' rights. "You can do your *help the people* thing in Washington, but that's not how it's going to work down here." Black and brown workers ended up excluded from programs like Social Security, unemployment, and protections afforded under the National Labor Relations Act, as agricultural workers and domestic servants were often excluded, and those were jobs most often occupied by Black Americans. According to *Social Science History*, "The most prominent explanation for these exclusions is they originated in a Southern-dominated congress and were deliberately designed to exclude a majority of African-American workers from the emerging welfare state."

The American people were suffering miserably under the tragedy of the Great Depression, and if you don't think government can be a force for good, then you don't know FDR's New Deal. In the first three months Roosevelt was in office, a period that has since become known as the Hundred Days—the benchmark against which all future presidents would be measured—FDR's administration put 8.5 million people to work, started construction projects on "more than 650,000 miles of roads, 125,000 public buildings, 75,000 bridges, and 8,000 parks." It also offered emergency and short-term government assistance and put the youth of America to work in our national forests.

The New Deal also created the Federal Deposit Insurance Corporation (FDIC), which offered government-backed insurance for deposits made in member banks, so that the disastrous bank runs that happened from 1929 to 1933 could never happen again. The administration created the Securities and Exchange Commission (SEC) to regulate the type of behavior that led to the stock market crash in the first place and to restore investor confidence, and they passed the Agricultural Adjustment Act, a program to help farmers raise prices by offering cash subsidies.

FDR's policies were wildly successful, and he followed his first term with a second where he implemented even more elements to stabilize and rebuild the country. The New Deal changed governing practices for how business worked, who they could hire (not children), what hours they could work (a standard eight-hour workday, then you'd be paid overtime), how much they should be paid (the federal minimum wage). It supported unions and created the National Labor Relations Board (NLRB) to have the federal government back collective bargaining. It also enacted Social Security, where employer and employee contributions funded the provisions for old age and widow benefits, and it created unemployment insurance.

So many things modern-day Americans accept as normal were created between 1933 and 1939. It was an inspirational administration, and a testament to the power of government to make positive change should it have the vision to do so, and a Congress that won't hold them back. This doesn't mean there weren't checks or balances on FDR. He overstepped the mark when he tried to expand the Supreme Court and increase the number of justices (which people thought he was doing to stack the courts to back up the New Deal) and Congress shut him down. It tarnished his reputation but didn't affect his legislation or legacy. In fact, FDR won four terms as president, seeing America through the Depression and World War II, dying in office in the first year of his fourth term when he would be replaced by his vice president, Harry Truman, who would continue his work after the war with the Fair Deal, which included advocating for the program that would eventually become Medicare.

FDR's years in office were an unmitigated success for the American people, but it was also the time that branded the

Democrats as "socialists" and the Republicans as the party of fiscal conservatism, small government, and states' rights. In fact, we only have the Twenty-second Amendment because of FDR. He was far too successful in making progressive change for conservative activists. They hated that he was able to steer the country in one direction for so long after winning four presidential elections in a row, so in 1951 after years of work, America ratified the Twenty-second Amendment limiting presidential terms to two.

Since this period, the Republican Party has opposed almost every social program Democrats have ever suggested by painting them as socialist and fighting them in court. However, we need to be clear that social programs, and a social safety net, are light-years away from "socialism." As Thomas Alan Schwartz, a Vanderbilt University history and political science professor, defines it, socialism is a "political system in which the state is in charge of the economy and provides not only social welfare services such as health care, but where all sorts of other things, including the large sections of the private economy, are in state control." There is not now, nor has there ever been, a Democrat who has ever proposed a government-controlled private sector.

Yes, Democrats believe the federal government should be more involved in regulating the economy through legislation, but that's more in line with "responsible capitalism" than "socialism." Republicans keep fighting for less regulation on everything from corporate profits to environmental protections, from how you treat your workers to the age those workers can be, but that's how we end up with toxic waste dumped in our cities' drinking water, credit card companies charging consumers secret interest rates, and the big banks failing in 2008. Unregulated capitalism only serves a select group at the top and the politicians they pay to do their bidding.

While left-wing darlings like Senator Bernie Sanders and representatives like Alexandria Ocasio-Cortez might identify as "democratic socialists," their ideas more align with the Scandinavian countries like Denmark and Sweden, which are not socialist but where universal health care, paid family leave, free college, and a wide range of social benefits are the norm. Yes, those countries pay higher taxes for those benefits, but capitalism is still the prevailing economic system, and democratic socialists would argue, the quality of life in those countries is rated far higher than the quality of life in America. As Jon Stewart said, "We're not going bankrupt in this country because of our taxes. We're going bankrupt because of all the things we pay for out of pocket that other countries pay for with taxes." Contrast the democratic socialism of the Scandinavian countries with those of actual socialist countries like Venezuela, where the state does control all major industries and authoritarians are in charge, and you see a vast difference between the two.

The renegotiated "Green New Deal" proposal that was part of President Biden's 2020 platform was actually a compromise between the different factions of the Democratic Party to address the existential crisis of climate change while creating new jobs in the private sector for working Americans—this is pragmatism, not socialism. President Biden argued America could lead the world in innovation and manufacturing at the same time it helped the planet. As of this writing, nothing close to the Green New Deal has passed. The best the country can hope for—without filibuster-proof numbers in the Senate and the Republican Party still claiming that the 97 percent of actively publishing climate scientists are wrong—is the environmental protections Democrats were able to include in the 2022 Inflation Reduction Act, which was the most progress we've ever made on climate legislation, and still nowhere near where we need to go.

We have to believe that this country can set itself on a new path, and we must understand a new path is nonnegotiable if we want to continue to live in a functioning nation with upward mobility on a sustainable planet. If everyone is supposed to have the opportunity to rise in America, then why are so many of us unable to do so, and what can the government, which is supposed to be responsible for the collective good of its people, do about it?

★ ★ ★

To find our way out of this New Gilded Age, we need to break up these giant monopolies and oligopolies that we've allowed to run our society and encourage far more corporate competition. We need to fund the IRS and get the missing tax revenue that the richest fail to pay every year. If we really wanted to reduce the deficit and debt, we would do things like repeal the Trump-era tax cuts and raise taxes, or at the very least, close all the loopholes in the tax code that allow people like Jeff Bezos to pay less taxes than his Amazon employees.

And if you think raising taxes on the wealthy amounts to class warfare, consider what Massachusetts senator Elizabeth Warren said when she was first running for Senate back in 2011:

> *There is nobody in this country who got rich on his own. Nobody. You built a factory out there? Good for you. But I*

want to be clear: You moved your goods to market on roads
the rest of us paid for. You hired workers the rest of us paid
to educate. You were safe in your factory because of police
forces and fire forces that the rest of us paid for. . . . Now look,
you built a factory and it turned into something terrific, or a
great idea? God bless. Keep a big hunk of it. But part of the
underlying social contract is you take a hunk of that and pay
forward for the next kid who comes along.

This is where we get the idea for a windfall tax for people who quadrupled their money during the pandemic, or a wealth tax for people who have such extraordinary amounts of money that it just begets more money, or a stronger inheritance tax so we're not just making another hereditary ruling class in a nation built in opposition to the very thing. This country also requires some form of campaign finance reform. Most Americans are tired of corporate money in politics. We recognize it doesn't serve us, and we have to vote with that in mind. We must continue to support our unions and the collective bargaining of our workers, and we have to work together to reverse *Citizens United*—the Supreme Court decision that ruled that corporations are people and money equals speech—in order to get corrupt, self-serving, almost unlimited money out of politics.

Now of course none of this will be easy. The very richest and most conservative Americans have spent the past five decades consolidating power both in the markets and the government, and now they're allowed to spend unlimited money influencing politics. However, it's something we absolutely must try, because having so much of the American economy and government in the hands of so few only hurts the American people, and continuing down this path will only serve to exacerbate income inequality and expand the chasm between those with wealth and power and the rest of us until, at some point, the divide will simply become too big and the system will break. What we're doing here is unsustainable.

★ ★ ★

The "American Dream" became a catchphrase when historian James Truslow Adams wrote *The Epic of America*. Adams was attempting to diagnose what had gone wrong after the Gilded Age and during the Great Depression. He believed the country had gone off track when it became too concerned with material well-being, abandoning its higher founding aspirations. The American Dream was not supposed to be the pursuit of individual wealth, but as Adams wrote, "That dream of a land in which life should be better and richer and fuller for everyone, with opportunity for each according to ability or achievement." He expanded on this idea by writing that the American Dream "is not a dream of motorcars and high wages merely, but a dream of social order in which each man and woman shall be able to attain to the fullest stature of which they are innately capable, and be recognized by others for what they are, regardless of the fortuitous circumstances of birth or position."

This idea of judge me on who I am and what I've done, not who my parents are and how much money we have, is a very American attitude. Like I said, other countries were very concerned about your parentage and the circumstances of your birth, but America was doing something different, something new. Of course, being an Astor or a Carnegie meant something, but it didn't stop people like the aforementioned Edison, the self-taught and youngest of seven, from a destitute family, to go on to be one of the world's greatest inventors, founding General Electric and inventing, among other things, the phonograph and the incandescent light bulb.

As the *New York Times* points out, the decades following *The Epic of America* saw the dream Adams imagined became a reality. "America had rapid, and widely shared, economic growth. Nearly all children grew up to achieve the most basic definition of a better life, earning more money and enjoying higher living standards than their parents." However, this idea of living up to your best self, of not being held back by anything but your own moxie, was redefined in the 1950s as the idea of the American Dream became commercialized and sold to people. If the earlier version had focused on the principles of a liberal democracy and pulling yourself up by your bootstraps, the 1950s version was its shiny, materialistic younger sister.

As people entered the job market in the 1970s, growth began to slow, partially credited to the energy crisis of the time. You might remember, or have seen pictures of, lines of cars parked outside service stations because of gas shortages. Still, more than 79 percent of the people born in the 1950s would ultimately make more than their parents, but in the 1980s, thanks to globalization, advances in technology, and deregulation (like the removal of antitrust laws), economic inequality began to rise. This is around the time education started to become more expensive and the workforce started asking for higher skill levels. This is when college became a thing you "had" to do rather than something you might want to do. All these elements together started to deeply affect the income of the poor and middle class.

Then we had a recession, a tech boom, a housing crash, and a pandemic, and the divide became even greater.

Only half of people born in the 1980s will make as much money as their parents. Going backward has become the norm. We have limited access to the things we were "promised" and the dream we were sold, and this trend toward lower economic mobility has made people angry. There are vast numbers of people around this country who understandably feel as if the American Dream has been stolen from them. Research shows that people's happiness is directly influenced by how they're doing in life, and since Americans have created a culture based around financial success, if you aren't financially successful, you feel like a failure. You can tell people the economy is "doing well" all you want, but they're not feeling it. Many of us look at our parents and grandparents and think, *I'll never have that*, and when Americans stop believing in the American Dream, or start seeking a better life in *other* countries, you know something's gone wrong.

As the writer David Leonhardt notes, the irony of electing someone like Donald Trump in 2016, someone who tapped into the nostalgic anger of the fading American Dream, is that he might have actually put that dream further out of people's reach. It's his party working to remove business regulations, Social Security, Medicare, the Affordable Care Act, and support for public schools, while continuing to cater to the richest Americans. Today's American Dream seems to be about unbridled capitalism and mass consumption, and it puts us all on a hamster wheel of working endless hours to make other people rich. As the wealth gap continues to grow, it starts to feel as if you'll never have the life you want, unless you were already born into it.

There is a shift happening in the American consciousness, where the idea we all bought into, this idea that if we just work hard enough we'll make it, is starting to feel like a bit of a scam. It's time to acknowledge that the trials Americans face, the struggles we deal with just to make ends meet, are not necessarily the result of our own actions or shortcomings, but rather the by-product of living in an oppressive system that's been rigged against most of us for the past forty years. This is not to say that people aren't personally responsible for their actions, of course they are, but there was a time in the not-so-distant American past where we had both a thriving middle class *and* a booming economy. Where people had pensions and benefits and Social Security was enough to live on rather than one more thing for politicians to take, but through political policy and voter ambivalence we've allowed a corporate takeover of the American Dream.

How do you rise if you work a full-time job and still can't afford a place to live? How do you rise if you're starting a career drowning in debt from a school you were told you had to attend? Are we succeeding if we're putting off having children or buying real estate because we simply can't afford it? Getting sick is the number one cause of bankruptcy in this country. It's no wonder America's suicide rates are so high.

The American people are increasingly miserable trying to live a dream that is so far from ever becoming a reality. Yet we struggle to change because a fair number of politicians and justices in charge of passing and upholding the laws that could protect us from predatory capitalism are, in many cases, bought and paid for by predatory capitalists.

There's a reason billionaires are now trying to control our

government and media. It serves them and their bottom line of course, but also because they've convinced themselves, and us, that they're smarter because they're richer. That they, capitalism's winners, know better by the very fact that they've thrived while the rest of us were left behind. They believe it's a testament to their talent, not just a reflection of a system that was built to protect and serve a certain class.

As former labor secretary Robert Reich said, "Wealth inequality is eating this country alive and concentrated wealth is endangering our democracy. Wealth doesn't just beget more wealth, it begets more power. It's a vicious cycle that destroys our economy and democracy at the same time."

If you're the "land of opportunity," you should offer opportunities. Educate your people. Take care of them when they're sick. Don't force them into debt for having children. If you want them to stay home with their kids, subsidize it, or subsidize daycare if you want them back at work. Look at countries like Germany, Denmark, Norway, and Spain, which all have excellent public education, free college, universal health care, and affordable childcare. Look at France. You can hustle as much as you want in that country, but you get a month off a year and if you work for a company of more than fifty people, your boss can't email you after 6 p.m. because that's your time. And France isn't an outlier. Many Europeans take a full month off and have strict rules for work/life balance. A large number of nations see time off from work as essential to the mental health of their population. Plus, these cultures aren't drowning in medical debt, or the cost of education. There's so much Americans could learn and adopt if we stopped saying we were "the greatest country in the world" and started trying to be it.

If we want to return to the original dream of a "better, richer, fuller life" for everyone, we need a new New Deal. New public works projects, new factories, new housing, new regulations and worker protections, more union support. We need investment in clean energy and renewables to protect our environment and the future of our planet. We need regulations on corporate greed and consolidation. We need more government investment in education and housing, but this time for everyone. We need childhood tax credits not billionaire tax benefits. We need to elect leaders who see the country as a whole. Who don't just think about the economy, but about the *people* who live and work in that economy. As FDR himself said, "The test of our progress is not whether we add more to the abundance of those who have much; it is whether we provide enough for those who have too little."

We don't need to make America great *again*. We need to make America great, and that starts with living up to its promise that everyone should have the opportunity to rise.

★ ★ ★

EVERY CITIZEN SHOULD HAVE A VOTE, AND THAT VOTE SHOULD COUNT

There is nothing more sacred in America, or any democracy, than the right to vote.

When I first considered writing this book a close friend of mine asked, "If you could leave your readers with only one thought, what would it be?" and I said, "Vote in every election." People have no idea how important their vote is. What an opportunity it is to live in a country where you get to choose and replace your leaders. To be a part of a nation where if you want change, change is possible. Where representatives are elected to move the country in the direction the people want it to go. Which is why, as our country has become more populous, more multicultural, more open-minded, we should be concerned that there are people actively working to limit who gets to vote.

America likes to think of itself as the shining star of democracy, but every battle to extend the vote in this country has been hard won. We think of American democracy as one person one vote, but we founded this nation with only one group having that vote—white male landowners over twenty-one. It was extended to all white men by the 1820s, but we had to fight an entire Civil War before we extended that right to Black men, and American women wouldn't get federal voting rights until 1920, with Native Americans having to wait until 1924. Even with the expansion of voting rights, every group that wasn't in the original group was often prevented from voting due to state laws or customs, and as mentioned earlier, eighteen-year-olds could fight for this country long before they were allowed to vote in this country.

To quote the late, great congressman and civil rights leader John Lewis: "The right to vote is precious, almost sacred. It is the most powerful nonviolent tool or instrument we have in a democratic society. We must use it." Which is why we should be incredibly alarmed that our voting rights are currently under attack across the nation. If you want to vote in America, you should be able to vote. If you do vote, that vote should count. Yet we find ourselves in a time where this most basic American tenet is no longer a given because one of our two major political parties has discovered it has a better chance of winning if fewer people have their voices heard.

Again, this is not new. There have been people in this country who have been against extending voting rights since voting began, and even as society changed, even as we progressed and improved, there were people who put up every possible roadblock between those they deemed lesser and their access to the polls. After Congress passed the Fifteenth Amendment in 1870, the last of the three Reconstruction Amendments, to make it clear that you could no longer deny or limit the right to vote by race, color, or having previously been enslaved, the Southern states still resisted. We shouldn't really have needed the Fifteenth Amendment, as the Fourteenth Amendment gave anyone born or naturalized in America citizenship, and by the nature of that citizenship African American men over twenty-one should have been allowed to vote. However, since most were not, Congress passed another amendment to make it crystal clear who had the right to vote, along with a slew of laws to enforce it. Yet the Southern states continued to resist by designing laws to specifically disenfranchise Black men. The claim was they weren't *denying* Black men the vote, they were simply adding prerequisites like literacy tests and poll taxes, and the particularly egregious "whites only" primaries, which had the desired effect of ensuring that any candidate a Black man could vote for was already white-approved.

It wouldn't be until 1965, after the assassination of President John F. Kennedy and the passing of the Civil Rights Act in 1964, that we would pass the Voting Rights Act to truly address many of these weapons against democracy and to secure legal protections against discrimination across America. Which is why, *again*, we should be alarmed as we watch the Voting Rights Act continue to be gutted by our current Supreme Court, while today's Republican Party refuses to vote for any and all federal voting rights protections, while simultaneously passing hundreds of voter suppression laws across the states that it controls.

As democracy's super-lawyer Marc Elias, whose firm the Elias Law Group fights most of these oppressive laws in courts across the country, reminds us, "You can't fight voter suppression unless you know it's happening." So, let's talk about what's happening.

In *Shelby County v. Holder* (2013), the Supreme Court ruled that jurisdictions with histories of racial prejudice in voting no longer needed federal approval to change their voting practices. This approval, which had been referred to as "preclearance," had been used as a guardrail against discriminatory voting practices across the country. Suddenly states were unshackled, free to implement massive voting restrictions without any federal agency acting as a check. The *Shelby* decision sent the message to the nation that the federal courts would no longer be playing the role of protector of voting rights, and since that decision, the Supreme Court has repeatedly confirmed this assumption by rolling back even more of the Voting Rights Act and turning a blind eye to some of the most egregious voter suppression laws at the state level.

Since the *Shelby* decision, the Republican Party has been extremely busy erasing decades of hard-won gains for disenfranchised groups and passing new laws to prevent the ever-changing face of the American electorate from affecting its preferred power structure. There are many reasons the conservative movement turned its eye on the federal courts and this is one of them.

Another tactic used to suppress votes is called gerrymandering. US House districts are based on population, and as a result of the census taken every ten years, some states lose population and some states gain population, and because of that all fifty states are required to redraw the boundaries of their House districts based on those new numbers. The goal being to have the House districts better reflect the population and demographic changes in their states. Districts, which in the majority of states have to be approved by state legislatures, can be drawn by a partisan group, a nonpartisan group, a bipartisan group, or an independent commission. However, when districts are drawn by a partisan group—with the express goal of assuring one party has a better chance of winning over another—that process is called gerrymandering.

The term "gerrymandering" (pronounced "Jerry") comes from Massachusetts governor Elbridge Gerry, whose administration passed a law in 1812 to divide up their new state Senate districts in such a way as to consolidate his power. He squished his opposition's votes into as few districts as possible, giving his party a disproportionate representation in the state. One district was so oddly shaped that people said it looked like a salamander, and a cartoonist for the *Boston Gazette* drew it, calling the animal a "Gerry-mander," solidifying the name for this kind of behavior in America's cultural vernacular. Gerrymandering can be done at the federal level, for US House seats, and also at the state level, for assemblies or legislatures.

Gerrymandering can be used to either push as many voters who might vote against you into the smallest number of districts (a practice called "packing") or break up your opponent's voting power by spreading voters across as many districts as possible to dilute their vote (a practice called "cracking"). Either way, the action gives the party in charge a competitive edge, with the doctored maps providing widespread victories to the party who drew the maps rather than the party who got the most votes. If you look around the country, you'll see districts that look like a blindfolded child drew a duck in a moving car. They're all over the place. "I'll take this voter, not these voters. Carve out that neighborhood, it's not good for us. I'll take this whole section of town—but not them, get them out." It's ridiculous.

While the Supreme Court has ruled that racial gerrymandering (drawing districts to favor one race over another) is unconstitutional, it has ruled that partisan gerrymandering is basically fine. You can see the power of partisan gerrymandering in a state like Texas, where the Republican Party has had complete control for nearly twenty-five years and has been able to keep its congressional representation reliably conservative and rural despite the fact most of the population growth over the past two decades has been liberal, minority populations in city centers. Gerrymandering has allowed the Republicans to offset the changing demographics so they aren't reflected in the districts' voting power.

Now, gerrymandering is something both parties do, but the Republican Party uses it far more readily than the Democrats. Republican legislators are responsible for drawing the maps in nineteen states whose 117 districts make up 41 percent of seats in the US House of Representatives, while Democratic state legislatures are only responsible for drawing 49 districts in seven states whose representatives make up about 11 percent of the House. Democrats have big states like California, which could easily use partisan gerrymandering to its advantage, but California—like Arizona, Colorado, and Michigan—uses what are called independent commissions, which means the legislators aren't directly involved in how the maps are drawn. The maps are created by an independent body that can't favor one party over another. We have a few states who use political commissions, which is a mix between partisan and independent map drawing, and Maine has split control of the maps so they end up with one Republican district and one Democratic district.

Finally, we have districts that are decided by the state courts, and those can be just as highly partisan as if they were drawn by state legislators. Recently North Carolina's 5–2 right-wing state Supreme Court approved district maps for 2024 that will likely give Republicans control of ten out of their fourteen House districts despite the fact that Republicans are less than one-third of registered voters. In 2020 Donald Trump only won North Carolina with 50.1 percent of the vote, but their House representation is going to look like Republicans have almost 72 percent of the state's support. Ohio Republicans proposed a congressional map that would give them 86 percent of the House seats in a state Trump only carried by 53 percent. Wisconsin Republicans recently attempted to pass a congressional map that would have given them 75 percent of the House seats in a state that went to President Biden in 2020, but they lost the election for the deciding vote on the state Supreme Court, so now the maps will be fairly drawn for 2024. Not drawn for Democrats mind you, just fairly drawn, so a fifty-fifty state has the chance to get fifty-fifty representation in the House. So when you hear people say "both sides gerrymander," know that while this is technically true, the frequency and results are not remotely the same.

In fact, in the fall of 2021 the Princeton Gerrymandering Project gave North Carolina's congressional, state Senate, and state House maps an F for partisan fairness because "all three maps were likely to decrease the number of districts where communities of color could elect their preferred candidates." Not only were the maps approved by the Republican legislature, but the legislature also passed a series of laws to limit the powers of the Democratic governor to do anything about it. He can't veto them. He can't call for a ballot measure so the people can weigh in, and the Democratic secretary of state and Democratic AG are powerless because the Republican state Supreme Court approved it all.

You could go down a rabbit hole with everything the Republicans have been doing to democracy in North Carolina, and you'd find it heartbreaking and morally and ethically wrong, but it's also currently completely legal, and just one of the Republican-controlled states that participates in this behavior.

When President Obama was reelected in 2012 and Mitt Romney lost the popular vote by over five million people, the Republican Party had a "come to Jesus" moment when Republicans conducted sweeping audits and research into their party's potential moving forward. They did a deep dive into their base, their potential voters, the popularity of their positions and policies and found that if they didn't adjust, or start reaching out to new voters, they would continue to lose. There was talk about changing party positions and policies to appeal more to young people and minorities. They considered reaching across the aisle and embracing more popular-leaning socioeconomic viewpoints, but when it came right down to it, they just couldn't pull the trigger and commit to that kind of change, and frankly, the people who wrote their checks wouldn't allow it. Ultimately, they decided against reaching out, and chose instead to look within. To double down on the Christian, nativist rhetoric, on the "these people are your problem" finger-pointing grievances, and "traditional values" which, if we're being honest, really just means keeping women and "the other" in their place, while white men—particularly for the Republican Party, rich white men—remain on top.

Republicans have realized they can no longer win purely on ideas or candidates, so instead of adjusting their unpopular policies, or picking better candidates, they've turned their attention to voting itself and are engaging in a multipronged attack on our democracy. If you can't win based on the rules, change the rules so your opponent can't win. They have chosen to lead, or more specifically rule, without input from the people, and are doing everything they can to erode our democratic norms and civil liberties to keep power in their own hands.

Republicans are purging voters from the rolls, challenging certified election results, restricting mail-in voting, banning drop boxes, limiting drop boxes, and attacking signature-matching rules. We have states where you have to drive for hours to get to a polling location or wait for hours to cast a ballot. We have electronic scanners being shut down in primarily minority neighborhoods before everyone in line has the opportunity to vote. We even have at least one state where it's illegal to give people any food or water while they're waiting in line to vote, and often these hurdles to cast a ballot are far more prevalent in *strategic* counties with *specific* voters. Just as states with strict voter ID laws tend to favor one "type" of voter over another, the Venn diagram of the states who refuse same-day registration seems to line up directly with the states who randomly purge voters from their rolls. So, when people arrive to vote on Election Day to find they're no longer registered, there's absolutely nothing they can do about it. It's just an endless onslaught of deceitful tactics to make it harder and more miserable for certain voters to make their voices heard, and most of this started *before* 2020, when everything changed after President

Donald Trump told the country the election was rigged and he'd won when he'd actually lost.

I can't overstate the damage Donald Trump and his enablers have done to this country, and our faith in democracy, by sowing the idea that our elections are not secure and claiming, without evidence, that the wrong person had become president.

As Barton Gellman, writer for the *Atlantic*, wrote, "The prospect of [a] democratic collapse is not remote. . . . Trump and his party have worked to convince an alarmingly large number of Americans that the essential workings of our democracy are corrupt, that their made-up claims of fraud are true, that their opponents cheat to win, and that tyranny has taken over."

As of 2024, we've had 446 restrictive bills passed by a legislative committee, and 119 voter-suppression laws enacted since 2021. Many of the states enacting these laws are states where voting was already restrictive, and prior to the Supreme Court gutting the Voting Rights Act, they would have required "preclearance" to change their voting laws. To be clear, the Republican response to record voter turnout in 2020 was to make sure it never happened again. To unleash a tsunami of bogus "election integrity laws" at the state level that will restrict access to voters they don't want voting and throw out or overturn votes they don't want counted. In fact, for a powerful network of conservatives, voting restrictions are now viewed as the political life-or-death debate.

Marc Elias has been sounding the alarm for years, claiming, "The United States is witnessing a slow-motion insurrection that has a far better chance of success than Trump's failed power grab in 2021." As Elias points out,

There are zero Republicans in Congress who support voting rights. ZERO. And the sooner we recognize and accept that the Republican Party is the party of voter suppression and election subversion, the better chance we have to proceed with the steps necessary to save democracy. Which means we must focus on protecting free and fair elections with at least as much intensity as those who are plotting to undermine them.

The Republicans argue they simply want "fair" elections, but if they were truly concerned about voter integrity, they wouldn't have voted against the John R. Lewis Voting Rights Advancement Act, which would have shored up the voter protections that had been stripped from the Voting Rights Act by the Supreme Court. If they were really concerned about protecting the vote, they wouldn't have voted against the For the People Act, which would have expanded voter registration and voter access, addressed campaign finance reform, beefed up election security, addressed ethics concerns in all branches of government, required a code of conduct for Supreme Court justices, prohibited members of the House from serving on for-profit corporate boards, and required the president and vice president to disclose ten years of tax returns.

If the fate of American democracy was really on Republicans' minds, they would have voted *for* the Freedom to Vote Act, which was a multipronged, multilevel plan to improve the health of American democracy and make all aspects of our elections— beginning to end—fairer and more transparent. The bill included making Election Day a public holiday, banning extreme racial and partisan gerrymandering, automatic voter registration, online voter registration, same-day voter registration, improving voter list maintenance so fewer people are unnecessarily purged from voter rolls, protecting election records, infrastructure, and ballot tabulation to ensure safer and more easily audited results post-election, recruitment and training of nonpartisan election officials, actively combating dark money* groups including foreign nationals who interfere in our elections, and working to stop dark money from influencing the election process itself. Even if you believe, despite all evidence to the contrary, that the 2020 election was stolen, the Freedom to Vote Act would have addressed all of your concerns. The only people who wouldn't want to support a bill like that would be those who directly benefit from the process remaining unfair and unaccountable. To put a final point on it, the Democrat-controlled 117th Congress introduced all three of these election integrity and voter protection bills and passed two in the House with little to no Republican support, but all three died in the Senate because the Republicans refused to vote for them.

So, are the American people supposed to accept that we only have fair elections if the Republican candidate wins, or that truth only exists if we like it? This is the fallout of Trump's Big Lie. Even after the Trump campaign lost every court case challenging the 2020 election, after Fox News had to pay $787 million for lying about the election being stolen, after Trump's lawyers and his chief of staff admitted they knew he'd lost but wanted to keep power anyway, we still have a third of the country's voters who believe Joe

---

* *Dark money* is election-related spending where the source of the money is secret, which, thanks to the *Citizens United* decision, allows big-money donors to spend unlimited amounts of cash affecting elections without scrutiny.

Biden didn't win and hundreds of state laws passed to stop people from voting under the pretense that the last election wasn't fair.

If the Republicans' 2020 election strategy was all about undermining turnout, particularly mail-in voting, which was seen as the democratic way to vote during the pandemic; and 2022 was all about limiting who could vote through gerrymandering, voter suppression, and court cases; strategies for 2024 lean hard not just on election suppression, but on election subversion. Not just using redistricting and deceptive tactics to manage *who* can vote, but also limiting which votes *count*. According to the election integrity experts at Democracy Docket, Republican states have been suing to empower more partisan poll watchers and to limit the ability of county officials to allow voters to fix simple errors on their mail-in ballot to ensure their vote is counted. You might remember hearing about armed vigilantes with video cameras harassing people at drop boxes in Arizona in 2022, or groups of armed men harassing secretaries of state to change the results after the 2020 election. The official RNC position is that it now wants more of that. An "army of poll watchers" to contest elections is the new plan.

The Republican Party seems to have given up on reaching out to new voters, it has given up on governing, and quite frankly, it has given up on democracy. Today's Republican Party, the MAGA party, Trump's party, has simply decided to retain power through fear and hate, weaponized misinformation, and the rigging of the election system itself. I shouldn't have to tell you that redrawing district lines to make it impossible for you to lose, or making voting so hard for your opposition that you win, does not reflect the will of the people. These are processes and protocols that allow the minority to tip elections in its favor. As David Frum, political commentator and speechwriter for George W. Bush, noted, "If conservatives become convinced that they cannot win democratically, they will not abandon conservatism. They will reject democracy." This is exactly what is happening in America right now.

Now, perhaps you hear all this and think, Well that's okay. That's my party, they want what I want—a whiter America, fewer immigrants, not teaching Black history, an end to gay people, women in the home, a Christian nation... whatever the Republican Party means to you—but, understand that by supporting the party that limits the power to vote, you're supporting voter disenfranchisement, and I hate to be the one to break it to you, but *you're* a voter. If you give people the power to strip others of their vote, you're giving them the power to do the same to you. No one in this country is served by disenfranchisement. If you can take the vote from one group, you can take the vote from all groups. It might seem as if it's working for you now, but eventually it won't.

I understand it's confusing for people because Republicans have tied "election subversion" up with a bow of "election integrity." They keep saying something's wrong with the election system and they're just trying to fix it, but *they're* what's wrong with the election system. Even when they lose their lawsuits that should prove to the American people that nothing was wrong, that they're actually trying to break the system rather than fix it, they use the loss to claim it's only further proof the system is rigged. It's a lose-lose for people's faith in democracy.

Losing faith in democracy is another way to drive down

voter turnout. In fact, one of the most efficient ways to get people not to vote is to convince them their vote doesn't count. In 2016 the nonvoters actually won the election. More eligible voters didn't vote than voted for Hillary Clinton or Donald Trump. So, when the media floods the airwaves with polls and commentary convincing you that an election has already been decided, or there's no point in weighing in because you can't change anything, know it's a form of voter suppression, and you shouldn't fall for it.

Think of all the people who believe their vote doesn't matter because their state always goes one way or the other. By not voting, they're giving away their power. Throwing up their hands and allowing the states to continue to not represent them. The most obvious way voters see this is through the Electoral College.

When deciding how the country would be run, the Framers outrightly rejected the idea of a national popular vote for president, not just because of the compromise with the smaller states, but because they didn't entirely trust the voters. They saw the general population as under-educated and unsophisticated, and felt it was more likely to be manipulated by someone who told it what it wanted to hear but would ultimately be bad for the country's leadership. So, they decided, much like had been done in ancient Rome, that they would choose a "body of wise men" to deliberate over the leading presidential candidates, and pick the best man for the job.

In the end, the Framers established an independent group, chosen by the states, called the Electoral College, and gave the electors in this group the power to choose the president based on the candidates the voters had chosen. The original plan gave each elector two votes for president. Whoever got the majority became president, and the runner-up would become vice president.

To this day, we still don't vote directly for president in America. We vote for the candidates, and our state electors vote for the president at a meeting held in December. There are 538 total electors, one for each House member and US senator, plus three electors to represent the District of Columbia (DC), which, since the ratification of the Twenty-third Amendment, has had federal representation despite the fact it isn't a state. A candidate must win 270 electoral votes (just over half of the 538 total) to win the White House.

In all but two states,* electoral votes are awarded on a winner-take-all basis. So, if a presidential candidate wins the majority of votes in the state, they get all the Electoral College votes for that state. However, state elections can be incredibly close—let's say, four hundred thousand votes to four hundred and ten thousand votes—but every electoral vote goes to the winner. This is how America ends up having winning presidential candidates who didn't win the majority of the votes in the country. Hillary Clinton won more than sixty-five million votes in 2016 while Donald Trump won only sixty-two million, but because of the Electoral College Trump won the presidency with 304 electoral votes to Clinton's 227.

---

* Maine and Nebraska have what's called a "district system," where electors are appointed depending on who won the popular vote in each congressional district, and then the two extra electors (who are there to represent the senators) are pledged to the overall winner of the state's popular vote. As this book goes to print, Nebraska is considering moving to a winner-take-all system.

AMERICA 101: HOW TO BECOME AN ELECTOR

Article II of the Constitution is clear that electors can't be members of Congress or hold federal office, but the Framers left choosing electors up to the states. The most common way of choosing electors is by state party. Electors are chosen by political parties at state conventions and are typically picked as reward for their service, support of the party, or because they have a personal or professional connection with the party's presidential candidate.

When American voters vote for president and vice president, they're actually voting for the slate of electors who have pledged to cast their votes for that party. Then, on the first Monday after the second Wednesday in December, members of the Electoral College meet (usually at their state capitals) and cast their official votes for president and vice president.

We usually know who won each state's popular vote on election night, so we know which slate (group) of electors will be sent to cast their votes, but the process of choosing the president isn't actually *complete* until the Electoral College votes in December, and the results are sent to Congress, where the president of the Senate (the vice president of the United States) presides over the certification and count of the electoral votes on January 6 (unless that day happens to be a Sunday and then the date to certify is changed by Congress).

The counting of the electoral votes was what was happening on January 6, 2021, when supporters of President Donald Trump stormed the US Capitol. Without the president of the Senate counting the electoral votes and declaring the winner, the next president of the United States is not actually confirmed. So, along with the protestors breaking into the building and causing members of Congress to flee and hide, disrupting the official proceeding declaring the next president (shout-out to the Senate aides who had the wherewithal to save the box with the electoral votes and get them somewhere safe), we also had senators from certain states calling electoral votes into question. Though the senators' objections were never acted on, as the rioters interrupted the process, the question remains: Were these senators asking for recounts in certain states to confirm the popular vote winner, and therefore the electors who could cast their vote for president, or did they want those state votes to be disqualified altogether and have the electoral count go forward without them?

We should remember that leading up to the official counting of the electoral votes in 2021 there had been multiple accusations of election interference and stolen elections, but the results had been certified by every secretary of state, with many of them being thoroughly investigated and recounted. Every legal case that had been filed challenging the election had been lost or dismissed, and there simply wasn't any proof of what the lame duck* president was claiming, or what the senators were challenging in Congress, but this didn't stop Donald Trump from encouraging his supporters to

---

* The "lame duck" period or label applies to any outgoing politician, such as the president, who is serving their final months in office because they didn't win reelection or are retiring. It's a wrapping-up period.

"fight like hell" or they "wouldn't have a country anymore" before unleashing them on the Capitol.

What happened on January 6, 2021, was a tremendous break in American tradition, American law, and in what most of us believe to be American values. We'll never know what would have happened if the electoral votes had been kicked back to the states, if the riot had been put down before the rioters breached the Capitol, or if the vice president had allowed certain states to be omitted and had counted the electoral votes without them.

Constitutionally, we know that if neither presidential candidate receives the majority of the Electoral College votes (which could have happened in 2021 if we'd removed certain states from the count) that the president is determined by the House of Representatives, with each state getting a single vote, a process that does not represent the will of the people. All 435 representatives only get fifty votes total, one for each state. So, despite the fact that Democratic representatives represented states with millions more voters than Republican representatives, there were numerically more Republican states than Democratic ones. So, notwithstanding the fact Joe Biden had legally won both the Electoral College and the popular vote by more than seven million people, he would have lost the vote for president in the House. That's a glaring problem that needs to be addressed.

You can understand the Framers' logic in setting up the Electoral College the way they did. The question is, does it still work two centuries later? People who defend the Electoral College say it's an important part of American democracy. That the institution was created to make sure that large states didn't dominate small ones and that power between Congress and state legislatures was balanced, but many scholars are challenging this idea because it's become quite obvious the Electoral College is not being used as intended, and may even have become a destructive force in American politics.

People started really paying attention to the Electoral College in 2000 when the race between George W. Bush and Al Gore was so close that the election came down to Florida's twenty-five electoral votes. The ballot design itself even came into question in certain counties, and the Florida Supreme Court ordered a manual recount. The Bush team filed a lawsuit to stop the recount, and the US Supreme Court ruled for them. Without recounting all the votes in the state, the Supreme Court allowed the Florida Electoral College votes to go to George Bush, making him, not Al Gore, the president. To rub salt in the wound, Gore had won the overall popular vote by more than half a million people. So, more people in the country voted for an Al Gore presidency, but the job itself came down to one state (where I should note George Bush's brother Jeb was the governor) and a Supreme Court decision to stop counting votes, and it made the American people go, *Hmmmmm . . .*

It's not that we hadn't had contested elections before, or presidents who had lost the popular vote but gone on to win the presidency. It just happened so rarely, and this was such a weird combination of circumstances, that it felt wrong. Usually, the Electoral College operates pretty smoothly. Voters cast their ballots and the presidential candidate with the most votes in that state gets the electors. We've only had a handful of contested elections in our history, and until the Bush/Gore election, it hadn't happened since just after the Civil War.

AMERICA 101: CONTESTED ELECTIONS

In 1800 Thomas Jefferson and Aaron Burr received the same number of Electoral College votes and the election went to the House. The House voted thirty-six times before Jefferson came out as the winner with Aaron Burr to be his vice president. The Twelfth Amendment was ratified in 1804 to avoid this kind of ballot confusion again, by more specifically laying out the rules around the Electoral College and to stop the process of having the vice president be the presidential runner-up.

In 1824 the Twelfth Amendment was used when four candidates all from the same party (the Democratic-Republicans) ran for president. Each candidate had their own regional popularity, but none received the majority of the electoral votes, so the election went to the House, where, once again, each state was allowed to cast one vote. Andrew Jackson had come closest to the majority, with ninety-nine electoral votes, but the fourth-place winner, Henry Clay, made a deal with the second-place winner, John Quincy Adams, to have his people vote for Adams if Adams would make him secretary of state. The deal was struck, and when the House voted, John Quincy Adams became president, and Andrew Jackson and his people accused Adams of stealing the election.

While America was still recovering from the Civil War, Rutherford B. Hayes ran against Samuel Tilden in the election of 1876. On Election Day, Tilden won the popular vote, but was one vote short of an Electoral College majority. Hayes claimed he would've won Florida, Louisiana, and South Carolina if there hadn't been voter intimidation against African American voters, and the Oregon electoral votes, which Hayes *had* won, were in dispute.

Since this was the first time Congress was dealing with *disputed* Electoral College results, where both parties were claiming victory in the same states, it had to figure out what to do. It wavered for about six weeks with things getting extremely heated, with another civil war even being suggested, before it eventually created a temporary bipartisan electoral commission to deal with the states in question. This commission had five members from the House, five from the Senate, and five Supreme Court justices, and it was tasked with deciding the twenty contested electoral votes.

The electoral commission ultimately gave all the outstanding electoral votes to Hayes, but only after his people made a deal with Tilden's people to give Hayes the presidency if he would agree to withdraw all federal troops from the South. According to the Brookings Institute, this agreement would go on to have "far-reaching consequences" as the withdrawal of federal troops would pave the way for Jim Crow laws, "including vigilante violence against African Americans, and the denial of their civil rights." It was also an incredible betrayal of the Black voters who had believed in Hayes, and called into question the Framers' idea that a small group of wise men would make better decisions than the voters.

The most recent controversy around the Electoral College arose when Donald Trump lost the popular vote to Hillary Clinton by almost three million votes in the 2016 election, making him the fifth president to win the presidency without winning the majority sentiment of the nation. This election drew a lot of attention to the Electoral College, and once again called into question the effectiveness of the Great Compromise now that the country's population was so much bigger. Having presidents who continue to lose the popular vote undermines both electoral legitimacy and democracy, as the Electoral College gives the states a disproportionate voting power over the will of the voters.

Advocates for the system say that this uneven power forces politicians to pay attention to the smaller states that would otherwise be ignored, but in practice, that's not what's happening. Despite the system's best intentions, the Electoral College doesn't encourage politicians to campaign in every state. Lots of states are still excluded from presidential campaigns, but they're not small states, but rather states that are no longer viewed as competitive.

Since almost all states allocate their votes in a winner-take-all method, there's no reason for candidates to campaign in states that clearly favor one candidate over another. For years it made little sense for the Democratic presidential candidate to campaign in Texas, despite the fact there were plenty of Democrats living there. A Democrat simply couldn't win the state's electoral votes. The same goes for the Republican candidate campaigning in a solidly Democratic state like Massachusetts. Candidates would rather spend their time in what are called "swing" or "battleground" states like Michigan and Pennsylvania, which are still considered toss-ups. So, states are still being ignored, just not for the reason the Framers thought they'd be.

Plus, the winner-take-all rule lowers voter turnout in states where one party is dominant, because individual voters feel like their vote doesn't count. In many ways they're not wrong on the presidential level, but voters forget those ballots also include the people who can hold the president accountable, namely their congressional representatives, not to mention state and local representatives, who are responsible for the laws that affect their daily lives.

It's also deeply undemocratic that the Electoral College allows for what are called "faithless electors" or electors who choose not to follow the will of the voters in their state but vote how they want. There's actually no law that requires electors to cast their ballot for the popular vote winner in their state. More than thirty states (and DC) have laws that bind electors to their state's vote, but they're pretty piddly punishments if you don't follow through. The rest of the states have no legal requirements over their electors, so despite the election's outcome, electors are theoretically free to vote for whomever they choose, including choosing not to vote.

America has never had faithless electors decide an election, but the idea that they could is something our country should address. This didn't used to be something parties worried about, but in 2016 seven electors broke with their state on the presidential ballot, and six broke with their state on the vice presidential ballot. The most in modern history.

We have to acknowledge our country is not functioning as it used to, and we've found ourselves in a position where we have to reconsider how we're doing things. At the very least we should be turning our "norms" into laws because we can no longer take for granted things will go as they've always gone. In this highly polarized political environment, it's quite possible to see a future where faithless electors, voting how they want, not how the voters decided, could tip a presidential election. Faithless electors could render an entire state's votes obsolete and, as we know from the 2000 election, one state can change who wins the presidency.

The Electoral College is simply no longer democratically fair. In a country with more than 330 million people and only 538 electoral votes, the small and medium states are overrepresented at the expense of the large ones. There's also an economic imbalance. The fifteen most prosperous states in the nation generally have the largest populations whose House members represent hundreds of thousands more people than smaller-state House members, and they have a total of thirty senators, which equates to thirty electoral votes. While the thirty-five states with smaller economic activity and populations, have seventy senators, which equates to seventy electoral votes. So the smaller, less prosperous states have disproportionate power to not only dictate national policy, but to choose the president.

The way we're headed, there's only going to be bigger and bigger discrepancies between the popular vote and the Electoral College vote. We're very close to a time when the candidate the majority of American voters want will always lose. We're dangerously close to ushering in an anti-majoritarian era, where a small number of votes in a few states can block all the legislation the majority of the country wants. It's what happens all the time in the Senate with the filibuster, which we'll talk more about in Principle 4, but inflicted on the entire country.

We have to accept that in modern-day America the Electoral College is a major problem for democracy, and if we want our votes to truly count, it's something we should seriously be rethinking. Now, I'm certainly not the first person to say this. Over the last two hundred years, there have been more than seven hundred proposals to either eradicate, or modify, the Electoral College. In 1934, in response to public concerns over the disparity between the popular vote and the electoral vote, Congress was just two Senate votes short of getting rid of the entire thing. Since then, legislators have continued to debate the elimination, or at least the reform, of the process.

In 1967, 58 percent of the country favored abandoning the Electoral College. In 1979 a vote to establish a direct popular vote failed to get the requisite two-thirds majority in the Senate by fifteen votes. In 1981 the number of people who wanted a direct popular vote was up to 75 percent, but still nothing changed. The most recent polling shows that despite the majority of the country wanting it gone, support for the Electoral College has become incredibly partisan. Republicans want to keep it, while Democrats want it removed.

In 2000, while the Bush/Gore election was still being decided, 73 percent of Democrats said they supported abolishing the Electoral College and making the move to a direct popular vote, while only 46 percent of Republicans said the same. When polled after the 2016 election 81 percent of Democrats wanted to abolish the Electoral College, but only 19 percent of Republicans agreed. Republicans have calculated, quite rightly, that the Electoral College helps them, and it would be very difficult for them to win the presidency without it.

The most permanent solution would be to amend the Constitution, which, as I laid out in the beginning, is not an easy process as it requires two-thirds of the House, two-thirds of the Senate, and then three-quarters of the fifty states (thirty-eight states) to ratify, but the Republicans have no incentive to make that kind of a change, so that's not going to happen the way Congress is set up now.

There are a number of states that support what's called the National Popular Vote Interstate Compact, which is a multistate, bipartisan agreement to award the state's electoral votes to the presidential candidate who won the national popular vote, even if that candidate lost the popular vote in their state. The NPVIC would become effective only if enough states vote to ratify it, and to do that they would have to reach an electoral majority of 270 votes, which they are currently well short of. Even if they reach 270 electoral votes, the NPVIC would face the same questions about what would happen if its electors decided not to vote for the national popular vote winner as faithless electors. And even if the NPVIC could get enough electoral votes to put this into effect, there would be constitutional challenges that would end up at the Supreme Court. However, I like the fact that people are thinking outside the box to make change. Democracy's not a spectator sport, and the NPVIC is trying to find solutions to make things more fair.

The best thing individual voters can do right now is work within our broken system. Yes, the deck is stacked for one party over another, and I understand if you're in that party that might feel like winning, but no one wins in a democracy that ignores the will of its people. The country should be going in the direction the majority decides and led by the people the majority chooses. We have simply become too powerful a nation to be held back by a regressive minority opposed to change, especially when its power comes from a system that gave the minority an outsized voice for the sake of compromise. The Great Compromise, just like the Three-Fifths Compromise, no longer works, and we need to elect leaders who understand this fact and are willing to try something new.

I understand why people feel like the game is rigged—in many ways it is—but that doesn't mean there's nothing we can do, and if we don't do *something*, then those who are rigging it will find their way to permanent power and we'll lose our chance to ever turn the tide. The thing is, the more voters who turn out, the more powerful our votes become. The 2020 election had the highest voter turnout in decades, with more than two-thirds of eligible voters casting a ballot, but some age groups and states voted at far higher rates than others. Minnesota had almost 80 percent of its electorate turn out, while Oklahoma only had 55 percent. In 2016 young people (age eighteen to twenty-nine) came out at 39 percent, by 2020 they were voting at 50 percent—sadly that number dropped to 23 percent in the midterms, because we've all been gaslit into thinking midterms are less important because we aren't voting for president, forgetting that every House member, a third of the Senate, and many state and local positions are on the ballot.

There are approximately nine million American voters abroad in any given election year, and while 8 percent of them voted in 2020, just 3 percent voted in the 2022 midterms. Three percent! American citizens abroad could change every election if they wanted, just like the youth of America could change every election if they understood their power. In fact, by 2024 we will have forty-one million eighteen- to twenty-seven-year-olds eligible to vote. That's eight million more than were eligible in 2022. Those are election-shifting numbers. Trend-changing numbers. Those are numbers that could make red states blue if they voted on the issues that really mattered to them. People simply can't conceptualize how important their vote really is.

Texas came out at around 66 percent for the 2020 election, but its attorney general was caught on tape saying his actions to limit mail-in ballots in highly Democratic areas was what won the election for the Republicans. Now whether that's true or not, the question is, could a state like Texas have different election results if 20 percent more people simply came out to vote? I believe it could. We literally don't know what the Electoral College map would even look like if we all voted at 80 percent like Minnesota. The bottom line, despite all the shenanigans around our elections—the suppression, the drama, the legal cheating—our vote counts. If it didn't, people wouldn't be trying so hard to take it away.

We must take our elections incredibly seriously. It matters that you come out to vote. It matters who you vote for. It matters who your state secretary of state is because they run your elections. It matters who your state attorney general is because they're the ones who will litigate your voting rights. If your state is making it difficult to vote, you should ask yourself why. Why don't you have universal mail-in ballots? Why not have weeks of early voting? Why wouldn't they want same-day registration and easy access to a ballot box? Who are they trying to stop from voting? And even if it's people you don't like, why would you support a system that silences the voter's voice when you're a voter?

AMERICA 101: SPOILER CANDIDATE

A spoiler candidate is a nonwinning candidate whose very presence on the ballot affects which candidate wins. In America, third-party candidates are typically spoilers because they end up taking votes from the majority party they most closely align with. So, for example, the Green Party will end up siphoning votes from Democrats. This is what happened in the 2016 election with Green Party candidate Jill Stein. Stein received just over 1 percent of the vote and had no legitimate chance of winning the presidency, but the votes that went to her in the swing states of Michigan, Pennsylvania, and Wisconsin arguably pushed the Democrat vote down just enough to allow those states' electoral votes to go to Donald Trump. So Green voters wanted a more environmental candidate, and ended up with the guy who gutted the EPA.

Americans deserve the opportunity to exercise their fundamental right to vote. They deserve representatives at the state and federal level who respect their "sacred duty" and vote to protect it. We need to be investing in our voting mechanisms at all levels. We need to have the tools, technology, and laws to protect our vote and make the system trustworthy. We have to ensure people have faith in the voting process from beginning to end.

When we talk about "secure elections" and "access to the ballot box" it ultimately comes down to people. Elections don't work unless we have people. Not just people to vote, but people to help us vote. We have to respect the poll workers and staff who are volunteering their time. We need to appreciate our secretaries of state and AGs and make sure we vote to put smart people in those jobs. Smart people who will protect the votes of *all* people, not just the people of *their* party. We currently have a shortage of election talent. Everyone wants to invest in election results, but no one wants to invest in the infrastructure of running the elections themselves. We need way more people who understand how the system works and want the process to be both efficient and fair. It might not be sexy, but it's essential. Election clerks all over the country are retiring because they're exhausted. They no longer want to deal with the pressure and harassment and many of them just quit after the 2020 election. There are states that have all brand-new clerks. Clerks who have never run an election before because we didn't have a backbench of talent ready and waiting to take those positions. That's something we need to rectify and something donors need to be funding.

We need to build a pipeline of talent for county clerks, election administrators, deputy secretaries of state, and poll workers for every election. There is currently only one election law clinic in the entire country that teaches you how to properly run an election, and it's at Harvard Law School. We need way more of those. Running elections is a legitimate job that our democracy requires, and we have to encourage more people to be part of the institution.

Above all, we need to vote. We need to vote to keep democracy's head above water in 2024, and then we need to vote for the long-term health of our democracy moving forward. That means voting for representatives who will prioritize voter rights and protections, who will vote to end partisan gerrymandering and dark money in politics. It means supporting backbenches of trained professionals ready to run elections and protect our right to cast a ballot. These should all be universal bipartisan agreements. Everyone should want this, and if they don't, again, ask yourself why.

Sometimes when you've had something for a long time you start to take it for granted. Think of America and democracy as a couple in a long-term marriage. We've been together for so long we just kind of figured democracy would always be there for us. We neglected the relationship, and I don't think I need to tell you that when you neglect a relationship, that's when you can lose it.

Governments don't just stay democratic. It doesn't take the majority of a population to change a system of politics. In fact, history shows us that it often just takes a determined and well-organized minority who think that their ideas are better and go for it. Republican leadership understands this moment. Quite frankly, they've played a big part in bringing us here. If Democrats have taken democracy for granted, the Republicans have kicked it out of bed. You only have to read the *Mandate for Leadership*, which is nothing short of an authoritarian manifesto, to see the plan in black and white. Project 2025 is not just a list of stated ideals, but a detailed strategic playbook on how to dismantle the government so the far right can effectively enact its extremist agenda without interference. This isn't hyperbolic, it's what all the Republican presidential candidates signed on for.

We have to remember that democracy is more than just getting a vote or being ruled by the majority. As philosopher Bernard-Henri Lévy argues, "Democracy is a style of behavior, of consent, of values, of a certain way of engaging in public debate, and believing in truth." Kori Schake, the director of foreign and defense policy at the American Enterprise Institute, defines democracy as the "building of a civil society. A society with free media, civic tolerance, and institutions of government that are able to buffer bad decisions." She says, "Democracy is a consensual relationship of accountability where we agree on how laws will be passed and how we will enforce those laws."

Ultimately, democracy is the grand idea that the people control the government, the government doesn't control the people. There is an old Winston Churchill quote that says, "No one pretends that democracy is perfect or all-wise. Indeed it has been said that democracy is the worst form of Government except for all those other forms that have been tried."

We stopped paying attention. We didn't always fill out the census, we didn't notice when the Federalist Society* stacked our courts with right-wing justices, we didn't get up in arms when our districts were gerrymandered to favor one party over another, we didn't do anything when lobbyists started writing our laws, or big money started taking over our elections. We took our eye off the ball, and let our relationship with democracy slide. Now we find ourselves frustrated, asking how the system is so broken. Well, it's broken because we stopped taking care of it, and now our democracy is in real danger. We must acknowledge it's something that can, and will, be taken away from us if we don't address the

---

* The Federalist Society is an influential nonprofit for conservative and libertarian lawyers that serves as a pipeline for federal judges. All three of President Donald Trump's nominees—Neil Gorsuch, Brett Kavanaugh, and Amy Coney Barrett—were personally handpicked by longtime Federalist Society leader Leonard Leo, though Leo also takes credit for installing John Roberts and Samuel Alito.

problem. We let it get bad and now we have to do major damage control. We need to put the power back in the hands of the people, and that starts with protecting the right to vote. As Georgia senator Raphael Warnock said, "The most powerful words ever uttered in a democracy are 'the people have spoken.'" So, we need to be sure we are heard.

PRINCIPLE 4

★ ★ ★

REPRESENTATIVES SHOULD REPRESENT THE PEOPLE WHO VOTED FOR THEM

We're in a tumultuous time in human history. The world is changing so fast because of technology and globalization and that's creating a real sense of anxiety for people about what the future is going to look like—the longevity of our jobs, the stability of the social order, the state of the climate—and that's putting a lot of pressure on our institutions. Institutions that were created to deal with different problems in a different time.

Many in America are angry at a political system that's perceived to be letting them down, and they're not wrong to feel that way. As Yascha Mounk, Johns Hopkins professor and author of *The People vs. Democracy*, points out, "The standard of living for the average American has stagnated. From 1945 to 1960 it doubled, from 1960 to 1985 it doubled again, but from 1985 to today it's flat-lined. Capitalism has become an unrestrained, and seemingly unchecked, burden on the American people." Only a small group of people in this country seem to be truly prospering, and those people have an outsized and growing influence on our government and its laws, and that makes people justifiably resentful. We're also a country that was founded on a strict racial hierarchy that we're attempting to evolve into a working multiracial democracy, and there are still a fair amount of people who don't want that. The demographics of the Western world are changing due to immigration policies and geopolitics and that makes some people feel uncomfortable, scared, and defensive. Whether they're right or wrong is irrelevant, their feelings are dictating their behavior, and if we don't start addressing some of these issues, we'll only have more protest votes or more apathy, and either one leaves the door open for an alternative to democracy to take over.

The problem with our democracy is that even when people vote, they feel as if they're not being heard. How can 85 percent of the country believe we need a higher minimum wage, but we don't have it? Or how can a vast majority of the country be in favor of common-sense gun legislation, but we're still getting shot up every day? Isn't America supposed to be a representative democracy? So why doesn't it feel like we're being represented?

Well, like many things in this country, we have to look back before we can move forward. From 1790 to 1910, the House of Representatives added seats to Congress after every census. Back then redistricting wasn't just about drawing new district lines, it was about adding new districts (seats) to Congress to accommodate population growth. However, in the early twentieth century, when the population was skyrocketing, mostly driven by immigration in urban areas, lawmakers in rural America began to feel very hesitant about the growing power of the cities. They were worried that if they didn't do something, the cities would end up with all the voting power and no one would listen to them. It was the same sentiment that drove the Great Compromise at the country's founding. So, after the 1920 Census the House stopped growing, and by 1929 Congress made it permanent by passing a law to cap the size of the House of Representatives at 435 seats. The House size grew temporarily when America added Hawaii and Alaska as states in 1959, but after the census of 1960, it went right back to divvying up 435 seats. So even as the population of America has continued to grow, the size of the House has remained the same. We had fewer than 100 million people living in the United States in 1910. In the 2020 Census, America had over 330 million people, but we still have the exact same number of representatives.

That means a single congressmember who used to represent around 200,000 people now represents approximately 700,000 people, with some congressmembers representing close to a million people. Which means that most of our congressional districts have a population larger than the city of Las Vegas with one person to represent them all. Not only does that insane ratio separate lawmakers from the people they represent—with that many constituents there's no way they could ever meet with all of us, read all our letters, or answer all our calls or emails—but it also means House members are representing an extremely diverse group of people with incredibly different issues, concerns, and perspectives.

Most countries have a lot more representatives per person. The UK has 650 members of Parliament, which comes out to be about one member per 100,000 people. The same goes for Japan, Mexico, South Korea, and Australia, whose representatives all represent between 160,000 and 270,000 citizens. America is simply not in line with our peer nations. If US House representatives represented the same amount of people as British members of Parliament we'd have 3,300 House members, which would clearly be unwieldy. But there has to be a happy medium.

There was a time when New York had forty-three representatives in the House. Today it has twenty-six. California lost a House member after the 2020 Census, despite having a population of almost forty million people. For reference, it would take twenty-two states with the smallest populations to even get to forty million people, which means California is hopelessly underrepresented in the federal government. But this isn't just a big-state problem. Take Delaware, for example. In 2020 it had a population of 989,948, while Montana had a population of 1,084,225. However, because of how representatives are allotted, Delaware stayed at one House seat, while Montana was given a second. So, despite the fact that the two states have almost the exact same population, Montana has double the House representation.

Plus, the difference between keeping and losing a House seat can be extraordinarily small. In 2020 Minnesota kept its eight congressional House seats by eighty-nine people. If the census hadn't counted those eighty-nine people, Minnesota would have only qualified for seven House seats, but now it's locked in at eight for an entire decade. This is why it's so important we count everyone in the census, and why people who mess around with census results—not counting *these* people or *those* people—are manipulating how our entire government works.

House size is one of those things no one talks about, but which drastically affects how our government functions and how much our voices are heard. In January 2023 Democratic representative Earl Blumenauer from Oregon introduced a bill to address this issue, House Resolution 622 (H.R. 622), a bill that would grow the House to 585 seats for the 2030 redistricting. This would dramatically impact how many constituents were in each congressional district, making each district approximately 200,000 fewer than it is today—closer to what House representation looked like in 1990. Under H.R. 622, states like Delaware and the Dakotas might gain one extra seat, while states like Alaska and Vermont would probably stay the same with one seat each. On the other end of the spectrum, big states like California, Texas, Florida, New York, and Pennsylvania would greatly increase their House representation, which would allow them to be more in line with the number of people who live and work in those states.

Critics will, of course, look at the numbers and say, "We can't possibly have ten more seats in Democratic New York, or thirteen more seats in Republican Texas," but we have to imagine these new districts would also be drawn with new voter protections that absolutely must pass in the next decade if we want to stay a functioning democracy. With a bill like H.R. 622 California would likely get close to eighteen more seats, but since California doesn't partisan gerrymander, that would mean the state would have more districts for conservatives and Republicans to actually feel represented. A bill like H.R. 622 would also expand the Electoral College votes, so if we were still using the Electoral College in 2030, it would make that system far more representative as well. As Thomas Paine wrote in *Common Sense*, "A long habit of not thinking a thing wrong, gives it a superficial appearance of being right," and locking our House districts at the same number they were in 1910 is definitely not right.

Now you may say, but even with the House districts at their ridiculous sizes, the House still gets bills passed all the time. Well, maybe not the 118th Republican House, it can't seem to get it together, but the 117th Democratic House passed, among other things, the American Rescue Plan, the Infrastructure Investment and Jobs Act, the PACT Act (for veterans), the CHIPS and Science Act to bring manufacturing back to America, and the Inflation Reduction Act that made America's recovery after the pandemic the best in the developed world, so what's the problem? Well, first of all, those two examples beautifully illustrate the importance of House leadership and cohesion, as both the 117th and 118th Houses had the same slim majority, but totally different leadership and priorities, and it shows you what can be accomplished when the majority works together for the good of the American people rather than fighting among themselves to gain approval from their base, or notoriety from the media and outside influences. The job of a congressmember is to write and pass legislation to improve the lives of the American people, to keep the government running, and to pass budgets and allot money. If they're not doing that, they're not actually doing their job.

In our current political environment, we have an "us versus them" thing happening to the detriment of the entire country. As mentioned, America primarily functions as a two-party system and those two parties are supposed to represent different points of view and the diversity of the political spectrum, but both parties are supposed to play for Team Democracy. Today's Republican Party is all obstruction and defense. Republicans have made the calculated decision that anything terrible that happens to America is a win if it's blamed on the Democrats. They have cynically chosen the destruction of the rival party over the success of America. The Republicans are actively betting against our economy, blowing up international relations, and fundamentally abandoning our democratic principles to regain power.

Which takes me back to the questions from the beginning of this principle. If our representative's job is to represent us, then why don't we have common-sense gun legislation? Why haven't we raised the minimum wage since 2009? We understand our elections are clearly problematic, so why didn't those voter protections become law back with the 117th Congress? Ultimately, why do our leaders keep getting elected to office making promises they can't keep? The answer to all these questions is sabotage. Sabotage, with an assist from the Senate filibuster.

The filibuster is an old-school parliamentary procedure, made possible by a Senate rule change in the early nineteenth century, that's used to prevent a bill from being brought to a vote. It usually happens when one or more senators try to delay, or block, a vote on a bill by extending debate on that bill in a process called filibustering. It's basically when they talk and talk and talk until the time runs out to vote. It's what that old Jimmy Stewart film *Mr. Smith Goes to Washington* is about.

However, that's not how the filibuster works anymore. It used to be difficult to filibuster. Physically and mentally draining for the senator or senators. You had to really want to delay a bill to go through all that trouble. It didn't used to just be senators reading *Green Eggs and Ham* on the Senate floor. Senators used to talk about the issues in the bill, why they opposed it, why they thought the bill would negatively affect people. The point was to give senators a way to waylay voting until their point could be sufficiently made. They were there to represent their state's voice and doggonit, they would have their say.

The Senate, like the House, was designed to pass legislation with a simple majority. The House would debate and pass a bill and send it to the Senate. The Senate would debate and pass the bill and send it to the president. The president would then sign or veto the bill, and the judiciary was there to act as a check on the constitutionality of the law itself. All three branches had the opportunity to step in if there was a problem, but things moved along. That's how the American government was designed to work.

AMERICA 101: SPEECH AND DEBATE CLAUSE

One of the reasons it seems like congresspeople can say pretty much whatever they want, true or not, with very few consequences is because of a clause in the Constitution called the Speech and Debate Clause. The main purpose of this clause was to protect members of Congress. To be sure something they said during "purely legislative activities" wouldn't implicate them in a lawsuit and disrupt their ability to do their job. However, that "purely" part has fallen by the wayside, which has left a lot of congressmembers feeling as if the Speech and Debate Clause gives them free rein to do or say any number of truly deceptive things—in hearings, on television, in fundraising emails—and get away with it because, they claim, it's within the "course of their legislative activities."

The filibuster was not in the Framers' plan for the Senate. They didn't say, "And if senators don't like a bill, they can just talk on the Senate floor until the time runs out to vote." Talking a bill to death was something senators discovered organically. This process of overtalking bills so no one could vote wasn't even given an official name until 1853, and there was no way to stop it until 1917, when senators adopted a rule (Senate Rule 22) that would allow a two-thirds majority to stop the filibuster and force a vote, calling it "cloture." Even with cloture it was still hard to stop senators from talking bills to death, so in 1975 the Senate lowered the cloture threshold to sixty votes. Today you don't even need to speak, let alone speak for hours or days, you simply need to send an email to the majority leader to say you're going to filibuster and the majority party needs cloture to stop it. This is the filibuster as we know it in modern America.

No one has to talk for seventeen hours. No one has to prepare a winning argument to change hearts and minds. No one has to wear a diaper on the Senate floor to make sure they don't have to leave and the vote's taken while they're in the bathroom. Today's filibuster is a simple email saying, "Hey man, we're filibustering. You need to convince however many of us you need to get to sixty votes, or your bill is dead."

This is one of the major reasons our legislators can't get things accomplished. It's one of the reasons the majority of the country can want something and not get it. It's why an amazing bill like the Freedom to Vote Act can pass in the House and then die in the Senate. It's the reason wildly popular things like paid family leave, expanded Medicare, border funding, and affordable college die on the Senate floor. Not because the American people aren't behind these game-changing pieces of legislation, but because it's not in the minority party's interest to give the majority party a win. That's how you get back into power. You say, "Look, they promised you all this, and they did nothing." You don't say, "We were the ones who stood in their way," you just point to the failure, and it works.

One of the biggest misconceptions about the filibuster is that it promotes bipartisanship, and perhaps in another age, where the representatives might have listened more to each other and really had debates, that might have been true; but in our day of modern, polarized politics, the filibuster has the exact opposite effect, because it gives the party *out* of power the ability to block the party *in* power from getting anything accomplished.

Adam Jentleson, the deputy chief of staff to the late Senate majority leader Harry Reid, and author of the brilliant, albeit depressing, book *Kill Switch: The Rise of the Modern Senate and the Crippling of American Democracy*, reminds us that in *Federalist Paper* No. 22,* Alexander Hamilton wrote against the idea of requiring a supermajority for votes (like the sixty votes the filibuster requires today) because it would provide "an irresistible temptation for the party out of power to make the party in power look bad." Hamilton uses the words "to embarrass the administration, to destroy the energy of the government," and I think that's exactly what the filibuster does.

---

* After the Constitution was written, Framers James Madison, John Jay, and Alexander Hamilton wrote *The Federalist Papers* to further defend the Constitution against criticism. Any question someone might have had regarding the articles of the Constitution, they wrote explanations and answers to. Madison wrote twenty-nine of the eighty-five essays, Jay wrote five, and as you probably know from the musical *Hamilton*, Hamilton wrote the other fifty-one.

The filibuster has been used frequently since the civil rights era to allow a minority of predominantly white, predominantly reactionary conservatives to block everything the increasingly diverse majority of the country wants. At this point it's a relic of a different era and something that gives undue power to a minority that's already overrepresented in the Senate. Senators don't even have to tell us who's for or against a bill anymore. If the majority can't convince the minority to help it get sixty votes nothing happens, and we blame the majority for nothing getting done.

This is why presidents in the modern era have started using so many executive orders. It's a way to bypass Congress and get something accomplished. However, as mentioned, an executive order isn't the same as a law, because an EO can be overturned in many different ways, the easiest being by the next president with a different executive order. This is also why the majority party often tries to jam as much as it can into the budget reconciliation bill because that bill only needs a simple majority to pass.

AMERICA 101: BUDGET RECONCILIATION

Budget reconciliation is a special parliamentary procedure set up to make certain federal budget legislation move faster, particularly in the Senate, because it overrides the filibuster and allows the bill to pass with just a simple majority. However, budget reconciliation can only deal with three things: spending, revenue, and the debt limit. The origins of budget reconciliation came in the 1970s when Congress was concerned about America's growing deficit, and what was seen as too much presidential influence over the budget process. To counter this, Congress created a new type of legislation—a final budget reconciliation bill—that could be used to ensure budget-related bills would fall within the overall spending target passed by Congress.

In the past, budget reconciliation was rarely used, but polarization, gridlock, and the filibuster have made it an important workaround to get things accomplished in our modern-day American Congress. Reconciliation is now most frequently used when the same party controls the presidency, the House, and the Senate, but does not have the sixty-vote majority needed to overcome the filibuster. There are, however, limits to what can go in the bill and how many times a year it can be used (usually only once). Theoretically, spending, revenue, and debt could be three separate bills, but that almost never happens.

The limits of what can be included in the bill are set by something called "the Byrd rule," which allows senators to block things in the reconciliation bill they believe to be unrelated to spending, revenue, or the debt limit. A good example of this is when the Democrats attempted to add an amendment to the American Rescue Plan to raise the federal minimum wage to $15 an hour during its passage in 2021. Despite the fact that the Congressional Budget Office (CBO)—the nonpartisan federal agency that provides independent analysis of all economic and budgetary issues to Congress—claimed the wage increase would increase the budget deficit and should therefore fall within "reconciliation," the Senate parliamentarian—the formal expert on everything US Senate—ruled the minimum wage increase was "merely incidental," therefore in violation of the Byrd rule, and could not be included in the bill. Technically, the Senate majority leader could have fired the parliamentarian and hired someone more likely to give them the answer they wanted, but that's not typically how it's done. There have only been six parliamentarians since the position was created in 1927. It's a long-term position as there are so few people who have that level of expertise that they tend to stick around. The Trump administration used budget reconciliation in 2017 to bypass the filibuster to pass its major tax cuts, and the Obama administration used budget reconciliation in 2010 to bypass the filibuster to significantly amend the Affordable Care Act.

Provided the majority party has its people in line, the passage of the reconciliation bill can't be stopped, but you can make it miserable at the end with something called a "vote-a-rama," which happens after the period of time for debate has expired—in budget reconciliation's case twenty hours—when senators can offer an unlimited series of amendments to the bill and then vote on each amendment one by one. It's a painful and relatively pointless process, but it does allow the minority party to force the senators to vote on all kinds of measures they can't typically just bring to the floor.

The Senate is broken. In many ways the Framers designed the government with the idea that Americans' first loyalty would be to their home state, and that each state, with their own regional identity, should get equal say in the US Senate. If the House was to be based on the people's voice, the Senate would be there to represent the state's voice. However, we're so far away from that in modern-day America that many people's first loyalty now seems to be to their political party, not their state, or their country, and the filibuster allows that polarization to thrive. The Senate is far too easily paralyzed when the majority is forced to get a certain number of votes from the minority to get anything accomplished.

Keep in mind most of the states didn't even exist when the Constitution was written, and as states were added over the years, their population growth wasn't consistent. Some states, like California and Texas, had population explosions while others, like North Dakota and Wyoming, have stayed relatively small. Just like with the Electoral College, there's also an economic imbalance in how the Senate is set up. Most of the country's economic activity comes from the East Coast, the West Coast, and a few metropolitan areas in between. As I said before, the most prosperous parts of America include about fifteen states with thirty senators, while the thirty-five less prosperous states have seventy senators. So, the citizens paying the most into the federal government via taxes actually have less political power in the federal government via representation.

Now, this might feel a little more democratic if the Senate still voted by simple majority, without the filibuster, as it did when the country was founded, or if we had continued to add more senators as our territories and populations expanded like we did in the past, but we don't. There are almost 700,000 people who live in Washington, DC. That's a larger population than Wyoming and Vermont, and in line with states like Alaska and North Dakota, and yet Washington, DC, has no Senate representation. America also has territories like Puerto Rico and the US Virgin Islands, which send nonvoting members to the House but have no real representation. Our government simply stopped evolving to best represent its people. Much like our amendments, the rules of how it all works seem frozen in time. Locked in to benefit minority rule and the status quo, this lack of representation only gets worse the more our votes are suppressed. We're not keeping up with the times because to do so we'd need Congress to vote on it, and too many people in Congress benefit from things staying the same. It's a logical decision. If the system is rigged to favor you, why would you vote to make things more fair but limit your own power? Sadly, few do the right thing because it's the right thing to do. It didn't happen with the end of slavery, it didn't happen with the expansion of worker's rights, or women's rights, or civil rights. The truth of the matter is, sometimes those who benefit from the status quo simply must be forced to do the right thing. That's where we are with American democracy and what the people are responsible for insisting their government start to do.

Suspending, amending, or abolishing the filibuster is something America really should consider. Without the filibuster, each senator would once again be responsible for their own vote. As I see it, abolishing the filibuster would reboot the Senate and make politicians accountable to their constituents again. Currently, politicians from both parties can hide behind the filibuster to pass blame when things that were promised aren't accomplished. "It's not our fault, we couldn't get to sixty votes." The House even uses it to shut down more progressive or extreme points of view. "There's no point in taking this up, it'll never get sixty votes in the Senate." This is simply not how Congress was intended to function.

Without the filibuster, we could conceivably put bills on the Senate floor that Republicans and Democrats could vote on together because they didn't need to vote as a bloc to represent their party; they needed to vote as individuals to represent their state. That's a far better process than what we have now. We've seen what happens when you protect your party over your people. It's gridlock, lying, nothingness. Eliminating the filibuster would put the people, not the parties, back in charge. If we could pass legislation using a simple majority, the majority party would have far more opportunity to accomplish what it was put there to accomplish, and the voters would be able to decide if it did a good job or not.

AMERICA 101: DISCHARGE PETITION

While the Senate has very little recourse to get past a majority leader who doesn't want to bring bills to the floor, there is a process in the House called a "discharge petition," which can force a bill to the floor for a vote. It's typically used by the minority party when it thinks it can get a handful of the majority to vote with it on a bill that might otherwise not come to the floor. It works like this: Thirty days after a bill has been introduced to a subcommittee, a Member of the House (MoH) can file a motion to have the bill released (discharged) from the committee. To do this, they need 218 members to sign a "petition to release the bill." Once the bill has been discharged, the House has twenty minutes (!!) to debate and take a vote, the assumption being it should pass quickly since it needed 218 votes to discharge it in the first place. To be clear, this rarely ever happens since a bill that could get 218 votes would usually just come to the floor, but sometimes the minority party uses a discharge petition to draw the public's attention to a bill that is deliberately being hidden from the people. A prime example of this would be in 2014 when the Democrats, who were the minority at the time, filed a petition to discharge for a bill they had filed to increase the minimum wage. Even knowing they probably couldn't get enough Republicans on board for 218 signatures, they filed the petition anyway to show the public what was *not* being voted on.

Eliminating the filibuster is often referred to as the "nuclear option," as people say getting rid of it would "blow up" the Senate and assure the mutual destruction of both parties. The Democrats suspended the filibuster (i.e., changed the rules) when it came to nominating executive branch positions—including cabinet members and federal judges—after the Republicans refused to confirm any of Obama's nominees. When the Republicans were back in charge they suspended the filibuster for Supreme Court justices, which allowed them to stack the court during Trump's time in office. At this point there is a strong argument to be made that it's worth abandoning the filibuster in its entirety to pass voter protections and shore up voting rights—including getting dark money out of politics and putting an end to partisan gerrymandering. Quite frankly, if Democrats regain the House and keep the Senate and the presidency, I believe this is something they should do. It feels worth it to make our elections safer and more secure, to stop the endless flow of money in politics, to pass congressional ethics laws, and maybe even reform the Supreme Court. Now, you can't go back from abandoning the filibuster, but they could, theoretically, suspend it and put something else in its place. The Constitution doesn't set out the Senate rules. The power is in the hands of the senators themselves. If the Democrats get complete power of the executive and legislative branch again, I believe they should be bold with what they do, for the good of the country and the better functioning of our government.

Now, to be clear, I understand it may not be prudent to eliminate the filibuster with authoritarianism—in the form of Donald Trump and/or Project 2025—knocking on America's door. Giving a deliberately undemocratic body the power to solidify minority rule might be a mistake in this particular political climate. So, until we can be sure we can protect voting rights and ensure that minority rule and disenfranchisement can't be locked in at the federal level, it might be too risky to allow the Senate to function by simple majority. Too much damage could be done. The filibuster may be archaic, undemocratic, and absolutely in the way of progress, but it's also the only protection we have to hold off some of the most destructive laws the country could face should the current Republican Party—with its desire to eliminate Social Security, pass a national abortion ban, and solidify the power of the federal government around the president—take control of the Senate.

The Republican Party is incredibly close to solidifying minority rule and it knows it. Which is why most Republicans don't care how bad Trump is, or how insanely someone like Marjorie Taylor Greene behaves. It doesn't matter how compromised someone like Paul Gosar or Matt Gaetz is. It's why they didn't put forward an official party platform in 2020, and why any member who speaks out against the party is primaried or ostracized. It's why any reasonable Republicans are leaving the party, and why anyone who's left is fine with actively embracing the violence that occurred on January 6, and isn't ashamed of how incompetent their legislators are. It's why MAGA Republicans have shifted their focus almost exclusively to conspiracy theories, culture war issues, and blaming the villain of the day. They can't stand behind their policies because they offer none. They can't stand up for their records because they aren't accomplishing anything. They're not interested in turning out more voters or making a better argument for the future of America. Their goal is to consolidate power by whatever means necessary.

We live in a system that already favors one party over the other. Joe Biden won the 2020 election by more than seven million votes, but the way we elect our president, he only won the Electoral College by about eighty thousand votes in a handful of swing states. The Senate favors the Republicans with tens of millions more voters on the Democratic side but the chamber numbers come out to an even split. Republican state houses have been using their power to gerrymander states for years to limit which groups have the ability to elect the candidates of their choice, and now we have hundreds of new voter suppression laws in red states to limit who can vote and which votes count.

Which is why many Republican politicians don't even have to pretend to care about the people anymore. In certain districts they can win no matter what they do. They can be the worst people in the world—pedophiles, sexual assault enablers, insider traders, incompetent, compromised self-dealers—and you stick them in a gerrymandered, voter-suppressed, safe red state and they can literally take a last-minute vacation to Cancún while people freeze to death thanks to bad policy, and not even consider losing the next election. That's not a functioning democracy.

Republicans know the Democrats are better for the economy. A quick Google search will tell you that. They know Democrats are ultimately better at governing. Case in point, the 117th vs. the 118th Congress. They know Democrats have popular ideas for how to improve the country, like expanding our healthcare system, affordable college, and universal pre-K. They know if the Democrats shored up Social Security, voting rights, and protected the environment it would be almost impossible to roll those improvements back. They know the economic success we're going to see in the next ten years will be based on legislation President Biden passed in his first two years, and they know that eventually people will catch on that none of it came from them.

The Republicans are also aware that the majority of Americans are done with the old way of doing things—of shunning people who are different, of allowing white men with means to hold all the power while keeping everyone else out of the room where it happens. They understand most of us want to see an end to money in politics and lying for profit. They know our population strongly favors gun legislation, better public education, and affordable health care. They understand only a tiny group of people actually believe the government should get to decide what we do with our bodies. I even think they know saving the planet is not only the right thing to do, but could be a gold mine for new industry, but they are so deeply beholden to their donors, to the big-money power brokers who have kept them alive long after they ran out of ideas that they're stuck. They need the evangelicals, the racists, and the oil and gas industry. They need the corrupt, self-serving billionaires and the fear and anger of their voters to keep them afloat because it's all they have left. If you can't win on what you plan to do, then you need to lie about what your opponent plans to do, and you can only spin those lies so far without big checks, and when you take big checks, you owe big favors. I believe the Republican Party is caught in a web it spun for itself, and it needs to be soundly defeated so it can be free.

The door to excessive money in politics was first opened back in 1976 with the *Buckley v. Valeo* Supreme Court decision that ruled that while the government can limit how much individuals can contribute to political campaigns, it can't place limits on campaign expenditures, expenditures by a candidate from their own personal resources, or by independent groups supporting the campaign. This was the first time the court made the argument that under the First Amendment, money equaled speech. This helped pave the way for the rise of political action committees (PACs)* in the future.

---

* Political action committees are organizations that raise and spend money for campaigns, and support or oppose political candidates, legislation, or ballot initiatives.

Following *Buckley*, America got the *First National Bank of Boston v. Bellotti* ruling in 1978, which decided the First Amendment allows all speakers, whether individuals or corporations, to "publicly discuss all matters of public concern." This decision laid the foundation for the "corporate personhood" argument that thirty-two years later would be used in the *Citizens United* decision. The *Citizens United* decision (*Citizens United v. Federal Election Commission*, 2010) was a travesty for democracy as it left the door wide open to corruption in politics, allowing big spenders to exploit the lack of transparency in our elections, and took dark money donations from less than $5 million in 2006 to over $300 million in 2012. I think it's fair to say the *Citizens United* decision was the tipping point event that shifted American political influence away from the people and toward wealthy donors and corporations.

Now, we're not going to be naive and pretend wealthy donors, corporations, and special interests haven't always had an outsized influence in American politics, but *Citizens United* supersized it. In a 5–4 decision, the justices ruled that limiting "independent political spending" from corporations and other groups was a "violation of the First Amendment right to free speech," so corporations could now spend unlimited money on political campaigns so long as they weren't formally coordinating with a candidate or political party. If you're someone who cares about the fairness of American elections, this decision was a real kick in the teeth. As a Brennan Center for Justice report pointed out: "In a time of historic wealth inequality, the [*Citizens United*] decision has helped reinforce the growing sense that our democracy primarily serves the interest of the wealthy few, and that democratic participation for the vast majority of citizens is of relatively little value."

The justices who ruled for *Citizens United* reasoned that unlimited spending by wealthy donors and corporations wouldn't distort the political process, because the public would be able to see who was paying for the ads, but in reality, voters have no idea who's behind campaign spending. That's why all these dark money groups have such ambiguous names like Citizens for a Healthy America. Would that be a pro-healthcare group or a white nationalist organization? Unclear, and that's the point.

In 2014, 71 percent of outside spending in eleven of the most competitive Senate races came from dark money, and those numbers have only continued to grow. Immediately after *Citizens United* passed, PAC money was pouring into elections. From 2010 to 2018, super PACs* spent approximately $3 billion on federal elections, with most of the money coming from just a few individual donors. In the 2018 midterms, 74 percent of contributions came from donors giving at least a million dollars. So, a hundred individuals were just out there picking and choosing leaders who worked best for them. The *Citizens United* decision allowed the very richest to buy a chunk of American lawmakers, so it's not surprising that when those lawmakers get into office, they don't work for the people, they work for their donors.

Finally, because dark money can hide the identity of its donors,

---

* The same year *Citizens United* was decided, a federal appeals court heard the case *SpeechNow.org v. FEC* and, using the precedent of *Citizens United*, ruled that outside groups could accept unlimited contributions from both individual donors and corporations so long as they didn't give directly to the candidates. Traditional PACs are permitted to donate directly to a candidate's official campaign but are subject to campaign limits both in terms of what they can receive from individual donors and what they can give to candidates, but super PACs have no such rules. While super PACs are still required to disclose their donors, their donors could include dark money groups, which make the original source of the donation unclear.

it's also a back door to foreign influence in American elections. Technically law enforcement is set up to protect us from foreign interference, but it can't follow dark money, or it could, but it doesn't seem to have the will or teeth to do so. *Citizens United* is one of those decisions, much like *Dobbs*, which overturned *Roe v. Wade*, that has caused a major disruption in American life and makes anyone paying attention feel rather hopeless. This isn't what the majority of us want, so why is it like this?

If we want our government to work for us, we need to get money out of politics. At the very least, we need Congress to write new legislation that limits outside influence in our elections, perhaps even considering publicly funding elections like they do in other countries. Then we need to vote for the people who are going to vote for those changes. Right now, running for office is dependent on cash, and if you aren't independently wealthy, you need sugar daddies like lobby groups or PACs, or you have to overrun everyone's inbox begging for money. A moderately aware person is now bombarded with anxiety-inducing correspondence from candidates just to keep the donations rolling in. It's necessary for the candidates, but frustrating for the people. Especially since what the people want so infrequently makes it to the president's desk to become a law.

The United States doesn't even have an official campaign season. Our election season is never-ending. Lead-up to the midterms, the primaries, the presidential election year, special elections, local elections. It's just one into another into another, and they all need cash and a way to get on our radar, which is usually some political stunt that induces fear and anger. It's absolutely exhausting and no wonder so many people hate politics.

Other countries have laws dictating how long a campaign can be. In Canada the election period must be a minimum of thirty-six days and a maximum of fifty days. Mexico's election season starts ninety days before election day and must stop three days prior to the election. American elections have no set time limit, and because of that they've become an industry. We've made the election of our leaders part of the economy, and that does not serve the people. For-profit elections with unlimited money is damaging our democracy, the same way for-profit health care damages our health.

You can't advertise for two years straight without millions in the kitty. So the fat cats end up with all the power. A publicly funded, shorter US election season would benefit everyone—it wouldn't exhaust voters or require tens of millions of dollars per candidate to run. It would level the playing field for candidates of different backgrounds, and free up time for lawmakers to do the job of governing instead of constantly shilling to keep their jobs, or showboating to stay in the news.

The hustle doesn't even end after the election—once congressional members are in office, they have to raise money to stay there, and fundraising takes up far too much of their time. People have tried to address this problem, but they've yet to come up with a good solution. For example, there are laws around congressmembers raising money, one of them being, you can't raise money from your office because that's considered interfering with your congressional duties. Which means congresspeople must use separate "off campus" locations to make fundraising calls and efforts. Now lawmakers are literally using time to travel from Capitol Hill to another location to ask people for the money they need to keep them on Capitol Hill. It's absurd.

Keep in mind, most of our congressmembers don't live in DC full-time. They're supposed to have active offices in their home districts as well. So, if a congressperson wants more time to actually do their job, what makes more sense? Take hours or days to secure funding from thousands of small donors, or take a huge check from one big donor? It's a catch-22. Theoretically, the big check would free you up to do your job, but more often than not, taking the check changes how the job is done. People who write big checks don't do it for nothing. Now, there are some representatives who don't accept that kind of money. They're the ones who tell you they're "grassroots funded" or don't take money from super PACs, but most end up having to fold in some way to compete with the people who have no problem taking the money.

We also know there are congressional members who are actually in the job *for* the money. You only have to look at the personal wealth of some congressmembers to realize they aren't getting rich on their $174,000 a year salary. This will be an unpopular opinion, but when you consider that congressmembers have to have at least two residences, constantly travel, fundraise, and legislate, they're probably not getting paid enough. If we paid them more, we could also justify not allowing them to trade stocks while they are in office, or sit on for-profit boards of companies their laws will affect. There is an uncomfortable conflict of interest between our lawmakers and those who benefit from their laws that we have yet to properly address, and it often shows up in lawmakers' bank accounts and stock portfolios.

So many politicians end up being sellouts because they can't lose their donors without losing their job. The amount of money it takes to become a politician is also a major reason we end up with so many unqualified yahoos. Famous, infamous, or super-rich people all think they should be in government now. The job has become about power and money, not service or scruples. It's become about personality, not ideas. We built a wonderful system, but it's been corrupted, and no matter your political persuasion, it's impossible not to see money as one of the main corrosive elements.

Just look at the 2023–24 Republican-controlled House. Instead of passing bills and writing legislation to deal with the many concerns facing the nation—health care, the rising cost of living, the unfortunate border crisis—the speaker of the House, in a role that has changed hands multiple times in one congressional term, has instead approved numerous fishing expeditions and congressional hearings to better feed the culture wars the party believes give it the best chance of being reelected. It's bad government but smart politics. Most people don't understand who's to blame for the lack of progress, so they end up blaming the Democratic president, which makes it good for the Republican Party even if it's bad for the American citizen.

This is how we get congressional members refusing to vote for bills they negotiated themselves. It's how we end up with representatives who have been in Congress for decades without drafting a single piece of legislation. This is why tactics like gerrymandering and voter suppression are so destructive to our faith in government. Someone can literally do nothing to help their constituents, but provided they please their donors, they'll end up as the only one who can win the seat again. That serves no one except the person in that seat and the people who bought it for them.

The Republicans of the 118th Congress are on track to pass

the fewest number of bills since the Great Depression, thirty-four bills total after their first year of leadership, but most people don't hear about that. We just hear the drama that gets all the press. This is why modern-day American politicians talk about things like Mr. Potato Head or the Trump trials. It's all part of distracting the public from what is, or isn't, getting done and we keep falling for it.

Being a member of Congress is a serious job that should go to serious people. There's so much that goes into a bill, or a law, before it ever gets to the president. These are the people who can declare war. They fund organizations like the FDA and FAA, government agencies that make sure our food doesn't poison us or our planes don't fall out of the sky. There are 535 people who are supposed to be doing the job of managing America's problems. We need to be paying more attention to who they are and what they're doing, and if they aren't doing their job we should be voting them out, regardless of how good their social media feed is or how often they get on television.

Accomplishments, or lack thereof, of congressmembers aside (and to be fair there are a lot of wonderful, qualified members), the bottom line is Americans are less represented every year. House members have far too many constituents for us to truly be considered a representative democracy, the filibuster is a destructive force in the Senate acting as a roadblock to progress, and special interests and big money play far too outsized a role in our politics for anyone to be comfortable. It's a broken system, and it shouldn't matter what party you belong to—if it's broken, you can't use it either.

PRINCIPLE 5

★　★　★

THE LAW APPLIES TO ALL OF US

Everyone in this country is supposed to live under the same set of rules. We are supposed to have equal justice under the law. The basic premise of "no one is above the law" is that both the government and the citizens know the rules and they obey them. That the law applies to everyone both equally and fairly. That it shouldn't matter your gender, race, religion, or culture. It shouldn't make a difference if you're rich or poor, young or old, we should all be treated fairly under the law, without discrimination or a special set of rules.

The form of authority we use in democracies is what's called "rational-legal," or "the rule of law." This is the kind of government that strives for fairness but knows things won't always be fair because the institutions themselves are made up of people, and people are flawed. The rational-legal form of authority is also very slow because the power is spread out to make sure nobody has too much of it.

A few centuries ago the criminal justice system was quite

simple. A person could quickly go from being accused of a crime to a hanging. James Madison was deliberate when he laid out the people's rights in many of our early amendments. He gave us specific search-and-seizure rules in the Fourth Amendment, and the right not to incriminate yourself or be tried twice for the same crime in the Fifth. The Fifth Amendment is the one that says you can't have your life, freedom, or property taken from you without "due process." The Sixth Amendment is all about your rights in a criminal trial, including your right to a speedy trial by a jury of your peers (which is also where we get jury duty), the right to confront those who accuse you in court, to have witnesses to testify on your behalf, and your right to a lawyer. The Seventh Amendment is like the Sixth but for civil trials—usually involving a dispute over money. The Eighth Amendment is about how bail can't be excessive and how we can't have "cruel and unusual" punishment for a crime. The Eighth Amendment is one of those amendments that really needs updating as we have major problems with bail in this country, with poor people rotting in prison for small crimes, while rich people because of their financial success get out on bail for things that are far more egregious. There is also the question of what "cruel and unusual" means when you consider the way some prisoners, or even accused, are treated in this country. Not to mention the US is one of only fifty-five countries in the world that still have the death penalty, but twenty-three of them haven't used it in ten years, which puts us in a group with Saudi Arabia, Iran, China, and Egypt. Is the death penalty not cruel and unusual? These are the type of things people consider when they talk about "criminal justice reform" because the system we're living in uses elements that are potentially unconstitutional, unethical, and often ineffective and expensive.

Now, even saying that, it's important to acknowledge we've come a long way in criminal justice reform over the years. As legal scholars point out, in the nineteenth and early twentieth centuries, it didn't take long to gather evidence. Police could beat confessions out of people or search your house without a warrant. Before the Fourteenth Amendment, everything in the Bill of Rights applied only to the federal government. Local governments and law enforcement could do whatever they wanted.

It was twentieth-century civil rights activists like Thurgood Marshall and legal scholar and theorist Pauli Murray who looked around and saw the criminal justice system needed attention and recognized how hard the law came down on Black men. Their idea was to create a series of procedures to make it harder to put people in jail. As legal scholar Teri Kanefield says, "Their goal was to turn a straight path into an obstacle course by implementing a series of procedures and safeguards that would help achieve due process for *everyone*, not just the rich and well connected."

This is why we should be careful about complaining about how slow justice can be. The whole idea of "He's guilty! Just throw him in jail already" is understandable when someone's crimes seem so obvious, but they still deserve due process and their day in court. It doesn't serve us to take shortcuts. If we want to function under the rule of law, then we need to allow the rule of law to play out. Checks on power, whether in government or law, make it harder for the powerful to take advantage. We don't want citizens wrongly imprisoned or falsely accused of crimes. We don't want autocrats to be able to take over simply because we abandoned checks and balances when we wanted to speed things up. Slow is preferable to unjust.

Autocracy is attractive to people because of the speed. A dictator doesn't need to follow the rules or ask for permission. They do what they want when they want, and that control thrills people. The whole idea of "Lock her up!" falls into the authoritarian camp. During the 2016 election, the Republican base wasn't interested in looking into what Hillary Clinton had actually done, putting her on trial, and punishing her if she deserved it—they just wanted her gone, rule of law be damned. And Trump and the current right-wing leaders are making it very clear that if they return to power, that's exactly how they plan to run our government and Department of Justice.

As Kanefield points out:

> *For most of American history we've lived in a hierarchy. Before 1920 there were no regulatory agencies or regulations to prevent powerful, and let's be honest, white men from taking what they wanted. Before the women's movement, and the modern Civil Rights movement, we had democratic institutions, but they were primarily run by these men. Through the hard work of many people over many years we have been making the transition from a form of government ruled entirely by a certain group for a certain group, to a form of government that's far more pluralistic, and big surprise, some people don't like it.*

When the world has revolved around you for so long, having the universe expand to include others can feel unsettling. You've probably heard the famous quote "When you're accustomed to privilege, equality feels like oppression." This idea of sharing power, wealth, and decision-making with others, especially others deemed lesser, has always been something certain people were going to fight. These are the people who were pro-slavery, pro–Jim Crow, who liked the age of the robber baron and hated the New Deal. You can still see them in today's white supremacy movement. They're your antisemites and misogynists. They're the people still mad about desegregating schools, and angry about diversity initiatives. It's families like the Trumps, Kochs, Sacklers, Devoses, and Kushners. These are the folks still working to get back to "the way it was." To make America Great AGAIN. When the system was run *by* them for *them*. The Republican Party embodies this sentiment now. The very idea that Donald Trump could suggest that the rule of law doesn't apply to him, the majority of the Supreme Court could agree, and his own party, the self-described "party of law and order," doesn't care, tells you exactly what this group is willing to abandon to keep their place at the top.

This is the group actively talking about rounding people up into camps, mass deportations, having religious tests, and locking up political enemies. This isn't something just for Putin to do in Russia, or Xi Jinping to inflict on the people of China, this is something that a fair number of American leaders are looking to do right here at home. The Republican Party is deliberately using hardball tactics and glorifying lawbreaking because Republicans don't want to live in a rule of law government that's stopped serving their interests. They want something new, and if they have to bring down the entire system of government to do it, so be it. This is why the idea that Democrats should "fight like Republicans" is misguided, because it only plays into their hands.

If you want to save the rule of law you can't use the same

tactics as those who want to destroy it. This takes us back to the old expression about "Democrats bringing a knife to a gun fight," because if you bring a gun, and I bring a gun, we just upped the chances someone gets shot. I understand, not having a (metaphoric) gun feels frustrating and unfair when you want action and results—why do they get to cheat if we have to play by the rules?—but we have to play by the rules if we want to live in a society with rules. Once we've abandoned the rules, we can't get them back. Which is why what's happening with the court system in America is such a disaster for the rule of law.

Laws, government, and the courts only have power because we collectively agree they have power. Just like money only has value because we collectively agree it has value. Kori Schake of the American Enterprise Institute defines democracy as a "consensual relationship of accountability where we agree on how laws will be passed and how we will enforce those laws." Schake argues that when the Founding Fathers wrote "We hold these truths to be self-evident . . ." in the Declaration of Independence, it meant the people have these rights innately and we loan them to the government on our behalf.

While the legislative and executive branches enact our laws and carry them out, the judicial branch—the federal courts—is the one that interprets the law. The judiciary determines the law's constitutionality and how it applies to individual cases. If Congress has the power of the purse (it's in charge of our money), and the president has the power of the sword (they're in charge of our military), the courts are dependent on the power of the public. Their authority comes from our believing what they do is legitimate, that they are acting on behalf of the law and not in their own interests.

Unlike the other branches of government, the judicial branch is deliberately undemocratic, as many of the judges and justices who preside over the federal courts are unelected and appointed for life. The people given this responsibility are supposed to be such legal standouts, so above reproach, that our government trusts them to take a job they can't be fired from. According to the White House, the courts were designed to be insulated from "the temporary passions of the public," which "allowed them to apply the law with only justice in mind, and not electoral or political concerns." Wouldn't it be wonderful if that's how it was playing out?

AMERICA 101: PARDONS

The Constitution gives the president "Power to grant Reprieves and Pardons for Offences against the United States, except in Cases of Impeachment." So, the president has the authority to grant a legal pardon to a person convicted in federal or military court. The Framers included the power of the pardon as a way for the highest office in the land to grant mercy for a miscarriage of justice. Governors in most states also have the power to pardon prisoners convicted of state crimes, depending on their state constitutions. Some governors are allowed to pardon independently, some require partnership from clemency boards or advisory groups, and in some cases the discretion is given directly to the advisory group and the governor just acts as a rubber stamp.

I shouldn't have to say this, but the power of the pardon wasn't included as a way for the president to use it on himself, it wasn't supposed to be used as a thank-you to the president's friends and donors, and it definitely wasn't designed to be used as a moneymaking scheme for the president to sell pardons for cash. This seems obvious, but without these clarifications written down as law (which they should be), the right to pardon can be, and recently has been, deeply abused.

As mentioned, the Framers were concerned the country would eventually splinter, with each state deferring to its own set of rules. For this reason, they believed it was essential to have one overarching set of laws to be overseen by an independent judiciary that sat above all others. States could have their own constitutions, and their own ways of doing things, which the federal government would have no right to review or veto, but the Framers also included the Supremacy Clause (Article VI, paragraph 2 of the Constitution), which states that when in question, federal laws will take precedence over state laws, and prohibits state governments from interfering while the federal government is exercising its constitutional powers. States are also not allowed to assume any job that is exclusively entrusted to the federal government.

So, that standoff between Texas governor Greg Abbott and the Biden administration around border patrol at the beginning of 2024, when the federal government told the state government to stand down, was the Supremacy Clause in action. When Governor Abbott said he wouldn't back down, the Supreme

Court ruled what he was doing was unconstitutional. The fact that the governor went on to ignore the court's ruling and continued his control of the border—a federal power, not a state one, and explicitly against the final word of our top court—wasn't brave, it was illegal, and it put our country in a very dangerous position. When leaders start picking and choosing which laws they follow and which they don't, it throws the entire rule of law into question. Are court decisions optional? Can we just decide we don't agree with the Supreme Court and make our own laws? A lot of people were outraged that *Roe v. Wade* was overturned, but so far we've agreed that the decision stands, because you have to play by the rules if you want to live in a nation of rules. However, the legitimacy of the court itself is now being called into question, and if we can't trust the courts then how do we trust the law?

The Supreme Court's power comes from the idea that it's above politics. That the law itself is its own living, breathing thing, and the justices are only there to interpret it. Our entire legal system is based on the foundation that there is something greater and more substantial than the personal preferences of a political appointee. Being a Supreme Court justice is an extremely consequential job that affects the entire country, which is why they have to go through a nomination period and be questioned and confirmed by the Senate. It's essential the people have faith in the institution of the court and are confident that its interpretations of the law and constitution are not simply political acts.

The Supreme Court is the last place someone can appeal a decision and the final word in matters of federal law, and although the Supreme Court may hear an appeal on any question of law, it doesn't typically hold trials. The bigger part of its job is "to interpret the meaning of a law to decide whether a law is relevant to a particular set of facts, or to rule on how a law should be applied." Lower courts are then obligated to follow the precedent* set by the Supreme Court when making their rulings.

It's amazing how many things we take for granted in this country that our courts have decided. Laws are written, actions are taken, and often they end up in front of a judge to decide if they are *allowed*. Once they end up at the Supreme Court, the justices have the final word until the justices themselves decide otherwise. This is how Americans ended up with the right to possess a firearm at home for self-defense (*District of Columbia v. Heller*, 2008), or the right to die if you've signed an advanced directive (*Cruzan v. Director, Missouri Department of Health*, 1990). The court is the reason we can no longer lock people up for mental illness unless they pose a danger to themselves or others (*O'Connor v. Donaldson*, 1975). Believe it or not, there was a time when we were just sending people, particularly women, away to facilities against their will. Even the right for same-sex couples to engage in sexual acts was a right the court ruled on (*Lawrence v. Texas*, 2003) because many of the states still made those consensual acts illegal. Even the right to burn the flag in protest was something that required a decision (*Texas v. Johnson*, 1989).

---

* Our entire legal system is built on precedent, or decisions, made by the Supreme Court. Lawyers all over the country use cases the court has decided as examples of why a judge or jury should rule in their favor. Supreme Court decisions are the foundation of the entire rule of law, and because of this, you must have a really good reason to overturn a settled decision. So, unless some grievous injustice has been made, the court is supposed to uphold its previous rulings in order to give our justice system a sense of stability.

To be clear though, there's actually nothing in the Constitution that gives the Supreme Court the exclusive right to decide what the Constitution means and impose that on the other two branches of government or the American people. The court actually gave *itself* the power to be the final arbiters of the Constitution in a case called *Marbury v. Madison* in 1803, when it created something called "judicial review." Most of us assume the courts have always had the right to decide what the law is, but the concept of judicial review caused quite a stir. President Jefferson was furious, claiming the ruling made the Constitution "a mere thing of wax" the judiciary could "twist and shape into any form they please." President Andrew Jackson completely ignored its self-appointed power and rejected a Supreme Court ruling, saying, "the opinion of the judges has no more authority over Congress than the opinion of Congress has over the judges," and Abraham Lincoln overlooked what could have been seen as the Supreme Court's expansion of chattel slavery in the 1857 *Dred Scott* decision by freeing all enslaved Americans with the Emancipation Proclamation in 1863, and following that up with the Thirteenth Amendment, making emancipation a national policy, before the court could weigh in again.

As Alexander Hamilton wrote in *Federalist Paper* No. 78, the courts were originally designed to be an "intermediate body between the people and their legislature," and although the courts have the power to "interpret the Constitution and our laws," this "did not put them above the legislative branch." In fact, Hamilton wrote, "The power of the people is superior to both [branches]," and "where the will of the legislature . . . stands in opposition to that of the people, declared in the Constitution, the judges ought to be governed by the latter rather than the former."

In that same paper, Hamilton wrote that judicial independence was the best way for the government to secure a "steady, upright, and impartial administration of the laws," and that if we wanted everyone living under the same rules, it was essential that we have a trusted court that would oversee those rules, and it worked for a long time. We had federalism and states' rights, but overall, despite our enormous size and regional differences, we moved forward in unity, because we were guided by a group of seemingly independent jurors acting as a separate but equal arm of the government upholding our constitutional rights.

However, over the past forty years, very powerful right-wing groups have been targeting the judicial branch of our government. The idea being if the court is the final word on our laws, then they would make sure the justices on the court would rule the way they saw fit. They may not be able to get the legislative branch to create the kind of laws they liked, but they *could* get the judicial branch to rule on the laws they didn't. Now that the Supreme Court has a 6–3 conservative majority, it's not even pretending to be unbiased anymore. Five of the justices, who in their own confirmation hearings agreed to uphold established precedent, are now upending established law willy-nilly in a "What are you going to do about it?" kind of way. The decision to effectively uphold Texas's obscene six-week abortion ban, against the precedent of *Roe*, was only the first step. They've now overturned the entire precedent of a woman's right to bodily autonomy. Fifty years of established law gone overnight. Why? Because the science changed? The facts changed? Our knowledge around abortion or pregnancy changed? No. Because the court changed. That's not a blind interpretation of the law.

That's the shaping of the law using a personal vision. The court has now done the same with the reversal of forty years' worth of precedent with the Chevron deference, stripping the power from the experts at federal agencies, and 250 years of precedent with their breathtaking decision on presidential immunity. And if the Supreme Court is no longer beholden to settled precedent, if it can just abandon precedents and change the Constitution as it sees fit, where does that leave us?

As sitting justice Sonia Sotomayor wrote in her dissent of the ruling in *Trump v. United States* (2024) after the six conservative justices gave legal immunity to US presidents, essentially making the American president a king, the decision "makes a mockery of the principle that no one is above the law" and allows a president who might use their power for the most corrupt purposes to be immune from criminal prosecution. She separately wrote, "Today's court . . . has replaced a presumption of equality before the law with the presumption that the President is above the law for all official acts." And she concluded her dissent with the chilling, "With fear for our democracy, I dissent."

Much like Justice Sotomayor wrote in her dissent to the *Dobbs* decision overturning *Roe v. Wade*, "Will this institution survive the stench that this creates in the public perception that the Constitution and its reading are just political acts? I don't see how that's possible."

She's right. Our faith in the law is shaken when the justices themselves appear to have ethics issues, if they're beholden to financial donors, their religion, or their personal desires. If you can get a different ruling on the same case, with the same facts, simply by changing who's on the bench, it throws into question whether the rulings are, in fact, based on the law or simply the will of the justices.

It's naive to believe that the Christian conservatives who built and support this current Supreme Court will stop while they're ahead. They're already talking about how *Griswold*—the case that acts as the backbone of privacy law in this country, the one that led to abortion rights, gay marriage, and contraception—"might not have been decided correctly." If any and all settled precedent can just be overturned, then our entire rule of law is up for debate if this activist court* feels it knows what's best for the country.

If our laws are only dependent on who sits on our highest court, and who sits on the court is dependent on politics, then how can the Supreme Court be seen as anything other than a political entity? And if we're dealing with a political entity, then why are these people not elected and why do they get lifetime appointments? Our country wasn't set up to give nine people the power to rule on all our laws, and yet, that's exactly where we've found ourselves. At a place where the Supreme Court—the interpreter of our nation's laws and guardrails for the other two branches—has become a corrupted organization, with the majority of its members seemingly installed to rule on behalf of the minority of our citizens.

It's also worth noting that today's court looks nothing like the

---

* The current conservative majority is what's called an "activist court" because it seems to be actively pushing the country in a particular direction. During the civil rights era, people called Chief Justice Earl Warren's court an activist court for the same reason. In this case, however, the court isn't moving the country forward to better represents all its citizens, or to expand the rights and protections afforded by the Constitution. This is a regressive court with five of the six conservative justices installed by presidents who didn't win the popular vote and who aren't reflective of the majority will of the nation.

American electorate. All six conservative judges—John Roberts, Samuel Alito, Clarence Thomas, Neil Gorsuch, Brett Kavanaugh, and Amy Coney Barrett have ties to the far-right, libertarian Federalist Society, and all three of President Trump's nominees—Gorsuch, Kavanaugh, and Barrett—were personally handpicked by Federalist Society mastermind Leonard Leo, though as I said earlier, Leo also takes credit for installing Roberts and Alito. All six justices are Catholic hardliners, or far-right Christians, and all six clearly make decisions based around their faith and politics—two things Supreme Court justices are not supposed to do. Our court is meant to reflect the country it presides over—and to be clear, our country is not 67 percent far-right Christian conservative with deep ties to dark money.

Senator Sheldon Whitehouse, a senior member of the Senate Judiciary Committee, has been telling us the court has been captured by dark money for years. That the far right turned its eye on the courts when it realized it was losing its handle on the will of the voters, and that it's only become worse since *Citizens United*. According to Federal Communications Commission (FCC) filings, the Judicial Crisis Network, now called the Concord Fund, is a web of allied dark money groups who have spent millions over the past few decades transforming the federal judiciary into a conservative force, having placed more than ten thousand ads since 2012 to get the Christian Right the control it wanted. Donors were giving $15, $17, $48 million at a time. What do you get for that kind of money? As Senator Whitehouse tweeted, "Here's the truth: dark-money court packing is a project by right-wing donors that's been supercharged by Republican justices and Republican defenders in the Senate." Former Senate majority leader Mitch McConnell was a huge force behind the plan to hijack the court for the far right, and like it or not, he did an exceptional job. Under McConnell's leadership the far right was able to fill three questionable seats on the court and turn what should have been a 5–4 conservative court into a 6–3 ultra-conservative court.

By 2020, the current Roberts's Court (named after Chief Justice John Roberts) had handed down more than eighty partisan 5–4 and 6–3 decisions that can be easily shown to benefit Republican donor interests. These wins have often come at the expense of everyday Americans—stripping protections from minority voters, reproductive rights, workers' rights, the environment, public health—and more often than not, these decisions also degrade our democracy: green-lighting gerrymandering, protecting dark money, and suppressing the vote.

By the end of the 2023–24 term, any perception we might have had that the court was still acting in good faith on behalf of the constitution has gone up in smoke.

The people who paid for this court, who spent forty years working diligently to reshape the judiciary in their own image, have been rewarded mightily. The goal was to turn back the clock. To gain control of the country without actually winning control of the country. To reverse the progress made on everything from voting rights to workers' rights, and they're succeeding. This is not a partisan statement. It's a factual observation. You can see it by asking, Is the court expanding or limiting who and what is protected. Is it *giving* rights to the people or taking them *away*? Is it liberty and justice for all, or liberty and justice for some? And why would these six people decide that the most powerful person in the country—arguably the world—would not have the law apply to them at all?

It might seem like what's happening with the courts is far away and won't affect you, but it's the courts who have shaped the face of our nation. We had been moving forward for nearly two and a half centuries—baby steps, but in the right direction—toward more freedom, more fairness, more equal rights. While most of us were assuming Dr. Martin Luther King Jr. was right when he said "The arc of the moral universe is long but it bends toward justice," the far-right, religious, corporate-aligned powers were working hard to make sure that wasn't true. To unravel the progress we've made and return the country to a place where the "right" people lived the "right" way. And this is not how the judicial branch is supposed to behave. What we're dealing with here is a bought and paid for operation by people who couldn't get their ideas codified through the legislative branch, so they're getting legislation overturned using the judicial branch.

While the courts of the 1940s through the 1960s were known for protecting minority or nondominant religions, it's mainstream Christian groups who most often claim minority status today. Rulings in favor of religion have increased from 46 percent in 1969 to 85 percent and rising today, the biggest leap occurring under current chief justice, John Roberts. The new story for Christians all over the country is they are a persecuted class. In fact, many Christians feel the separation of church and state itself is discriminatory. That keeping religion or prayer out of public schools is not neutral, but "imposes the religion of secularism" on our children. We see these ideas reflected in court decisions that allow religion to be the deciding factor like *Burwell v. Hobby Lobby*

(2014) or *Little Sisters of the Poor v. Pennsylvania* (2020), where the court ruled that employers could deny their employees birth control for religious reasons. You see it in *Masterpiece Cakeshop v. Colorado* (2018), where the Supreme Court ruled a conservative baker should be able to deny service to a gay couple because their marriage was against his religion, and again in *303 Creative LLC v. Elenis* (2023), where the court ruled a website designer could preemptively tell customers she would discriminate against gay people for religious reasons despite the fact that she had questionable standing to even bring the case before the court, as no gay couple had actually asked her to design a website. Under the current far-right Supreme Court, "religious liberty" is simply a way for far-right Christians, under the guise of freedom, to impose their will on those who don't share their beliefs. So, it shouldn't be a surprise that we now find ourselves in an America where people are banning books, and we're discussing the idea of abolishing contraception, as well as interracial and same-sex marriage, because it's all part of the same plan.

As Margaret Talbot wrote in her *New Yorker* article "Amy Coney Barrett's Long Game," though conservative justices now dominate the court, it is striking how firmly they hold to the notion of themselves as the persecuted figures. In fact, in 2020, after a series of court victories in favor of "religious freedom" lawsuits, Justice Samuel Alito gave a speech to the Federalist Society where he warned that "in certain quarters, religious liberty is fast becoming a disfavored right." He also asserted that the right to keep and bear arms was "the ultimate second-class right," linking Christianity and gun rights together, with the conservative justices as the last line of defense for the defenseless.

Sure . . . the "defenseless" with their $400 million ad budgets and stacked court. Justice Barrett gave a speech less than a year later at a private event in Louisville, Kentucky, where she said, "My goal today is to convince you that this Court is not comprised of a bunch of partisan hacks," but she said it from the stage of the McConnell Center with Mitch McConnell, the man who had brazenly and hypocritically strong-armed her onto the court eight days before an election, standing behind her. For a modern America that is statistically more open-minded, more pluralistic, and more tolerant than it's ever been, these court rulings have been a tough nut to swallow, with the presidential immunity ruling being an actual choking hazard. Which probably explains why the Supreme Court's public approval rating is at an all-time low.

★ ★ ★

America is huge, far bigger than our Founding Fathers could have ever imagined in both size and scope, which is why our courts, and our faith in the courts, have never been more essential. Every case this activist court overturns, every precedent it abandons, every decision it makes using the shadow docket, without arguments or publicity, throws our faith in the law into question. This court is abandoning the protections of the Voting Rights Act. It has overturned a woman's legal right to her own body. It has disposed of affirmative action and softened the rules around search and seizure. It even thinks *Brown v. Board of Education*, which desegregated our schools, is up for debate. It shouldn't matter your politics, this kind of partisan reading of the law should concern everyone. Justice is supposed to be blind, but this court has not only taken off the blindfold, it clearly knows exactly which direction it's marching.

AMERICA 101: SHADOW DOCKET

Supreme Court cases take one of two tracks: the merits docket or the shadow docket. While the merits docket is how we usually get rulings, the shadow docket is generally only used in emergencies when the Supreme Court needs to temporarily uphold or block a law, and unlike in a merits case, the parties involved file their briefs in days, not months, and the cases themselves are typically decided without oral arguments. To be clear, this is not how the court is supposed to function, just quietly changing laws off the public's radar without any extensive briefings or hearings, but our current conservative-majority Supreme Court has been using the shadow docket far more regularly these days to avoid scrutiny. According to the Brennan Center for Justice, the shadow docket has been used twice as often since Justices Gorsuch, Kavanaugh, and Barrett joined the court.

So how long does the court, and consequently the foundation for our rule of law, retain legitimacy if it continues to eliminate people's rights, or disregard the very principles of the Constitution it's meant to interpret? Especially, as Justice Sotomayor said regarding the presidential immunity decision, when the ruling has "no basis in law"? When the court is simply making decisions in favor of donors' wishes, corporate profits, or specific religious dogma? My guess is not long. Which is why the idea of "Supreme Court reform" has gained a lot of momentum in recent years. At this point court reform might be the only way to retain our country's faith in the rule of law. Otherwise, we're all going to be like Governor Abbott, just looking at rulings and saying, "No thanks." And where does that leave us?

The general sentiment seems to be that anything we try to do to counter the dark money influence in our judicial branch will be seen as a partisan maneuver, and that any lawmaker backing any sort of change will be accused of taking a partisan position. Which is why we need the *people* of the United States behind the mission to reform our courts. We need to give our lawmakers the support they need to fix this branch of government. If we could return the courts to a place of legitimacy, we would have a far better chance of fixing the other branches moving forward. So, let's look at the options, because based on where we are now, we clearly can't do nothing:

Can we limit the Supreme Court's power? Yes. Congress is the check on the judiciary. Congress could choose to pass legislation to limit the power of the court or, at the very least, expand its ethics rules. As the brilliant American writer and intellectual Thom Hartmann suggested, Congress could write regulation that says, "all decisions involving Constitutional matters must be decided by consensus, or with no fewer than 7 out of 9 votes," which would, at least temporarily, stop the six right-wing justices from steamrolling the rest. Or, as Hartmann proposes, perhaps make all Supreme Court arguments and decisions televised, bringing the entire process into the light, raising integrity through transparency, and increasing the power of the dissenting voices in the public consciousness. At minimum, Congress should pass a law insisting the Supreme Court follow the same ethics rules that every other federal court judge has to follow.

AMERICA 101: DISSENT

The Supreme Court votes on which cases it wants to take up. Verdicts on a case are typically decided after all parties involved have submitted months' worth of legal briefs explaining their position and, in many cases, after having argued the case before the court, where justices had the opportunity to ask deep, probing legal questions about how the Constitution applies to each argument. The justices then sign their verdict so it's clear how each justice voted in the case. If a justice doesn't agree with how a case was decided they can write a dissent, explaining why they disagree.

Can we force justices to recuse themselves from cases where they might be compromised? No. Article III of the Constitution lays out no rules for recusal, so the justices get to self-monitor. So even if, say, one of their wives is a known insurrectionist and they're ruling on insurrection, they don't have to sit out unless they choose to, or unless a majority of their fellow justices come together to insist they do, but usually the individual justices make the call.

Can we change their term limits so that they're no longer lifetime appointments? Yes and no. The Constitution says federal judges can "hold their office during good behaviour," so they have the job as long as they want unless we pass a constitutional amendment, which would be difficult with a normal functioning government but downright impossible in this polarized political environment. However, the Constitution doesn't specifically stipulate permanent status on the *Supreme Court*, only the *federal bench*. Theoretically, Congress could pass Supreme Court term limits—eighteen years has been suggested—and the justices could either retire at the end of their term, or return to a district or appellate court to finish out their career. With this solution we'd have more movement on the court and presidents would be more inclined to nominate justices with wisdom and experience, rather than simply trying to pick the youngest person they can to lock in that seat for their party for as long as possible. This would also serve to stop justices from having to basically work until they die to avoid the "wrong" president choosing their replacement.

FDR proposed moving all justices who were over seventy to an "emeritus status," so they could still participate in deliberations, but would no longer have a vote. Or, perhaps, all emeritus members' votes could be consolidated into one, if there was consensus. This way we wouldn't have seventy- and eighty-year-olds deciding the laws for the youth of America, without understanding the world those young people will have to live in.

Can we remove them if they are clearly compromised? Not really. The Constitution's check on judicial power is impeachment and removal, but that requires two-thirds of the Senate, and with our current Congress, that would be a nonstarter. The Constitution does say the justices "shall hold their Offices during good Behaviour," which could be questionable, now that we've seen justices like Clarence Thomas and Samuel Alito taking things like fancy trips and housing from donors who were seeking certain outcomes from the court, but it would take court reform from Congress to really define what "good Behaviour" means. If anything, it's a glaring reminder to be incredibly deliberate with our votes for Congress, because Congress is our only check on the court.

AMERICA 101: IMPEACHMENT

The Constitution says the president, vice president, and all "civil officers" of the US are subject to removal from office upon "impeachment" and "conviction." Impeachment was created to serve as a check mostly on the executive and judicial branches of government. To impeach someone, the House of Representatives brings "articles" (charges) of impeachment against the official. The House "adopts" the articles by a simple majority vote. Once this happens, the official has *been* impeached. The case then goes to the Senate for an impeachment *trial*. If it's the president who's been impeached, the chief justice of the Supreme Court presides over the trial.

If the impeached individual is found guilty by the Senate via a two-thirds majority, the official is removed from office and can never hold elected office again. If the Senate fails to get the requisite majority and the impeached individual is found not guilty, they are acquitted and may continue to serve in office. They will, however, always remain impeached.

As of June 2024, the House has initiated impeachment proceedings over sixty times and there have been twenty-two impeachments. This includes three presidents, two cabinet secretaries, and one senator. Although, as this book goes to print, there is talk of filing articles of impeachment against a few more Supreme Court justices. Of the twenty-two impeachments only eight were found guilty by the Senate and removed from office. All eight were federal judges. The presidents who have been impeached include Andrew Johnson in 1868, Bill Clinton in 1998, and Donald Trump in 2019 and 2021. All three remained in office following acquittal by the Senate. Former president Richard Nixon was not impeached—he resigned at the suggestion of his own party after Congress started the process against him in 1974.

State legislators can file articles of impeachment against their governor and other state officials, and many local governments have impeachment procedures in place as well.

What about expanding the court? Could we add justices to the bench and dilute the power of the compromised justices? The simple answer is yes. We only have a nine-member court because 155 years ago Congress matched the number of Supreme Court justices to the number of circuit court districts, which at the time was nine, but is now thirteen. So, there's already a precedent for matching justice numbers to districts. While adding seats to the Supreme Court would have once been considered extremely radical (FDR was deeply criticized for suggesting such a thing), what's going on with the court right now is already radical, so not considering this option might be the more extreme choice.

The expansion of the number of Supreme Court justices to match the number of appellate districts is the "easiest" and most popular proposed fix. Personally, I think we should expand the court far more extensively. Now that we know justices can be compromised partisan actors, I think it's prudent to limit the power of each individual justice. Plus, we need a way to force them away from Team Liberal or Team Conservative, to work as individual arbiters of Team Constitution.

I propose we expand the court to twenty-seven. The Supreme Court becomes either two courts of thirteen plus a sub, or three courts of nine. The justices pick their cases and fellow justices at random. They won't know which cases will be coming before them, or who they'll be working with from case to case. Cases like *Dobbs*, which overturned *Roe*, won't simply come before the court because the petitioners know ahead of time they have the votes to win. No one would know what the makeup of the court would be before they brought the case, and while the justices would continue to choose which cases came before them, they wouldn't get to choose which cases they would personally oversee. This would limit the ability for bad actors to buy or curry favors with a particular justice, so justices would be left to rule on the merits of the case, the quality of the argument, or the interpretation of the Constitution rather than simply personal bias or bribes.

Twenty-seven justices means justice could once again be blind. Justices could get sick, or retire before they died, because the laws of the country wouldn't come down to their one vote. One in twenty-seven doesn't make that much of a difference. That many justices picking cases and colleagues at random would mean we could stop pouring gasoline on the fire of partisanship and begin to have faith in the highest court again.

Obviously, there's a lot of nuance to this, and this isn't a legal book, so legal scholars will all have their thoughts, but if we don't do something about the Supreme Court, pretty soon we won't be able to do much about anything. Since the beginning of this nation, our courts have played an essential role in how the country functions. We started with a constitution and a bill of rights. Every big change that came after that, every game-changing piece of legislation that was written, every societal change weighed in on, even the power the government gave itself, has been checked by the court.

The most important thing to remember as we watch this far-right court attempt to fundamentally reshape the country, is that things can only change if we expand the majority in Congress who believe things *should* change. The legislative branch is the only check we have on the judiciary. Those who seek to take us backward and steal our freedoms are patient, calculated, and backed by billions, but we still have our voices, our vote, and the majority sentiment. At the end of the day the court only works if people believe in it, and the rule of law is dependent on people believing in the court. Without the legitimacy of the Supreme Court, we have a country without law and order, and without law and order we have no country at all. We win Congress, then we push Congress to expand the Supreme Court. This court doesn't speak for us, it wasn't elected by us, and as Alexander Hamilton said, if it comes down to the court or the people, we must always defer to the latter.

★ ★ ★

GOVERNMENT SHOULD BE A FORCE FOR GOOD

It's easy to criticize government, and candidly, there's plenty that deserves criticism. However, government is something we can not live without. There is so much the government does that we don't even consider. From local governments sending workers to remove that tree that fell across your street to Homeland Security stopping a potential terrorist attack. From weekly garbage pickup, to workers in our national parks, to government scientists approving the quality of our vaccines and baby food. If you call the police, that's the government. If you need the fire department, it's paid for by the government. If your state has a natural disaster, it will be the government who foots the bill to clean it up. Do you use public school? Government. Is mail delivered to your home? Government. Do your streetlights come on, and traffic lights work? That's the government. Government plays such a huge and essential role in our modern society that we couldn't live without it, yet we spend so much time complaining about it when we could be engaging with it to make it better.

Ronald Reagan inflicted a great wound on the country when he said, "The nine most terrifying words in the English language are: I'm from the Government, and I'm here to help." As president of the United States, Reagan used his authority as head of the government to undermine how essential government really is. The government *should* help its people, and if you don't believe that, then what are you doing in government?

There are legitimate reasons to be frustrated with the American government. Justifiable reasons to be angry at the way things have been going, but that doesn't mean we abandon the one form of government that offers us the power to change things. It means we redouble our efforts. We shore up our wonderfully flawed system, and put our time and energy into protecting that which people have fought and died for. There are people who dream of the ability to choose their leaders, who can't even imagine a nation of freedom and liberty. We owe it to them, and to ourselves, to not be so ungrateful that we let the amazing American experiment fail because it felt too hard or we were too busy. We can recognize the ridiculous excess in our government without defaulting to the idea that democracy itself doesn't work.

So how do we make it better? We start by raising expectations and accountability. Rather than expecting government to screw up, to be useless, to act selfishly, and to spend our money wastefully, we should demand our government be a force for good. We should make it clear that its job is to protect our rights, not take them away. To keep us safe, not put us in danger. To keep the government open, funded, and functioning. We need a government that's more New Deal and less "Art of the Deal." We need our lawmakers thinking about how to make life better for all Americans, not just better for themselves. We need leaders we can trust—upright, upstanding, honest people—who respect the American citizen and don't suppress our votes or rig our districts.

America needs leaders who don't trick us with deceptive advertising and blatant lies. A government that believes in the American Dream and will fight for what it stands for. Representatives who understand they speak for the *People*, not just their voters or donors. Long-term thinkers and big-picture planners. Leaders who acknowledge the reality of the future, who seek to address the problems ahead of time, rather than being reactionary and passing blame when they're caught unprepared. We need transparency and morality in government. If our lawmakers are passing laws so we can't see what they're doing, we need to assume what they're doing isn't right. If our legislators are behaving in ways we wouldn't allow our children to behave—lying, calling people names, passing the buck, not doing their work—we need to punish them for it at the ballot box. Not everyone is suited to public service, and we need to get far more comfortable kicking people out. No politician should have to tell you the horrible thing they said was "just a joke." This isn't high school. These people are responsible for the future of our nation and the world. Being an elected official is not a job just *anyone* can do. The people need to have faith in their leaders. Faith in a god belongs in the confines of your heart, but faith in government functions solely in the secular world of laws where our representatives are supposed to function.

I'm not going to argue for the two-party system in America. It is what it is. I have no loyalty to one party over another, but as a liberal, my values, needs, and morals are far more in line with the Democratic Party than the alternative. As John F. Kennedy said,

If by "Liberal" they mean someone who looks ahead and not behind, someone who welcomes new ideas without rigid reactions, someone who cares about the welfare of the people—their health, their housing, their schools, their jobs, their civil rights, and their civil liberties . . . if that is what they mean by a "Liberal," then I'm proud to say I'm a "Liberal."

People think government is lame, that legislation is boring, and all politicians are cheats and liars, but that's simply not true. Over time the American government has changed the lives of so many people for the better. From the Emancipation Proclamation to the Civil Rights Act, from the New Deal to Social Security, from workers' rights to regulated industries.

From a personal perspective, a government program saved my life. I have an incredibly rare lung disease and my husband and I work for ourselves. Without the protections of the Affordable Care Act to stop insurance companies from discriminating against people like me with preexisting conditions, I'd be dead. Dead. With that one piece of legislation, the Obama administration helped me, and millions of other Americans, stay alive, and the Republican Party continues to try to repeal it to this day.

President Joe Biden got the Infrastructure Investment and Jobs Act, the CHIPS Act, and the Inflation Reduction Act passed in his first two years in office with the smallest of majorities in Congress. Those bills will literally be rebuilding a crumbling America for the next decade, not just fixing our roads, bridges, and airports and bringing high-speed broadband to people across the country—which is essential to functioning in today's digital world—but returning high-tech manufacturing to the United

States and outfitting the country with climate initiatives to address our struggling planet. These bills will also create tens of thousands of well-paid jobs. Don't tell me government can't be a force for good. Even Republicans who voted against these bills are out there at ribbon cuttings taking credit for the money as it arrives in their state.

We have to recognize that government is a big, slow-moving machine, like an aircraft carrier that, going in the right direction, can be a force for good, but if used incorrectly, can be a danger to us all. Former president Trump has already told us that should he become president again, his first order of business would be retribution. To consolidate the power of the federal government around himself, to take control of the Justice Department, to purge the civil service of anyone who isn't a loyalist, and to make sure anyone who's ever stood against him is punished. Whether he's elected or not, his rhetoric is a reminder of why we can't get caught up in the promises of a populist who tells us what we want to hear, or believe that giving someone the power of a dictator would be a preferrable way to run our government.

Merriam-Webster defines public servant as "a government official or employee," and public servants are supposed to work for the public good. Government is not supposed to be a place for profit, greed, or personal power, and voters should remember that. Government should be there to serve the public and make people's lives better. It should be a job of great worth and respect. We should have people coming out of high school who want to grow up and go into government because that's where change is made. Government should be cool. A career for world shakers and visionaries, not power mongers and self-dealers.

The Framers founded our nation with the noble aspiration of a government *by* the people, *for* the people, and it's one we should return to. No, not everyone should get a say in how government is run. We should all get a vote, but that vote should collectively hire smart, capable, goal-oriented individuals who want to *do* the job, not just *have* the job. The voters should have to pay attention to who they elect, but not be responsible for monitoring everything they do. We should have our laws and the press for that. At the end of the day, we have to be educated citizens who vote in every election, but thinking about politics all day long is ridiculous. We all have lives and most of us would like them back, thank you very much.

In *Common Sense*, Thomas Paine described government as a "necessary evil" that exists to give people a structure so they can work together to solve problems and prosper. Paine argued that in order for a government to do this, it had to be responsive to the people's needs. That the British system failed America because it gave the richest and the most powerful too much power over the people's chosen representatives. Paine wrote that it was essential the individual colonies put aside their differences to form one powerful nation that better reflected the will of the people. I would argue it's essential the states put aside their differences now to do the same.

It doesn't matter if you're from California or Kentucky. We are all in this together and we live or die depending on how we handle things. If you live in a Southern state that's been controlled by Republicans for the last two to eight decades and you aren't happy with your life, the people in New York didn't do that to you. Your leadership has been making choices to favor themselves and letting you suffer. Then they tell you who to blame, and it's *never* them.

We've been taught to hate each other in America—programmed even—because it serves certain people in positions of power to keep our attention on each other and not on them. As historian Thomas Zimmer says,

> *Modern-day Republicans are single-minded in their goal to transform the current political system, which has gone too far towards true equality, back to something they feel more aligns with their world view and the power structure they're comfortable with, and they don't care if they have to hold that power without majority support, or even against explicit desires of the majority of the country.*

Zimmer makes it clear that there's no point in debating whether Republicans really want to abolish multiculturalism and open-minded democracy. The proof is there at the state level. They can't control the federal level as much as they'd like, so they act as obstructionists, but wherever they are in charge, Republicans are openly embracing an authoritarian version of American government.

Look around America. Look at what's happening in red states. It's all about regression, control, limiting the rights of people. We've got kids being paddled in school, children working overnight shifts in factories, pregnant women being left to go septic without medical treatment. We have IVF clinics shutting down, border patrol allowing refugees to drown, child marriage, violence against trans children, and people being shot every day just going about their daily lives. The red states are banning books and history and hairstyles. They're telling teachers what to teach and claiming just being gay grooms children. There is a legitimate theocratic takeover of state legislatures, quoting biblical scripture to pass secular legislation and forcing everyone in their state to conform to their narrow worldview.

So, what's our country's problem? Why can't we pull it together? How can we possibly be this divided and unable to hear reason or see truth? I believe it's identity, and the over-identification with our identities, that hinders our progress. We talk about "identity politics" all the time as if it's a bad thing. "Oh, here we go again with the identity politics. Why do you have to be so sensitive and woke and politically correct?" As if offering equal rights to everyone or treating every citizen with the same level of respect is some kind of overreach. The way I see it, the problem isn't what the marginalized, or minority, are asking for. The problem is what the un-marginalized have learned to expect without having to ask. People blame identity politics on Democrats, on women, on the LGBTQIA+ and BIPOC communities, but real identity politics doesn't come from those who have been forced into their identity through marginalization, but from those who put them in that box in the first place. Real identity politics comes from those whose identities have always run politics. Those who feel the ground shift under their superiority don't like the feeling. As I said before, "When you're accustomed to privilege, equality feels like oppression."

Humans get tied up when the problem we have to solve is linked to how we identify. It's the same phenomenon that keeps people in bad marriages, or jobs they don't like, or what keeps young people playing sports they no longer enjoy. Once your identity is tied to something, it becomes very difficult to let go or be objective. Now consider this concept on a macro level with the type of problems America deals with—racism, nationalism, religion, gender politics, politics/politics—whenever you try to solve any of these issues with someone who's tied their existence to the thing you're discussing, you're going to get pushback because you're no longer discussing the issue, you're discussing them. If your identity is fused to something, any criticism of that something will be seen as an attack. Consider yourself. Who are you? What is the thing you most identify with? Your race? Your color? Your citizenship? Your lack of citizenship? Your religion, gender, sexuality? Well, that's the thing you're going to have the hardest time discussing.

Say your identity is tied up with being American. It's how you see yourself. A member of the greatest country on earth, land of the free, home of the brave. Now it's likely you're going to take any criticism of America personally. "Don't come at me with 'Americans killed all the natives and is a racist country.' I didn't do that. I'm not like that." Well no one said you did, or you are. These are just discernible facts about the nation that you're unable to see clearly because it's wrapped up in how you see yourself. If you define yourself as being a Christian, a God-fearing person who follows the Bible, goes to church, and is going to heaven, then you're going to take any discussion around the history of Christianity, its contradictions, the validity of other religions, or taking "God" out of our national motto as an attack on your entire reality, and it will be, and often is, met with defensiveness and anger.

Which is why it's so hard to reason with Trump supporters, Second Amendment Warriors, or Evangelical Christians. Why it's so tough to get lifelong Republicans to see that the party they identify with is gone. To question the things people associate with is to question who they are. I can debate religion all day because my identity is not tied up in it. I can criticize America, because it's where I choose to live, not who I am. Certain Trump supporters can't understand how Biden could have won the election without having big rallies or seeing Biden flags everywhere. They can't conceptualize people who could vote for him without defining themselves by him. That if he was bad, his voters would criticize him, not follow him to jail.

The right wing has actively worked to tie people's identities tighter to things, that way it's able to play into people's fear of losing that identity. A certain subset of America has always been fixated on this idea of their identity being threatened or replaced. In the 1925 F. Scott Fitzgerald novel *The Great Gatsby*, the antagonist talks about how immigration is altering America's racial composition and destroying the country when he says, "The 'dominant race' is being 'swamped out' by immigrants." The book, which was published the year after Congress passed the Immigration Act of 1924, which set national origins quotas to limit the "less desirable" immigrants, reflected the sentiment of many in the nation, with the stated purpose of the law being to "preserve the idea of American homogeneity."

On Fox News Tucker Carlson spent years promoting the idea of people being "replaced" in America, although he often disguised it as just asking questions: "Who says diversity is a strength? Who says that?" But the truth is, the hosts of that network have made the fear of demographic change a central theme since 2016. Before Tucker was fired as part of the fallout from the lawsuit around Fox lying about the 2020 election, a *New York Times* investigation reported that Tucker had used the theme of white/American replacement in over four hundred shows.

This idea of "identity" is why all the dog whistles of white supremacy, xenophobia, and homophobia are so effective. It feeds the great replacement theory—"These people are trying to steal your way of life, change your way of being, of doing, of speaking . . ."— and gives it power. The Right leans hard on identity—"good" Christians, "real" Americans, "traditional" family values—because it sells. Fear sells. Bigotry sells. Hate sells. Identity sells. Identity is how we got to a place where people claim we can take their gun "from their cold, dead hands" because they've tied their identity so thoroughly to the Republican interpretation of the Second Amendment that it's become almost impossible to disassociate themselves long enough to realize we don't have to accept daily mass shootings. Our lives have simply become less worthy than their identity as a gun owner.

Which is why I don't see Democrats as the party of "identity politics." The far left of America, sure. You could make the argument that it also takes its identities to such an extreme that it can no longer see the bigger picture, or separate its sense of self from the reality of what's happening, but while Democrats might *talk* more about different identities, it's the Republicans who push their supporters to *base their politics* around identity. This is how we end up with self-described "patriots" wearing shirts that say they'd rather be Russian than a Democrat. That's identity politics, "Hey, can you use my correct pronouns?" is not. Requesting to be seen and referred to with respect has no bearing on anyone else's rights or freedom. Telling someone they can't be who they are, or that you're passing laws to stop hospitals from treating them, that's a completely different situation. Allowing room for different identities doesn't strip you of yours, but denying people their rights because their identity doesn't line up with your beliefs? That's a problem.

We need a thirty-thousand-foot view. To see the big picture and recognize the hypocrisy of leaders preaching the "dangers of tyranny" while publicly supporting autocrats and wannabe dictators. We need people to see the absurdity of believing they're the "party of freedom" while simultaneously passing laws that tell people what they can read, say, teach, and do with their own bodies. If you call yourself the party of "small government" but believe the government can just remove children from their loving homes because they don't personally agree with the parent's "lifestyle," or that teachers should out gay children to their communities against the child's will or safety, then you've lost perspective.

★ ★ ★

Stop telling us America is the greatest, richest country in the world and how lucky we are to live here without acknowledging what our actual lives are like. We can love this country and still acknowledge that the daily existence of many Americans is the opposite of the PR fantasy we've been sold. That we have an extraordinary chasm between the rich and poor, that our social safety net is minimal at best, and that medical crises are the leading cause of bankruptcy in this country. We have a mental health crisis and no way to deal with it because we don't have quality, affordable health care. We spend billions on police, but don't feel safe or protected. Trillions on defense, but we're surrounded by violence. And not for nothing, but we had over two hundred thousand preventable deaths during

Covid because we had leaders who chose to politicize the virus instead of uniting us against a common enemy.

We need a government full of people who not only want to do the job but are *capable* of doing it. As I said before, there are only a few hundred people who can pass federal laws. We can't be filling those seats with useless partisan showboats who do nothing but obstruct and denigrate the process. We need true representatives. Especially if they're supposed to be representing 800,000 people each. We need lawmakers who acknowledge today's problems rather than living in a preferred past. We need a government up to date on science and technology. We can't have eighty-year-old legislators asking tech giants how to update their Facebook account. We need representatives who understand the need to regulate technology for the safety of humanity, who understand the risk of AI, and are thinking of plans for the American people when the world's machines inevitably take our jobs. This isn't a game. It's a consequential profession for talented people and we need to vote with that in mind.

We need the government to properly fund our education. To make our kids, all our kids, open-minded and smart enough to solve the problems of tomorrow. To expand our public education dollars through college and trade schools. We need American children ready and able to compete in a changing global world, and that won't happen if we teach them different facts from state to state based on our personal bias and beliefs. To paraphrase a popular saying: Studying history will sometimes disturb you. It will sometimes upset you and make you angry. If studying history always makes you feel happy and proud, you aren't studying history. That's propaganda.

We need a government that understands the importance of protecting our environment, not just for our health, but for the world order. We can't have representatives willing to ignore the consensus of almost all the world's scientists because it's bad for a few of their donors' bottom line. Rescuing our planet should be nonnegotiable. We don't need 544 bills denying trans people their rights. We need 644 bills around everything from renewable energy to minimizing microplastics. Managing fake crises, rather than handling real ones, simply does not serve the people.

We need a government who listens to what we want. None of us are here to just pay bills and die. No one wants to worry about getting gunned down at the grocery store. We don't want the power to control our own bodies or family planning to be taken from us. We don't want to lose Social Security or Medicare, or to have to work until we're seventy while our children are on a factory floor at age twelve.

Covid-19 should've brought us together. It was as much a common enemy as any alien invasion we've seen in the movies. More than a million Americans died and most of us didn't even know because it was invisible and weaponized. It was hidden from our field of view and used as a cudgel to separate us. We should have seen the devastation splashed across our newspapers and social feeds like the Vietnam War, solidifying our perspective as to who the real villain was. Not doctors, or scientists, or mask wearers, or people trying to stay safe getting a vaccine, but the virus itself. The media did us a tremendous disservice by not showing us what was really happening, and it allowed those with nefarious intentions to use that space to sow doubt. Doubt in each other, in science, in facts, and in truth. We were divided at the very time we should have been united, and we had hundreds of thousands of unnecessary deaths because of it. What would Pearl Harbor have looked like if half the country had been told it wasn't real? Or that it was just a political enemy pretending to be the Japanese? Or the Japanese had been invited by "those" Americans? Who does it serve to make us hate each other? Who benefits?

Our country is divided and ignorant and racist and backward. We worship at the altar of celebrity and wealth but don't support our families, our poor, our working class. Churches have a ridiculously outsized amount of political power in a country that's supposed to be based on the separation of church and state. Children go hungry every day in this nation, and we have politicians voting against feeding them. We abandon our elderly and scapegoat our minorities. We've passed laws allowing neighbors to spy on neighbors and turn them in for cash bounties, rapists to file for custody, and had legislators seek to inspect children's genitalia under the guise of "protecting the kids." It's no wonder our life expectancy goes down every year. People are miserable. Most are one paycheck, or illness, away from homelessness. This level of stress is killing us, and we wonder why our people keep shooting each other? Is this really the America you want? I think not. I think we can do better. I think we need to *demand* better.

I believe the idea of American exceptionalism is waning. I think, despite the behavior of the loud and ignorant, white supremacy is on the decline. I believe the patriarchy has had its day and we're in a transition between how things were and how they're going to be moving forward. We're currently experiencing a massive shift in how the world works and that makes a lot of people uncomfortable, so they fight to hold on to what they know. Change is scary, and between one thing and the next there's a void, and people can't get their footing in a void, so they reach back to a time when they had a grounded sense of their place in the world, or they find something in the void to hold on to like a conspiracy theory or a political party that promises to keep them safe if they support them without question. There's purpose in fighting against satanic pedophiles or standing up against a stolen election. It doesn't matter if the facts don't line up. It makes people feel like they're part of something. The world is changing, but people aren't sure how they'll fit in, so they'd rather stick with what they know, or hold on to something they created, even if that puts them in direct conflict with the truth, or their own best interests. There's a small and powerful group who don't want things to change because it benefits them, but there's a far larger group who don't want things to change because they don't know how change will affect them and it's a risk they're not willing to take.

We have to remember American democracy is not promised to us. We could easily become like Russia. A nuclear superpower with the trappings of democracy, but what is in truth, a corrupt oligarchy run by criminally unscrupulous people. You don't think leaders like Donald Trump wouldn't love to lock up people who disagreed with him? You think he'd be above disappearing political enemies or journalists if it served him? You don't think he'd give public contracts to his friends, or rig elections and lawsuits? Because you could make the argument he's already done most of those things.

I question if the current Republican Party, what we would call MAGA, can even be considered an American party as they no longer seem interested in working within our system of government.

The Republicans seem more than willing to sell out American democracy to retain power. Addressing the loss of their dominance due to a changing demographic, they seem to have chosen not to evolve but devolve into an unethical, nefarious group of cowards who represent the very worst of us. They have *become* the party of Trump. The party of personal vengeance, of victimization and conspiracy. They represent racism, homophobia, xenophobia, misogyny, and power at all costs. They have abandoned American values and no longer deserve American respect. They can't even stand up to the worst among them. They are an embarrassment and a danger to our great republic, and anyone who doesn't have the courage to call them out is complicit. There's a reason democracies don't last that long. Somebody always wants more power and will abandon democracy to attain it.

To the people who would take us down this path: there must be a part of you that knows this is wrong. Not just wrong— unsustainable. A part of you that understands that when a minority takes power over a majority the only way to keep control is to become more militant and totalitarian. If you don't have the will of the people, or faith in the system, then you must rule with an iron fist. History is littered with how bloody and brutal these kinds of governments have been. All dictators eventually topple, but not without great cost to the people. America can't go down this road. Should we allow the Republican Party, as it stands, to achieve unchecked power in this country, then we will far more closely resemble Russia, or Hungary, or Turkey than the country we know and love. We only need to look at Iran to see what happens when rights are taken away. It's almost impossible to get them back. We can't afford to be complacent about how quickly things can deteriorate. We can't just assume democracy, the rule of law, and liberal values are just sticking around. We're being offered a choice, and we must choose correctly.

Is the Democratic Party perfect? God no. There's a bunch on their high horse, some unable to compromise, a handful that are too old and out of touch, and a few with real power who are basically in it for themselves, but it's still a diverse group of representatives out here getting things done. Everything might be a mess in America, but for the most part, the Democratic Party is still trying to make people's lives better. People can be salty that change isn't happening fast enough, or they're not getting everything they want, but it's important to acknowledge that even with ridiculously slim margins, positive change is still occurring.

The Democrats are a coalition. They have to bridge the divide between the corporatists, the centrists, the liberals and progressives, and the far left. That's not easy. The Democrats are basically a working parliamentary system under the umbrella of one party. You want more parties? They're already here. They're just all considered Democrats. Representatives talking about a wealth tax, universal health care, and the Green New Deal would not remotely be in the same party as representatives looking out for the coal industry and corporate profits in another country, and yet within our two-party system, the Democrats are somehow making it work. Quite frankly, if the system itself (*cough* filibuster) wasn't so screwed up, they could probably do an even better job. Every *reasonable* political stance in American history from right to left is currently represented under the Democratic banner, and then there's that other party and whatever it thinks it's doing.

I believe former Republican speaker of the House Kevin

McCarthy said it best: "When you look at the Democrats, they look like America. When you look at my party, we look like the most restrictive country club in America."

This is the moment for common sense. For your own sense of critical thinking and your own sense of self-preservation. Tell these people you won't be fooled into giving them authoritarian power no matter how appealing their message might seem to you. If liberty, justice, and freedom are America's founding ideals, we simply can't embrace anything that would destroy them. We must stand for the liberty of all if we hope to keep it for ourselves. As Thomas Paine said, "When republican virtues fail, slavery ensues." There are so many people who understand this. Which is why your classic conservative, old-school Republicans, like the folks at the Lincoln Project, are currently on the same side as your AOC/Bernie Sanders type Democratic Socialists. Both sides understand what's at stake, and what the alternative would mean to this nation we love.

When Trump was in office, he did everything he could to undermine our institutions. He stacked our courts, he pardoned his friends, he undermined the free press, and used, and continues to use, propaganda media networks to push his agenda. He created a world of "us versus them," of "alternative facts," and petty grievance and hate. He refused to submit to the peaceful transfer of power, and he and his enablers staged a coup that ended in a bloody insurrection. Years later that threat continues. The Republican Party is passing laws every day to undermine our elections. Free thought is no longer encouraged in right-wing circles. You tow the party line no matter how dishonorable or untrue, or you're out.

Look at Nikki Haley, the last candidate standing against Donald Trump in the 2024 Republican primary. She called him "mentally unfit," "unhinged," and "unqualified," but a month later she was telling people she was voting for him. That should be deeply concerning. As George Orwell wrote in his dystopian novel *1984*, "The Party told you to reject the evidence of your eyes and ears. It was their final, most essential command." That's not democracy and it should not be encouraged.

We got lucky that Trump and his original team were so incompetent. America dodged a bullet, but that doesn't make us bulletproof. The weaknesses in our system have been revealed, and MAGA Republicans are currently taking advantage of those weaknesses across the country. If they get full federal power again, they'll exploit those weaknesses to destroy our institutions from within, just as they're doing in the states. We won't dodge the bullet a second time because this time they know where to aim. The only thing left to do is disarm them. To fight and beat these authoritarian factions using the very thing they're trying to destroy. Democracy.

Kori Schake argues that while democracy might be "slow and messy, and we're almost always dissatisfied with the process or outcome," the point is we can *change* the outcome, and, as she puts it, "that seems to be a universal yearning." Every time people get a chance to *choose* their form of government, they choose democracy, and that's not something you just give away. That's the power we've been gifted with the American experiment, and it's a luxury we've taken for granted for too long. No one would actually choose to live in a dictatorship. You don't see people packing up and moving to authoritarian or communist countries because things are just so much more efficient, no matter what Tucker Carlson's Russian lovefest would have us believe.

People have the right to feel that Washington is unresponsive. To feel as if no one is listening, but the changes we have to make are to the institutions and representatives themselves, not the *form* of government. We need to fix how things are done, not allow democracy to be cast aside for something else. We need to get rid of the filibuster, so senators are responsible to the voters, not party leadership. We need to pass voter protections to stop gerrymandering and voter suppression, so people's votes are heard and counted. We need to consider how the Electoral College works, and if it's something we should move beyond in a country this big. Finally, we need to get money out of politics. Politicians should be working for the people, not the donors. They should be debating and passing legislation, not raising money for the next election. People have been driven toward populism because populism makes things seem simple. It makes things feel easy, as if they're going to get everything they want. But populists in power don't lead; they just consolidate more power until no one else is allowed to lead.

People who say they'd be fine with military rule would not actually be happy if they woke up in a military dictatorship. People who say they want a strongman leader would not actually be happy under an authoritarian regime. However, the fact that so many people seem dissatisfied with democracy, and are willing to try something else, is an important thing to note.

It has been said that democracy is three things: (1) the vote, (2) the rule of law, and (3) a society that includes freedom of speech, a way of behaving in a civilized way with "the other," and free debate that is out of the grasp of power. Modern American democracy is showing strain in all three categories. We must use our vote to protect our institutions and behave with decorum and civility in the face of ignorance and incivility. Finally, we must uphold the rule of law, which means holding everyone, no matter who they are, accountable for their actions.

To quote Barack Obama on the first anniversary of the January 6 insurrection:

> *A violent attack on our Capitol made it clear just how fragile the American experiment in democracy really is. And while the broken windows have been repaired and many of the rioters have been brought to justice, the truth is that our democracy is at greater risk today than it was back then. . . . If we want our children to grow up in a true democracy—not just one with elections, but one where every voice matters and every vote counts—we need to nurture and protect it . . . that responsibility falls to all of us . . . nothing is more important.*

AFTERWORD

★ ★ ★

When I started the PoliticsGirl Project, my intention was to educate and inspire. I wanted people to understand how things worked so they could get their heads around what needed to be fixed. Then I wanted them to care enough to want to fix things. I believe in the American experiment. I believe in a nation founded on the noble ideals of liberty and justice, built on the foundations of freedom, within the protection of the rule of law. I know we could be the country we tell people we are. We've simply lost our way and allowed the wrong people too much power. It's time we took that power back.

The Six American Principles are a map we can follow to a future of which we can be proud. If we know who we are, and what we stand for, then we move forward with intention, and we measure ourselves, and our leaders, against those benchmarks. Americans deserve to live in a free nation of opportunity where our vote counts and our leaders listen. We can't have different sets of rules for different sets of people, and those who have the honor of representing this country should be held to the very highest standard, because they are the ones responsible for protecting our right to a "better, richer, fuller life." A social order where every person has the opportunity to rise while being recognized for their inherent worth. This is the kind of country we *could* be. These are entirely possible goals. Everything we do moving forward should be measured against The Six. If your politicians don't believe in, or work to uphold, them, then they have no business in American government.

Change is possible, growth is possible, fixing this country is possible, and the fact that you've read this book means you're a part of the solution. It's people like you who understand where we could go and will work to get us there. We need you. We need you to reject leaders who tell us it's impossible or seek to divide. We need you to talk to your friends and family when they're negative or apathetic or just plain wrong. We need you to believe we can do better than this, and then we need you to vote for it.

What I've noticed while positioning myself in this "warrior for democracy" space is that I've struck a nerve, not just with the people who tell me I'm an idiot, or a communist, or hate it when women speak, but with important and powerful people. People with real influence and the ability to make change. People who, despite what we see on TV, in formal tweets, or what their general by-the-book demeanor may suggest, really do care about what's happening in this country and are passionate about fixing it. I say this because I want you to know if you speak up, if you vote, if you organize, that you will be heard. That there are people who recognize you are unhappy, and they are out here attempting to work within the system to fix it. Please know you have not been abandoned, and the louder and clearer we are about what we want and are willing to fight for, the more confidence and courage those people will have to make the changes this country truly needs.

We must address our flawed, but inspired democracy. To set

ourselves on a stronger, more intentional path, so we can rebuild this nation on more secure footing than we began on. It's my belief, as Paine argued all those years ago, that there's only one right way to go and if we fail to choose it, we'll lose the opportunity to choose again. So, put your anger and disappointment aside. What kind of country do you want to live in? What would bring you pride and allow you to pursue the happiness that you were promised? Then ask yourself if you're willing to work for it.

I am.
I hope you'll join me.

In the appendix of *Common Sense*, Thomas Paine speaks directly to the Quakers, whom he believed were speaking on behalf of an entire group without the authority to do so. In that spirit, I'd like to end this book by speaking directly to those who call themselves "conservative" or "MAGA," as I believe they have claimed the mantle of American patriot without proper authority:

Dear MAGA,

The number of you who see my work and are so sure I'm making things up astounds me. You're absolutely convinced that what I'm saying is wrong. That Democrats are liars and cheats. Woke, liberal monsters driving the country into the ground. Some of you throw around words like "communist" and "socialist," but many just go with "evil" or "typical." As in, "Typical a Democrat would say that." Say what? That Republicans are planning to take your Social Security? That's not something I'm saying. That's what they wrote down they're going to do. That's what they've been working on for years. I'm not telling you Republicans are coming for your rights. They're coming for your rights. They already took a woman's right to her own body in red states, and they're being very clear the plan is to expand that to the whole country should they get back in power. They're on record, and video, saying gay marriage shouldn't be allowed and contraception should be banned. That we're a Christian nation and people shouldn't be able to opt out of Christianity. So what I want to say to all the people who try to school and shame and undermine me is: What if I'm right?

*What if the news you listen to and the politicians you like
are the ones deceiving you? It's not hard to check what I'm
saying. I check what I'm saying. I research everything. I'm so
careful about making sure what I put out there is the truth.
Can you say the same about your sources of information? What
if it's not the Democrats trying to hurt you, but your own party
tricking you into hurting yourself? The right wing is counting
on you to just vote Republican without looking into what it's
doing, but if they win, I think you're going to be very surprised
when all the things you've been hearing from the "liars"
turns out to be true. When IVF really is banned. When your
prescription drug prices really do go up. When you're kicked off
your insurance, or your parents lose their Social Security and
have to move in with you. You're going to be pretty upset when
you find your rapist has more rights than you, or when the
Republicans default on your loans because crashing the economy
is how you build an oligarchy, and I think you'll be particularly
surprised when your party doesn't just suppress Black votes,
or liberal votes, but your vote because you gave them so much
unchecked power, they didn't need you anymore. I'm not asking
you to believe what I believe. I'm asking you to check. I'm
telling you democracy and human rights are on the line, and
I'm suggesting you make sure I'm actually lying before you vote.
Because what if you're wrong?*

*Here's the thing. The people of California don't hate the
people of Arkansas. The city doesn't hate the country. The
LGBTQIA+ community isn't trying to take anything from
the cishet community. Our religion has no bearing on our
morality, jut as our color doesn't reflect our humanity. People*

try to divide us because they want us on teams. They want us stuck in our identities, so that we don't realize we're all American and our futures are inextricably linked. The only people who benefit from the idea that our fellow citizens are our enemies are those in positions of power who are best served when we fight one another rather than collectively standing up to them. We must find a way to see each other's humanity before our personal "identity." As a friend of mine says, "I just want to be able to stop and help someone at the side of the road without first having to check their bumper sticker to make sure we're on the same side." We don't need an alien invasion or a global catastrophe to find our way back to each other, we need an agreed-upon set of ideals and a shared intention to make things better.

Please understand I wish you no ill. I hope you live out your days in this country in freedom and prosperity. Everything we liberals want for ourselves—from the freedom to love who we want to love, and be who we want to be, and to worship who we want to worship—we want for you. We want you to have clean air and clean water, a livable wage, quality health care, and a responsible, responsive government. None of this is just for us. An American pledges liberty and justice for all. If you can't get behind that, then maybe stop thinking you're the one who's the patriot.

With respect,
Leigh

ACKNOWLEDGMENTS

★ ★ ★

M y biggest thank-you goes to my husband, Sean, who takes all my big ideas and helps bring them to life. The PoliticsGirl Project would not exist without him, and I'm deeply grateful to have had his partnership and love all these years. Marriage isn't for everyone, but it's certainly for us.

★ ★ ★

To my incredible son, Lochlan, who all this is for, because our kids deserve a far better world than the one we're leaving them, and we need to do something about that.

★ ★ ★

To my driven friend Monique, who took our one dinner a year and made me write down the ideas for this book, and my brilliant friend Hilary, who helped synthesize those ideas. This book wouldn't exist without either of you. Thank you.

★ ★ ★

My gratitude to my editor, Jenny Xu, who took on an orphaned writer and understood exactly what she was trying to do. This book could have been an opus. You have Jenny to thank for the fact that it's not.

Big thanks to my agent, Byrd Leavell, who believed this political nerd could write a book when others were less sure. Our work together is far from done.

I'd like to thank my publicists, Tanya Farrell and Elena Stokes, and the wonderful team at Wunderkind PR. I've never done this before, and you guys made what could have been crazy-inducing such a pleasure.

Huge thank-you to Randy Dolnick for producing the audiobook with Elisa Shokoff for S&S Audio. I listen to most of my books these days, so making sure the audio was exactly right was so important to me. I really appreciate all your time, effort, and attention to detail.

And great thanks to my wonderful supporters at PoliticsGirl Premium. This book would have been impossible without your patronage. You kept my head above water, and I will be forever grateful for your generosity. I can only hope my work continues to be worthy of your time.

Finally, I'd like to thank my amazing mom, who inspired the creation of PoliticsGirl by asking her lost and disheartened daughter what she really cared about at the exact right time.

FURTHER READING LIST

★　　★　　★

Organizations you may, or may not, know worthy of your time and money:

Emily's List—emilyslist.org
Field Team 6—fieldteam6.org
Media Matters—mediamatters.org
Reproductive Freedom for All—reproductivefreedomforall.org
Run for Something—runforsomething.net
The States Project—statesproject.org
Swing Left—swingleft.org

Recommended books for the moment we're living through:

Battling the Big Lie by Dan Pfeiffer
The Great Questions of Tomorrow by David Rothkopf
Humankind: A Hopeful History by Rutger Bregman
The Light We Carry by Michelle Obama
OMG WTF Does the Constitution Actually Say? by Ben Sheehan
On Tyranny by Timothy Snyder
Project Hail Mary by Andy Weir
Red Rising Trilogy by Pierce Brown
Saving Democracy: A User's Manual for Every American by David
    Pepper
Scythe series by Neal Shusterman

An incomplete list of podcasts I listen to regularly and would recommend:

Amicus from Slate
The Daily
Daily Beans
The Ezra Klein Show

Mueller She Wrote
On with Kara Swisher
Pivot
Pod Save America & Pod Save the World
This American Life

Newsletters and substacks worth your time:

Democracy Americana—Thomas Zimmer
Democracy Docket—Marc Elias
The Hartmann Report—Thom Hartmann
Hopium Chronicles—Simon Rosenberg
Letters from an American—Heather Cox Richardson
The New Republic
OpentoDebate.org
Pepperspectives—David Pepper
Proof—Seth Abramson
Stuff That Needs to Be Said—John Pavlovitz
TeriKanefield.com—Teri Kanefield

Accounts on social media whose opinions/thoughts I follow and respect *(an incomplete list—politics and American issues, not including politicians)*:

Allison Gill
Angelo Carusone
Ann Applebaum
Asha Rangappa
Barton Gellman
Brennan Center for Justice
Brian Tyler Cohen
Center for Reproductive Rights
Dahlia Lithwick
Dan Rather
David Corn
David Rothkopf
Elie Mystel

Ian Bremmer
The Intellectualist
Jen Psaki
John Fugelsang
Joy Reid
Kara Swisher
Kate Shaw
Katie Phang
Laurence Tribe
Lawrence O'Donnell
Lindi Lee
Mandana Dayani
Mark Elias
Mark Greene
MeidasTouch
Melissa Murray
Michael Mezzatesta
Michael Steele
Mini Timmaraju
Molly Jong-Fast
Neil Katyal
Perfect Union
Rachel Bitecofer
Rachel Maddow
Rebecca Traister
Rick Wilson
Robert Reich
Roxane Gay
Ruth Ben-Ghiat
Sage Lenier
Seth Abramson
Shannon Watts
Sherrilyn Ifill
Steph Rhule
Stephanie Miller
Strict Scrutiny

Vote Vets

*PLUS everyone from my substack list

Quality journalists/news outlets I respect that you might not be as familiar with...

The Atlantic

BBC

CBC

Courier Media

The Guardian

Mother Jones

NOTES

★ ★ ★

Introduction

1 *Thomas Jefferson's biographer:* Joseph Ellis, *American Sphinx: The Character of Thomas Jefferson* (New York: Knopf, 2005).

1 *Thomas Paine came from humble beginnings:* "Thomas Paine," American Battlefield Trust, https://www.battlefields.org/learn /biographies/thomas-paine.

2 *a response to the popularity of Paine's call to arms:* "Creating the United States," Library of Congress, accessed April 16, 2024, https://loc.gov/exhibits/creating-the-united-states/interactives /declaration-of-independence/docindex.html.

2 *five-thousand-square-foot underground bunker in Hawaii:* Mallory Moench, "Mark Zuckerberg Is Reportedly Building an Underground Bunker in Hawaii," *Time,* December 30, 2023, https://time.com /6551188/mark-zuckerberg-underground-bunker-hawaii-report -reaction/.

2 *an infrastructure bill in 2021:* The White House, Fact Sheet: The Bipartisan Infrastructure Bill, November 6, 2011, accessed April 15, 2024, https://www.whitehouse.gov/briefing-room/statements -releases/2021/11/06/fact-sheet-the-bipartisan-infrastructure -deal/.

4 *Aaron Sorkin would call our "star-spangled awesomeness":* "We Just Decided To," *The Newsroom,* Season 1, Episode 1, directed by Greg Mottola, aired June 24, 2012, on HBO.

5 *"The cause of America is, in great measure, the cause of all mankind":* Thomas Paine, *Common Sense* (Canada: Broadview Press, 2004), 45.

6 *America is the world's biggest polluter after China:* Laura Paddison

and Annette Choi, "As Climate Chaos Accelerates, Which Countries Are Polluting the Most?," CNN, January 2, 2024, accessed April 16, 2024, https://www.cnn.com/interactive/2023/12/us/countries-climate-change-emissions-cop28/.

8 "*Common Sense . . . has come in seasonably*": Patrick J. Kiger, "How Thomas Paine's 'Common Sense' Helped Inspire the American Revolution," History, June 28, 2021, accessed April 16, 2024, https://www.history.com/news/thomas-paine-common-sense-revolution.

10 "*I offer nothing more than simple facts*": Paine, *Common Sense*, 61.

America 101: The US Government

13 *"Framers"*: "Meet the Framers of the Constitution," National Archives, https://www.archives.gov/founding-docs/founding-fathers.

13 *fought a war to make it true:* "Timeline of the Revolution," National Park Service, https://www.nps.gov/subjects/americanrevolution/timeline.htm.

14 *a political system called federalism*: "Module 6: Separation of Powers and Federalism," Constitution Center, https://constitutioncenter.org/education/constitution-101-curriculum/6-separation-of-powers-and-federalism.

14 *the Supremacy Clause:* "Supremacy Clause," Cornell Law School, https://www.law.cornell.edu/wex/supremacy_clause.

15 *devoted solely to updating it:* "Constitutional Amendment Process," National Archives, https://www.archives.gov/federal-register/constitution.

15 *Filmmaker Matthew Cooke notes:* Matthew Cooke, "The Ghost Who Wrote the U.S. Constitution," February 7, 2023, in *American Origin Stories,* produced by Realm, podcast, https://www.matthewcooke.com/aos.

18 *The House of Representatives has 435 members:* "U.S. House of Representatives," USA Gov, accessed April 16, 2024, https://www.usa.gov/agencies/u-s-house-of-representatives.

18 *House members are elected:* "The House Explained," United States House of Representatives, accessed April 16, 2024, https://www.house.gov/the-house-explained.

18 *The Senate 100 senators:* "U.S. Senate," USA Gov, accessed April 16, 2024, https://www.usa.gov/agencies/u-s-senate.

18 *To be a member of the Senate:* "Constitutional Qualifications for Senators," United States Senate, accessed April 16, 2024, https://www.senate.gov/artandhistory/history/common/briefing/Constitutional_Qualifications_Senators.htm.

18 *State Assembly:* "Wisconsin State Assembly," Wisconsin State Legislature, accessed April 16, 2024, https://legis.wisconsin.gov/assembly.

18 *House of Delegates:* "Virginia House of Delegates Member Listings," Virginia General Assembly, accessed April 16, 2024, https://virginiageneralassembly.gov/house/members/members.php.

18 *General Assembly:* "Under the Gold Dome," Georgia General Assembly, accessed April 17, 2024, https://www.legis.ga.gov/.

19 *Not only does the speaker of the House get:* "Salaries," House Radio Television: Correspondents' Gallery, accessed April 17, 2024, https://radiotv.house.gov/house-data/salaries.

19 *It's a big deal to be the majority party:* "The Legislative Process," United States House of Representatives, accessed April 16, 2024, https://www.house.gov/the-house-explained/the-legislative-process.

19 *responsible for budgets:* "History and Jurisdiction," House Committee on the Budget, February 16, 2023, accessed April 16, 2024, https://democrats-science.house.gov/about/history-and-jurisdiction.

19 *and impeachments:* "How Federal Impeachment Works," USA Gov, accessed April 16, 2024, https://www.usa.gov/impeachment.

19 *In the Senate the majority leader:* "About Parties and Leadership: Majority and Minority Leaders," United States Senate, accessed April 16, 2024, https://www.senate.gov/about/origins-foundations/parties-leadership/majority-minority-leaders.htm.

19 *the majority leader does get to decide . . . which bills come to the floor:* Parliamentarian John V. Sullivan, "How Our Laws Are Made" (House Document 110-49) (Washington, DC: U.S. House of Representatives, July 24, 2007), https://www.govinfo.gov/content/pkg/CDOC-110hdoc49/pdf/CDOC-110hdoc49.pdf.

19 *The Senate is responsible:* "Article III Judges," United States Courts,

accessed April 16, 2024, https://www.uscourts.gov/judges-judgeships
/about-federal-judges.

19 *president's cabinet:* "About Executive Nominations: Historical
Overview," accessed April 16, 2024, https://www.senate.gov/about
/powers-procedures/nominations/executive-nominations-overview
.htm.

19 *top military officers:* "Committee Actions: Nominations," United
States Senate Committee on Armed Services, accessed April 16,
2024, https://www.armed-services.senate.gov/committee-actions
/nominations.

19 *foreign diplomats:* "About Nominations," United States Senate,
accessed April 17, 2024, https://www.senate.gov/about/powers
-procedures/nominations.htm.

19 *and treaties:* "About Treaties," United States Senate, accessed April 16,
2024, https://www.senate.gov/about/powers-procedures/treaties
.htm.

19 *Congressmembers don't have term limits:* Ashley Lopez, "Term
Limits for Congress Are Wildly Popular. But Most Experts Say
They'd Be a Bad Idea," NPR, October 29, 2023, accessed April 16,
2024, https://www.npr.org/2023/10/29/1207593168
/congressional-term-limits-explainer.

20 *Congressional members only leave office:* "About Expulsion," United
States Senate, accessed April 16, 2024, https://www.senate.gov
/about/powers-procedures/expulsion.htm.

20 *Recall elections:* "Recall of State Officials," National Conference of
State Legislatures, September 15, 2021, accessed April 16, 2024,
https://www.ncsl.org/elections-and-campaigns/recall-of-state
-officials.

20 *Which explains why the state representative:* William Melhado,
"A Petition to Recall Dallas Mayor Eric Johnson Fails," *Texas
Tribune,* March 6, 2024, accessed April 16, 2024, https://www
.texastribune.org/2024/03/06/dallas-mayor-eric-johnson-recall
-petition-fails/.

20 *Neither state has that option:* Meghan Bragg, "No, There Is No
Process for a Recall Election in North Carolina," WCNC Charlotte,
April 5, 2023, accessed April 16, 2024, https://www.wcnc.com

/article/news/verify/recall-politics-cotham-political-parties
/275-b0cf2c76-e1ed-463a-b4a1-df043398cfd9.

21 *The executive branch of the federal government:* "ArtII.S1.C5.1
Qualifications for the Presidency," Constitution Annotated,
accessed April 17, 2024, https://constitution.congress.gov/browse
/essay/artII-S1-C5-1/ALDE_00013692/.

21 *The executive branch of the government is responsible:* "Executive
Office of the President," White House: President Barack Obama,
accessed April 17, 2024, https://obamawhitehouse.archives
.gov/administration/eop#:~:text=The%20EOP%20has%20
responsibility%20for,of%20the%20President's%20closest%20
advisors.

21 *The EOP is responsible for everything:* Seung Min Kim, "Chief of
Staff Exerts Quiet Power at Center of White House," Associated
Press, February 18, 2023, accessed April 16, 2024, https://apnews
.com/article/biden-politics-united-states-government-district
-of-columbia-mitt-romney-45c2ca5c526467eb29ce39891d
a60594.

22 *A less well-known position in the EOP:* "National Security Council,"
White House, https://www.whitehouse.gov/nsc/.

22 *the Office of Scheduling and Advance:* Lauren Egan and Daniel
Lippman, "Biden's Advance Team Is Rife with Turmoil and
Toxicity, Staff Allege," *Politico*, March 11, 2024, accessed
April 16, 2024, https://www.politico.com/news/2024/03/11
/bidens-advance-team-is-rife-with-turmoil-and-toxicity-staff
-allege-00146363.

22 *While the senior advisors in the EOP work in the West Wing:*
"Eisenhower Executive Office Building," White House, https:
//www.whitehouse.gov/about-the-white-house/the-grounds
/eisenhower-executive-office-building/.

23 *When the country was created, there were four cabinet positions:* "Cabinet
Members," George Washington's Mount Vernon, accessed April 17,
2024, https://www.mountvernon.org/library/digitalhistory/digital
-encyclopedia/article/cabinet-members/.

23 *there are fifteen executive departments:* "The Executive Branch,"
White House, accessed April 16, 2024, https://www.whitehouse

.gov/about-the-white-house/our-government/the-executive
-branch/.

23 *The cabinet secretaries are joined by other executive agencies:* "Director
of the CIA," CIA, accessed April 16, 2024, https://www.cia.gov
/about/director-of-cia/.

23 *both of which are not part of the cabinet:* "The Cabinet," The White
House: President Barack Obama, accessed April 16, 2024, https:
//obamawhitehouse.archives.gov/administration/cabinet.

24 *The Department of Justice is overseen by the nation's top lawyer:* "DOJ
Strategic Plan," U.S. Department of Justice, accessed April 16, 2024,
https://www.justice.gov/doj/doj-strategic-plan/doj-strategic
-plan-2022-2026

25 *Each commissioner serves a seven-year term:* Sheila F. Anthony,
"Remarks," Columbia University International Journalists Seminar,
March 2000, https://www.ftc.gov/news-events/news/speeches
/remarks-9.

25 *Other independent organizations for which the president:* "About the
FCC," Federal Communications Commission, accessed April 16,
2024, https://www.fcc.gov/about/overview.

25 *the National Aeronautics and Space Administration (NASA):* "Bill
Nelson," NASA, accessed April 16, 2024, https://www.nasa.gov
/people/nasa-administrator-bill-nelson/.

25 *We've had VPs who primarily served:* Aziz Huq, "Cheney and the
Constitution," Brennan Center for Justice, June 26, 2007, https://
www.thenation.com/article/archive/cheney-and-constitution/.

26 *The Constitution lays out the specifics of the job:* "About the Vice
President (President of the Senate)," United States Senate, accessed
April 16, 2024, https://www.senate.gov/about/officers-staff/vice
-president.htm.

26 *In 1793, when John Adams:* Rhonda Barlow, "The Day the Vice
President Showed His Strength," Beehive, July 29, 2021, accessed
April 16, 2024, https://www.masshist.org/beehiveblog/2021/06
/the-day-the-vice-president-showed-his-strength/.

26 *So, after four elections, Congress passed:* "12th Amendment," Cornell
Law School, accessed April 16, 2024, https://www.law.cornell.edu
/constitution/amendmentxii.

27 *The courts can't just weigh in on laws:* "About the U.S. Courts of Appeals," United States Courts, accessed April 16, 2024, https://www.uscourts.gov/about-federal-courts/court-role-and-structure/about-us-courts-appeals.

28 *Judges and justices serve no fixed term:* Kimberly Wehle, "How to Impeach a Supreme Court Justice," *Politico*, March 30, 2022, accessed April 16, 2024, https://www.politico.com/news/magazine/2022/03/30/impeach-supreme-court-justice-clarence-thomas-00021480.

29 *If Congress told you to show up and testify:* "In Committee," United States House of Representatives, accessed April 16, 2024, https://www.house.gov/the-house-explained/the-legislative-process/in-committee.

29 *mostly by congressional members themselves:* Luke Broadwater, "Republicans Signal Refusal of Jan. 6 Subpoenas, Setting Up a Showdown," *New York Times*, May 26, 2022, accessed April 16, 2024, https://www.nytimes.com/2022/05/26/us/republicans-jan-6-subpoenas.html.

30 *Each member who wants to speak is given:* "The Legislative Process on the House Floor: An Introduction," Congressional Research Service, December 14, 2022, https://crsreports.congress.gov/product/pdf/RL/95-563.

30 *This behavior is typically seen when senators:* "About Filibusters and Cloture," United States Senate, accessed April 16, 2024, https://www.senate.gov/about/powers-procedures/filibusters-cloture.htm.

31 *This is what's called a pocket veto:* "ArtI.S7.C2.2 Veto Power," Constitution Annotated, accessed April 17, 2024, https://constitution.congress.gov/browse/essay/artI-S7-C2-2/ALDE_00013645/.

32 *At our founding only certain people got to vote:* "Voting and Guardianship," SABE USA, accessed April 18, 2024, https://www.sabeusa.org/govoter/voting-info/voting-and-guardianship/.

33 *Some states even allow the voters:* "States with Initiative or Referendum," Ballotpedia, accessed April 19, 2024, https://ballotpedia.org/States_with_initiative_or_referendum.

Principle 1: America Is a Land of Freedom

39 *on the 2023 Human Freedom Index, America:* Ian Vásquez et al., *The Human Freedom Index 2023: A Global Measurement of Personal, Civil, and Economic Freedom* (Washington, DC: Cato Institute and Fraser Institute, 2023).

41 *The Founding Fathers . . . who mostly owned slaves:* Jeff Wallenfeldt, "How Many of the Signers of the U.S. Constitution Were Enslavers?," Britannica, https://www.britannica.com/story/how -many-of-the-signers-of-the-us-constitution-were-enslavers.

41 *James Madison . . . "Father of the Constitution":* "James Madison," The White House, accessed April 17, 2024, https://www .whitehouse.gov/about-the-white-house/presidents/james -madison/.

41 *"the great rights of mankind":* "The Bill of Rights: A Brief History," ACLU, March 4, 2002, https://www.aclu.org/documents/bill -rights-brief-history.

42 *the First Amendment says:* U.S. Constitution, amendment 1, December 15, 1791, https://constitution.congress.gov/constitution /amendment-1/#:~:text=Congress%20shall%20make%20no%20law ,for%20a%20redress%20of%20grievances.

43 *They argued that removing them was against:* Nikki McCann Ramírez, "Elon Brings One of America's Most Prominent Nazis Back to Twitter," *Rolling Stone,* December 2, 2022, https://www .rollingstone.com/politics/politics-news/elon-musk-twitter -reinstates-neo-nazi-andrew-anglin-account-1234640390/.

44 *"true threats":* Kevin Francis O'Neill, "True Threats," Free Speech Center, August 12, 2023, accessed April 16, 2024, https: //firstamendment.mtsu.edu/article/true-threats/.

44 *allowing people to hit protestors with their car:* Reid J. Epstein and Patricia Mazzei, "G.O.P. Bills Target Protestors (and Absolve Motorists Who Hit Them)," *New York Times,* April 21, 2021, accessed April 16, 2024, https://www.nytimes.com/2021/04/21/us /politics/republican-anti-protest-laws.html.

45 *Ida B. Wells:* Arlisha R. Norwood, "Ida B. Wells-Barnett," National Women's History Museum, https://www.womenshistory.org /education-resources/biographies/ida-b-wells-barnett.

45 *stopping giant corporations from consolidating:* Gilbert King, "The Woman Who Took on the Tycoon," *Smithsonian*, July 5, 2012, accessed April 16, 2024, https://www.smithsonianmag.com /history/the-woman-who-took-on-the-tycoon-651396/.

45 *severely rolled back during the Reagan administration:* Louis Galambos, *Constructing Corporate America* (New York: Oxford University Press, 2004), 149–67.

46 *fifty companies in charge of most American media:* Ashley Lutz, "These 6 Corporations Control 90% of the Media in America," *Business Insider*, June 14, 2012, https://www.businessinsider.com /these-6-corporations-control-90-of-the-media-in-america-2012-6.

46 *90 percent of the media in the United States:* Thomas Schatz, "How 2 Companies Came to Dominate the Media Business," *The Nation*, December 13, 2023, https://www.thenation.com/article/society /netflix-disney-media-consolidation/.

46 *the Reagan administration also got rid of the Fairness Doctrine:* Matt Stefon, "Fairness Doctrine," Britannica, April 9, 2024, accessed April 17, 2024, https://www.britannica.com/topic/Fairness -Doctrine.

46 *"obliged . . . to cover fairly the views of others . . . refrain from expressing":* Audrey Perry, "Fairness Doctrine," Free Speech Center, January 1, 2017, accessed April 17, 2024, https://firstamendment.mtsu.edu /article/fairness-doctrine/.

47 *There are differences between companies:* Jason Abbruzzese and Kevin Collier, "The FCC Could Choose to Act Against Rupert Murdoch for Fox News' Election Lies, but Few Expect It To," NBC News, March 9, 2023, accessed April 16, 2024, https://www.nbcnews .com/media/fcc-rupert-murdoch-fox-news-rcna74187.

47 *Tucker Carlson was in a defamation trial:* David Folkenflik, "You Literally Can't Believe the Facts Tucker Carlson Tells You. So Say Fox's Lawyers," NPR, September 29, 2020, accessed April 21, 2024, https:// www.npr.org/2020/09/29/917747123/you-literally-cant-believe-the -facts-tucker-carlson-tells-you-so-say-fox-s-lawye.

47 *NBC was in a defamation trial:* Jonathan Stempel, "Trump Ally Devin Nunes Can Sue NBCUniversal for Defamation—Judge," Reuters, November 28, 2022, accessed April 21, 2024, https://www

.reuters.com/business/media-telecom/trump-ally-devin-nunes-can
-sue-nbcuniversal-defamation-judge-2022-11-29/.

47 *30 percent of the electorate:* Martin Pengelly, "More Than a Third
of US Adults Say Biden's 2020 Victory Was Not Legitimate," *The
Guardian*, January 2, 2024, accessed April 16, 2024, https://www
.theguardian.com/us-news/2024/jan/02/poll-biden-2020-election
-illegitimate.

47 *Modern politicians are also taking major liberties:* Clark Corbin,
"Idaho GOP Won't Allow News Media Inside Upcoming
Republican Presidential Caucus," *Idaho Capital Sun*, February 14,
2024, accessed April 21, 2024, https://idahocapitalsun.com/2024
/02/14/idaho-gop-wont-allow-news-media-inside-upcoming
-republican-presidential-caucus/#:~:text=News%20reporters
%20will%20not%20be,concerns%20among%20some%20trans
parency%20advocates.

48 (*Eighteenth Amendment*): U.S. Constitution, Amendment 18,
January 16, 1919, https://constitution.congress.gov/constitution
/amendment-18/.

48 *his relationship with Frederick Douglass:* "Confronting a President:
Douglass and Lincoln," National Park Service, accessed April 16, 2024,
https://www.nps.gov/frdo/learn/historyculture/confronting-a
-president-douglass-and-lincoln.htm.

49 *African American voting rights:* "Abraham Lincoln and
Emancipation: Timeline," Library of Congress, accessed April 16,
2024, https://www.loc.gov/collections/abraham-lincoln-papers
/articles-and-essays/abraham-lincoln-and-emancipation/timeline/.

50 *was a strong proponent of states' rights*: "Andrew Johnson," The White
House, accessed April 16, 2024, https://www.whitehouse.gov
/about-the-white-house/presidents/andrew-johnson/

50 *the Black Codes:* "The Black Codes and Jim Crow Laws," *National
Geographic*, October 19, 2023, accessed April 16, 2024, https:
//education.nationalgeographic.org/resource/black-codes-and
-jim-crow-laws/#:~:text=Black%20codes%20and%20Jim%20
Crow%20laws%20were%20laws%20passed%20at,of%20whom%20
had%20been%20enslaved.

50 *limiting what they could do:* "Black Codes," History, June 1, 2010,

accessed April 17, 2024, https://www.history.com/topics/black
-history/black-codes.

51 *Jim Crow was a character:* Gilder Lehrman Center for the Study
of Slavery, Resistance, and Abolition, "The History of Minstrel
Shows and Jim Crow," July 6–12, 2014, Gilder Lehrman Institute of
American History Summer Teachers' Seminar, https://glc.yale.edu
/outreach/teaching-resources/teacher-professional-development
-programs/past-teacher-development-15.

52 *Black Americans, on the whole, more educated:* Andre M. Perry et
al., "Black Wealth Is Increasing, but So Is the Racial Wealth Gap,"
Brookings, January 9, 2024, https://www.brookings.edu/articles
/black-wealth-is-increasing-but-so-is-the-racial-wealth-gap/.

52 *Exception Clause:* U.S. Constitution, Amendment 13, December 6,
1865, https://www.law.cornell.edu/constitution-conan/
amendment-13/section-1/exceptions-clause.

52 *America has the highest prison population:* "Mass Incarceration,"
ACLU, accessed April 16, 2024, https://www.aclu.org/issues
/smart-justice/mass-incarceration.

52 *the University of Chicago reported:* Jennifer Turner et al., "Captive
Labor: Exploitation of Incarcerated Workers," ACLU, June 15, 2022,
https://www.aclu.org/publications/captive-labor-exploitation
-incarcerated-workers.

53 *have no choice but to work for little to no pay:* "Law School's Global
Human Rights Clinic, ACLU Examine Coercion, Exploitation in
Prison Labor," University of Chicago News, June 16, 2022, https:
//news.uchicago.edu/story/us-prison-labor-programs-violate
-fundamental-human-rights-new-report-finds.

53 *The Fourteenth Amendment:* U.S. Constitution, Amendment 14,
July 9, 1868, https://www.archives.gov/milestone-documents
/14th-amendment.

53 *It gave Black men:* "Landmark Legislation: The Fourteenth
Amendment," United States Senate, accessed April 16, 2024,
https://www.senate.gov/about/origins-foundations/senate-and
-constitution/14th-amendment.htm.

54 *The Fourteenth Amendment did not:* NCC Staff, "On This Day,
All American Indians Made United States Citizens," National

Constitution Center, June 2, 2023, https://constitutioncenter.org /blog/on-this-day-in-1924-all-indians-made-united-states-citizens.

54 *Congress had to explicitly add the Fifteenth Amendment:* "15th Amendment to the U.S. Constitution: Voting Rights (1870)," National Archives, accessed April 16, 2024, https://www.archives .gov/milestone-documents/15th-amendment.

55 *The debate ultimately split the women's movement:* "Why the Women's Rights Movement Split Over the 15th Amendment," National Park Service, January 14, 2021, accessed April 16, 2024, https://www.nps.gov/articles/000/why-the-women-s-rights -movement-split-over-the-15th-amendment.htm.

55 *While the amendment to let women vote:* "Voting Rights for Women," Library of Congress, accessed April 21, 2024, https:// www.loc.gov/classroom-materials/elections/right-to-vote/voting -rights-for-women/#:~:text=Since%201878%2C%20a%20 women's%20suffrage,Nineteenth%20Amendment%20on%20 June%205.

56 *"no religious Test shall ever be required":* "Article VI Supreme Law," Constitution Annotated, accessed April 17, 2024, https:// constitution.congress.gov/browse/article-6/clause-3/.

56 *"no law representing an establishment of religion":* U.S. Constitution, Amendment 1.

57 *The Founders were adamant:* Joseph Rosenblum, "Taxation of Religious Entities," Free Speech Center, August 8, 2023, accessed April 16, 2024, https://firstamendment.mtsu.edu/article/taxation -of-religious-entities/.

57 *"separation between church and state":* John S. Baker Jr., "Wall of Separation," Free Speech Center, August 5, 2023, accessed April 16, 2024, https://firstamendment.mtsu.edu/article/wall-of-separation/.

57 *This wasn't so much to protect the state from the church:* "History of Chaplaincy," Office of the Chaplain, accessed April 16, 2024, https://chaplain.house.gov/chaplaincy/history.html.

57 *a three-part test laid out in the 1971 Supreme Court case:* "The Lemon Test," Pew Research Center, May 14, 2009, https://www .pewresearch.org/religion/2009/05/14/shifting-boundaries6/.

58 *Putting "In God We Trust" on our money:* Margaret Wood, "In God

We Trust," Library of Congress Blogs, April 22, 2013, accessed April 16, 2024, https://blogs.loc.gov/law/2013/04/in-god-we-trust/.

58 *The secretary of the treasury put the motto on the two-cent coin:* "Why Do Coins Say 'In God We Trust'?" GovMint, December 7, 2021, https://www.govmint.com/coin-authority/post/why-do-coins-say-in-god-we-trust.

58 *In 1954, during the height of the Cold War:* Michael Lipka, "5 Facts about the Pledge of Allegiance," Pew Research Center, September 4, 2013, accessed April 21, 2024, https://www.pewresearch.org/short-reads/2013/09/04/5-facts-about-the-pledge-of-allegiance/.

58 *in 1957 the Treasury started printing:* Sarah Begley, "How 'In God We Trust' Got on the Currency in the First Place," *Time*, January 13, 2016, accessed April 21, 2024, https://time.com/4179685/in-god-we-trust-currency-history/.

58 *adopted as the official motto of the state of Florida:* "State Motto," Florida Department of State, accessed April 16, 2024, https://dos.fl.gov/florida-facts/florida-state-symbols/state-motto/.

59 *Not because the Constitution specifies that they use a Bible:* "Presidential Inaugurations: I Do Solemnly Swear," White House Historical Association, accessed April 16, 2024, https://www.whitehousehistory.org/presidential-inaugurations-i-do-solemnly-swear.

59 *John Quincy Adams used a book of law:* Joanna Lin, "'I Do Solemnly Swear . . .'" *Los Angeles Times*, January 18, 2009, accessed April 16, 2024, https://www.latimes.com/archives/la-xpm-2009-jan-18-na-inaug-religion18-story.html.

59 *President Theodore Roosevelt didn't use anything:* "The Swearing in of Theodore Roosevelt," Joint Congressional Committee on Inaugural Ceremonies, https://www.inaugural.senate.gov/swearing-in-of-roosevelt/.

60 *It should worry us that the speaker of the House refers:* Molly Olmstead, "Mike Johnson Claims That God Prepared Him to Be a 'New Moses,'" *Slate*, December 7, 2023, accessed April 16, 2024, https://slate.com/news-and-politics/2023/12/mike-johnson-christian-nationalist-lawmakers-moses.html.

60 *flies the flag of the far-right New Apostolic Reformation:* Molly Olmstead, "The Radical Evangelicals Who Helped Push Jan. 6 to

Wage War on 'Demonic Influence,'" *Slate*, January 6, 2024, accessed April 16, 2024, https://slate.com/news-and-politics/2024/01 /january-6-insurrection-mike-johnson-evangelical-christian -apostolic-reformation.html.

60 *outside his office:* Bradley Onishi, "The Key to Mike Johnson's Christian Extremism Hangs Outside His Office," *Rolling Stone*, November 10, 2023, accessed April 16, 2024, https://www .rollingstone.com/politics/political-commentary/mike-johnson -christian-nationalist-appeal-to-heaven-flag-1234873851/.

60 *Conservative think tanks like the Heritage Foundation:* Clyde Haberman, "Religion and Right-Wing Politics: How Evangelicals Reshaped Elections," *New York Times*, October 28, 2018, accessed April 16, 2024, https://www.nytimes.com/2018/10/28/us/religion -politics-evangelicals.html.

60 *Now, the Heritage Foundation:* "Project 2025 Reaches 100 Coalition Partners, Continues to Grow in Preparation for Next President," Heritage, February 20, 2024, accessed April 16, 2024, https://www .heritage.org/press/project-2025-reaches-100-coalition-partners -continues-grow-preparation-next-president?preview_id=2848 &preview_nonce=e270c3a857&preview=true&_thumbnail _id=2853.

60 *Project 2025 lays out the plan:* Russell Berman, "The Open Plot to Dismantle the Federal Government," *The Atlantic*, September 24, 2023, accessed April 16, 2024, https: //www.theatlantic.com/politics/archive/2023/09/trump-desantis -republicans-dismantle-deep-state/675378/.

61 *Project 2025 includes consolidating the power:* Michael Hirsh, "Inside the Next Republican Revolution," *Politico*, September 19, 2023, accessed April 16, 2024, https://www.politico.com/news /magazine/2023/09/19/project-2025-trump-reagan-00115811.

61 *Project 2025, which is supported by every:* Mark Wingfield, "Yes, Trump Has a 'Radical Agenda' If Elected Again, but Where's the Religious Talk?," Baptist News Global, November 20, 2023, accessed April 16, 2024, https://baptistnews.com/article/yes -trump-has-a-radical-agenda-if-elected-again-but-wheres-the -religious-talk/.

63 *A hospital can't even take organs:* "Organ Donation and Transplantation Legislation History," Health Resources and Services Administration, accessed April 16, 2024, https://www.organdonor.gov/about-us/legislation-policy/history.

64 *The Chinese government told its people:* Feng Wang et al., "The End of China's One-Child Policy," Brookings, March 30, 2016, accessed April 16, 2024, https://www.brookings.edu/articles/the-end-of-chinas-one-child-policy/.

64 *Concerned with overpopulation:* Yaqiu Wang, "It's Time to Abolish China's Three-Child Policy," Human Rights Watch, February 23, 2023, accessed April 21, 2024, https://www.hrw.org/news/2023/02/22/its-time-abolish-chinas-three-child-policy.

65 *It now has way too many adult men:* Waiyee Yip, "China: The Men Who Are Single and the Women Who Don't Want Kids," BBC News, May 24, 2021, accessed April 16, 2024, https://www.bbc.com/news/world-asia-china-57154574.

65 *For years, the one-child policy:* Yanzhe Zhang et al., "Empirical Research on Male Preference in China: A Result of Gender Imbalance in the Seventh Population Census," *International Journal of Environmental Research and Public Health* 19, no. 11 (June 2022): 6482, https://www.ncbi.nlm.nih.gov/pmc/articles/PMC9180325/.

65 *China is experiencing an epidemic of loneliness:* Juanjuan Sun et al., "Social Isolation and Loneliness Among Chinese Older Adults: Examining Aging Attitudes as Mediators and Moderators," *Frontiers in Psychology* 13 (December 2022), https://doi.org/10.3389/fpsyg.2022.1043921.

65 *Which is why sitting Supreme Court justice Samuel Alito:* Politico Staff, "Read Justice Alito's Initial Draft Abortion Opinion Which Would Overturn Roe v. Wade," *Politico*, May 2, 2022, accessed April 17, 2024, https://www.politico.com/news/2022/05/02/read-justice-alito-initial-abortion-opinion-overturn-roe-v-wade-pdf-00029504.

66 *Supreme Court justice Amy Coney Barrett suggested:* Mark Sherman and Jessica Gresko, "Justices Signal They'll OK New Abortion Limits, May Toss Roe," Associated Press, December 1, 2021,

accessed April 17, 2024, https://apnews.com/article/abortion
-donald-trump-us-supreme-court-health-amy-coney-barrett-a3b5cf
9621315e6c623dc80a790842d8.

66 *I could cite the growing homeless population:* Claire Thornton, "The
Number of Homeless People in America Grew in 2023 as High
Cost of Living Took a Toll," *USA Today*, December 15, 2023,
accessed April 16, 2024, https://www.usatoday.com/story/news
/nation/2023/12/15/homelessness-in-america-grew-2023
/71926354007/.

66 *young adults who simply aged out of foster care:* "HHS Releases
Guidance to Help Prevent Homelessness for Youth Who Have
Transitioned Out of Foster Care," U.S. Department of Health and
Human Services, January 17, 2024, accessed April 16, 2024, https:
//www.hhs.gov/about/news/2024/01/17/hhs-releases-guidance
-help-prevent-homelessness-youth-who-have-transitioned-out-of
-foster-care.html.

66 *I could horrify you with the reality:* Geoff Mulvihill, "Things to
Know About Efforts to Block People from Crossing State Lines for
Abortion," Associated Press, November 10, 2023, accessed April 16,
2024, https://apnews.com/article/abortion-texas-idaho-alabama
-state-lines-trafficking-d314933f3f7db93858561a0c6ad0b188.

66 *rapists getting parental rights:* Michaela Haas, "When Your Rapist
Demands Custody," *Mother Jones*, September/October 2019,
https://www.motherjones.com/criminal-justice/2019/08/rapist
-custody-abortion/.

67 *the LGBTQIA+ community theoretically shares the same rights:*
Kaitlyn Radde, "What Does the Respect for Marriage Act Do?
The Answer Will Vary by State," NPR, December 8, 2022, accessed
April 16, 2024, https://www.npr.org/2022/12/08/1140808263
/what-does-the-respect-for-marriage-act-do-the-answer-will-vary
-by-state.

68 *as Warren Burger, former chief justice of the Supreme Court:* John
Schwarz, "Right-Wing Supreme Court Continues Its 'Great Fraud'
About the Second Amendment," The Intercept, June 24, 2022,
accessed April 17, 2024, https://theintercept.com/2022/06
/24/supreme-court-gun-second-amendment-bruen/.

69 *At the end of the day, I consider freedom the "American way":* Megan Smith, "Norman Rockwell's 'Four Freedoms,'" Museum of Fine Arts, Houston, December 16, 2019, accessed April 16, 2024, https://www.mfah.org/blogs/inside-mfah/norman-rockwells-four-freedoms.

70 *In fact, when the* Four Freedoms *toured the country:* "Rockwell's Four Freedoms," Norman Rockwell: Imagining Freedom, accessed April 16, 2024, https://rockwellfourfreedoms.org/about-the-exhibit/rockwells-four-freedoms/.

73 *Thomas Jefferson once proposed revising:* "Thomas Jefferson to Samuel Kercheval," Monticello, July 12, 1816, https://www.colorado.edu/herbst/sites/default/files/attached-files/nov_2_-_constitution.pdf.

74 *Sure, we got the Twenty-seventh:* Matt Largey, "The Bad Grade That Changed the U.S. Constitution," NPR, May 5, 2017, accessed April 16, 2024, https://www.npr.org/2017/05/05/526900818/the-bad-grade-that-changed-the-u-s-constitution.

74 *The last amendment that really mattered:* "The 26th Amendment," Richard Nixon Presidential Library and Museum, June 17, 2021, https://www.nixonlibrary.gov/news/26th-amendment.

74 *Most people think the move to make this change:* "Twenty-sixth Amendment Timeline," Annenberg Classroom, accessed April 16, 2024, https://www.annenbergclassroom.org/resource/our-constitution/twenty-sixth-amendment-timeline/.

74 *Jennings Randolph, a Democrat from West Virginia:* "Jennings Randolph: 'Father of the 26th Amendment,'" Agribusiness Council, accessed April 16, 2024, https://www.agribusinesscouncil.org/JR-amendment.htm.

Principle 2: Everyone Should Have the Opportunity to Rise

79 *The UK has completely free health care:* Josh Chang et al., "The UK Healthcare System," Columbia University, http://assets.ce.columbia.edu/pdf/actu/actu-uk.pdf.

79 *Germany has a government fund:* Miriam Blümel and Reinhard Busse, "International Healthcare System Profiles: Germany," Commonwealth Fund, June 5, 2020, accessed April 16, 2024,

https://www.commonwealthfund.org/international-health-policy
-center/countries/germany.

79 *South Korea, whose healthcare system:* Duffie Osental, "Private
Health Insurance Still Booming in South Korea," Insurance
Business, December 8, 2018, accessed April 16, 2024, https://www
.insurancebusinessmag.com/asia/news/breaking-news/private
-health-insurance-still-booming-in-south-korea-118259.aspx.

80 *All the major Western nations:* "Foreign Countries with Universal
Health Care," New York State, accessed April 16, 2024, https:
//www.health.ny.gov/regulations/hcra/univ_hlth_care.htm.

80 *According to the 1619 Project:* Jeneen Interlandi, "Why Doesn't
the United States Have Universal Healthcare? The Answer Has
Everything to Do with Race," *New York Times*, August 14, 2019,
accessed April 16, 2024, https://www.nytimes.com/interactive
/2019/08/14/magazine/universal-health-care-racism.html.

80 *Black doctors were already barred:* Jonathan Sidhu, "Exploring the
AMA's History of Discrimination," ProPublica, July 16, 2008,
accessed April 16, 2024, https://www.propublica.org/article
/exploring-the-amas-history-of-discrimination-716.

80 *According to the 1619 Project:* Interlandi, "Why Doesn't the United
States Have Universal Healthcare? The Answer Has Everything to
Do with Race."

82 *While the Affordable Care Act has brought health insurance:* Nicole
Rapfogel et al., "10 Ways the ACA Has Improved Health Care in
the Past Decade," Center for American Progress, March 23, 2020,
accessed April 16, 2024, https://www.americanprogress.org
/article/10-ways-aca-improved-health-care-past-decade/#:~:text
=The%20ACA%20generated%20one%20of,since%20the%20
ACA%20was%20enacted.

82 *According to the National Bureau of Economic Research:* Sarah Miller
et al., "Medicaid and Mortality: New Evidence from Linked Survey
and Administrative Data," Nber Working Paper Series (January
2021): https://www.nber.org/system/files/working_papers/w26
081/w26081.pdf.

83 *Today there are ten states:* Douglas Conway et al., "Decline in Share
of People Without Health Insurance Driven by Increase in Public

Coverage in 36 States," United States Census Bureau, September 15, 2022, accessed April 16, 2024, https://www.census.gov/library /stories/2022/09/uninsured-rate-declined-in-28-states.html.

85 *Knowing the country's history:* "U.S. Education Timeline," Future Ed, November 11, 2023, accessed April 16, 2024, https://www .future-ed.org/u-s-education-timeline/.

87 *college wasn't always the precursor to success:* "Servicemen's Readjustment Act (1944)," National Archives, accessed April 18, 2024, https://www.archives.gov/milestone-documents/servicemens -readjustment-act.

87 *at the end of World War II:* "Born of Controversy: The GI Bill of Rights," U.S. Department of Veterans Affairs, accessed April 17, 2024, https://www.va.gov/opa/publications/celebrate/gi-bill.pdf.

87 *To this day, many people join the military:* "How the Military Helps Pay for College and Job Training," Military One Source, November 25, 2020, accessed April 17, 2024, https://www.militaryonesource .mil/relationships/support-community/how-the-military-helps -pay-for-college-and-job-training/.

88 *I often think of the author John Green's statement:* John Green (@sportswithjohn), "Public education does not exist to benefit parents, or for that matter students," Twitter, July 3, 2023, accessed April 17, 2024, https://twitter.com/sportswithjohn/status /1676074891475394560.

88 *a large amount of the financial backing:* Tyler Kingkade, "A Betsy DeVos-backed Group Helps Fuel a Rapid Expansion of Public Money for Private School," NBC News, March 30, 2023, accessed April 17, 2024, https://www.nbcnews.com/politics/politics-news /betsy-devos-american-federation-children-private-school-rcna76307.

90 *You're not allowed to actively discriminate in public schools:* Peter Greene, "How School Voucher Laws Protect Discrimination," *Forbes*, February 1, 2023, accessed April 18, 2024, https://www .forbes.com/sites/petergreene/2023/02/01/how-school-voucher -laws-protect-discrimination/?sh=15d04042d9c1.

91 *The Federal Housing Administration subsidized builders:* Terry Gross, "A 'Forgotten History' of How the U.S. Government Segregated America," NPR, May 3, 2017, accessed April 19, 2024, https:

//www.npr.org/2017/05/03/526655831/a-forgotten-history
-of-how-the-u-s-government-segregated-america.

93 *If you've met America:* Wil Del Pilar, "A Brief History of Affirmative
Action and the Assault on Race-Conscious Admissions," Education
Trust, June 15, 2023, accessed April 17, 2024, https://edtrust.org
/resource/a-brief-history-of-affirmative-action-and-the-assault-on
-race-conscious-admissions/.

94 *The original homes:* "Average Sales Price of Houses Sold for the
United States," FRED (Federal Reserve Bank of St. Louis), accessed
April 19, 2024, https://fred.stlouisfed.org/series/ASPUS.

94 *Which is why today, while Black income is about 60 percent:* Maggie
Davis et al., "Snapshots of Black and White Disparities in Income,
Wealth, Savings and More," LendingTree, February 5, 2024, accessed
April 17, 2024, https://www.lendingtree.com/debt-consolidation
/black-and-white-disparities-study/.

95 *According to the Center for Economic and Policy Research:* Dean Baker,
"CORRECTION: The Productivity Adjusted Minimum Wage
Would Be $21.50 in 2020 and $23 in 2021," Center for Economic
and Policy Research, March 16, 2022, accessed April 18, 2024,
https://cepr.net/correction-the-productivity-adjusted-minimum
-wage-would-be-21-50-in-2020-and-23-in-2021/.

98 *Millions of people died during this time:* "Immigration and
Overcrowding," Skyscraper, accessed April 17, 2024, https:
//skyscraper.org/housing-density/crowding/#:~:text=By%20
1900%2C%20the%20population%20of,(42%2C000)%20were%20
in%20Manhattan.

99 *The wealthy of the Gilded Age considered themselves American
royalty:* "In Pictures: Great American Castles," *Forbes*, December 10,
2010, accessed April 21, 2024, https://www.forbes.com/2010/12
/08/american-castles-palaces-lifestyle-tourism-architecture_slide
.html?sh=e4f849c4b3a5.

101 *By 1893, the Census Bureau:* "Overview of the Gilded Age," Digital
History, accessed April 17, 2024, https://www.digitalhistory
.uh.edu/era.cfm?eraid=9&smtid=1.

102 *In 1906 an exposé on the mistreatment of workers:* Christopher
Klein, "How Upton Sinclair's 'The Jungle' Led to US Food Safety

Reforms," History, May 10, 2023, accessed April 21, 2024, https://www.history.com/news/upton-sinclair-the-jungle-us-food-safety-reforms.

102 *This act would be further expanded:* "A Brief Overview of the Federal Trade Commission's Investigative, Law Enforcement, and Rulemaking Authority," Federal Trade Commission, accessed April 18, 2024, https://www.ftc.gov/about-ftc/mission/enforcement-authority.

103 *Reagan's whole concept of "trickle-down economics":* Juliana Kaplan and Andy Kiersz, "A Huge Study of 20 Years of Global Wealth Demolishes the Myth of 'Trickle-down' and Shows the Rich Are Taking Most of the Gains for Themselves," *Business Insider*, December 7, 2021, accessed April 18, 2024, https://www.businessinsider.com/how-bad-is-inequality-trickle-down-economics-thomas-piketty-economists-2021-12.

103 *From 1980 to 2016, income inequality in the US rose:* Juliana Menasce Horowitz et al., "1. Trends in Income and Wealth Inequality," Pew Research Center, January 9, 2020, accessed April 19, 2024, https://www.pewresearch.org/social-trends/2020/01/09/trends-in-income-and-wealth-inequality/.

103 *the highest wealth gap of all the G7 nations:* Katherine Schaeffer, "6 Facts about Economic Inequality in the U.S.," Pew Research Center, February 7, 2020, accessed April 19, 2024, https://www.pewresearch.org/short-reads/2020/02/07/6-facts-about-economic-inequality-in-the-u-s/.

104 *According to OxFam International:* "Ten Richest Men Double Their Fortunes in Pandemic While Incomes of 99 Percent of Humanity Fall," OxFam International, January 17, 2022, accessed April 18, 2024, https://www.oxfam.org/en/press-releases/ten-richest-men-double-their-fortunes-pandemic-while-incomes-99-percent-humanity.

104 *starting to consider policies that would reduce wealth inequality:* Tom Hancock, "China Needs More Tax Revenue, Risking Backlash from Middle Class," Bloomberg, June 14, 2023, accessed April 17, 2024, https://www.bloomberg.com/news/articles/2023-06-14/potential-tax-increases-in-china-risk-political-backlash-for-xi.

106 *Banks, broadband, pharmaceutical companies:* Gustavo Grullon et al., "Are US Industries Becoming More Concentrated?," https://www.stern.nyu.edu/sites/default/files/assets/documents/Michaely%2C%20Roni%20-%20Are%20US%20Industries%20Becoming%20More%20Concentrated.pdf.

106 *corporate profits are the highest:* Tobias Burns, "Corporate Profits Hit Record High as Economy Boomed in Fourth Quarter of 2023," *The Hill*, March 28, 2024, accessed April 19, 2024, https://thehill.com/business/4561631-corporate-hit-record-high-as-economy-boomed-in-fourth-quarter-of-2023/.

108 *According to* Social Science History*:* Richard Rodems and H. Luke Shaefer, "Left Out: Policy Diffusion and the Exclusion of Black Workers from Unemployment Insurance," *Social Science History* 40, no. 3 (July 25, 2016): 385, https://doi.org/10.1017/ssh.2016.11.

108 *In the first three months Roosevelt was in office:* "Public Works Administration," Britannica, March 29, 2024, accessed April 21, 2024, https://www.britannica.com/topic/Public-Works-Administration.

108 *The New Deal also created the Federal Deposit Insurance Corporation:* Robert Stammers, "The History of the FDIC," Investopedia, April 30, 2023, accessed April 17, 2024, https://www.investopedia.com/articles/economics/09/fdic-history.asp.

108 *The administration created the Securities and Exchange Commission:* James Chen, "Securities and Exchange Commission (SEC) Defined, How It Works," Investopedia, April 16, 2024, accessed April 18, 2024, https://www.investopedia.com/terms/s/sec.asp.

109 *It supported unions:* "1935 Passage of the Wagner Act," National Labor Relations Board, accessed April 18, 2024, https://www.nlrb.gov/about-nlrb/who-we-are/our-history/1935-passage-of-the-wagner-act.

109 *So many things modern-day Americans accept:* "New Deal Timeline," Living New Deal, accessed April 18, 2024, https://livingnewdeal.org/history-of-the-new-deal/what-was-the-new-deal/timeline/.

109 *He overstepped the mark:* NCC Staff, "How FDR Lost His Brief War on the Supreme Court," National Constitution Center, February 5, 2024, accessed April 18, 2024, https://

constitutioncenter.org/blog/how-fdr-lost-his-brief-war-on-the
-supreme-court-2.

110 *In fact, we only have the Twenty-second Amendment:* NCC Staff,
"FDR's Third-term Election and the 22nd Amendment," National
Constitution Center, November 5, 2020, accessed April 18, 2024,
https://constitutioncenter.org/blog/fdrs-third-term-decision-and
-the-22nd-amendment.

110 *As Thomas Alan Schwartz . . . defines it:* Brian Naylor, "Republicans
Blast Democrats as Socialists. Here's What Socialism Is," NPR,
August 25, 2020, accessed April 18, 2024, https://www.npr.org
/2020/08/25/905895428/republicans-blast-democrats-as-socialists
-heres-what-socialism-is.

110 *Republicans keep fighting for less regulation on everything:* Sewell
Chan, "Financial Crisis Was Avoidable, Inquiry Finds," *New York
Times,* January 25, 2011, accessed April 21, 2024, https://www
.nytimes.com/2011/01/26/business/economy/26inquiry.html.

111 *As Jon Stewart said:* "Where Is Our Tax Money Going?," *The
Problem with Jon Stewart,* Season 2, Episode 2, directed by Andre
Allen, aired October 14, 2022, on Apple TV+.

111 *The renegotiated "Green New Deal":* Emma Snaith, "What Is the
Green New Deal and How Does Biden's Climate Plan Compare?,"
Independent, October 30, 2021, accessed April 18, 2024, https://www
.independent.co.uk/climate-change/infact/green-new-deal-what
-is-biden-summary-aoc-b1790197.html.

112 *If we really wanted to reduce the deficit and debt:* Jesse Eisinger et al.,
"The Secret IRS Files: Trove of Never-Before-Seen Records Reveal
How the Wealthiest Avoid Income Tax," ProPublica, June 8, 2021,
accessed April 18, 2024, https://www.propublica.org/article/the
-secret-irs-files-trove-of-never-before-seen-records-reveal-how-the
-wealthiest-avoid-income-tax.

112 *And if you think raising taxes on the wealthy:* Lucy Madison,
"Elizabeth Warren: 'There Is Nobody in This Country Who Got
Rich on His Own,'" CBS News, September 22, 2011, accessed
April 18, 2024, https://www.cbsnews.com/news/elizabeth
-warren-there-is-nobody-in-this-country-who-got-rich-on-his
-own/.

114 *He believed the country had gone off track:* Mary Delach Leonard, "The Birth of the American Dream," NPR, February 16, 2011, accessed April 17, 2024, https://www.stlpr.org/economy-business /2011-02-16/the-birth-of-the-american-dream.

114 *The American Dream was not supposed to be:* Matthew Wills, "James Truslow Adams: Dreaming Up the American Dream," JSTOR, May 18, 2015, accessed April 18, 2024, https://daily.jstor.org/james -truslow-adams-dreaming-american-dream/.

114 *Of course, being an Astor or a Carnegie meant something:* "Edison Biography," National Park Service, accessed April 17, 2024, https://www.nps.gov/edis/learn/historyculture/edison -biography.htm.

115 *the phonograph and the incandescent light bulb:* Michael Levenson, "G.E., Which Traces Its Roots to Thomas Edison, Sells Its Lighting Business," *New York Times*, May 28, 2020, accessed April 17, 2024, https://www.nytimes.com/2020/05/28/us/General-electric -light-bulb-business.html.

115 *"America had rapid, and widely shared, economic growth":* David Leonhardt, "The American Dream, Quantified at Last," *New York Times*, December 8, 2016, accessed April 18, 2024, https://www .nytimes.com/2016/12/08/opinion/the-american-dream-quantified -at-last.html.

115 *However, this idea of living up to your best self:* Anna Diamond, "The Original Meanings of the 'American Dream' and 'America First' Were Starkly Different from How We Use Them Today," *Smithsonian*, October 2018, accessed April 18, 2024, https://www .smithsonianmag.com/history/behold-america-american-dream -slogan-book-sarah-churchwell-180970311/.

116 *As the writer David Leonhardt notes:* Leonhardt, "The American Dream, Quantified at Last."

117 *Getting sick is the number one:* Bill Fay, "Bankruptcy Statistics," Debt.org, July 20, 2023, accessed April 18, 2024, https://www.debt .org/bankruptcy/statistics/.

119 *As FDR himself said:* "FDR Biography," Franklin D. Roosevelt Presidential Library and Museum, accessed April 18, 2024, https: //www.fdrlibrary.org/fdr-biography.

Principle 3: Every Citizen Should Have a Vote, and That Vote Should Count

122 *To quote the late, great congressman:* John Lewis (@repjohnlewis), "The right to vote is precious," Twitter, July 26, 2016, accessed April 18, 2024, https://twitter.com/repjohnlewis/status /758023941998776321?lang=en.

126 *Republican legislators are responsible:* Chris Leavertown, "Who Controlled Redistricting in Every State," Brennan Center for Justice, October 5, 2022, accessed April 18, 2024, https://www.brennancenter .org /our-work/research-reports/who-controlled-redistricting-every -state.

127 *Donald Trump only won North Carolina with 50.1 percent:* "North Carolina Presidential Results," *Politico,* January 6, 2021, accessed April 18, 2024, https://www.politico.com/2020-election/results /north-carolina/.

127 *Wisconsin Republicans recently attempted:* Megan O'Matz, "Wisconsin Picks New Legislative Maps That Would End Years of GOP Gerrymandering," ProPublica, February 16, 2024, accessed April 18, 2024, https://www.propublica.org/article/new-wisconsin -district-map-gop-gerrymander-elections.

127 *the Princeton Gerrymandering Project gave North Carolina's congressional:* "North Carolina 2023 756 Congressional Map," Gerrymandering Project, accessed April 19, 2024, https: //gerrymander.princeton.edu/redistricting-report-card /?planId=recOeyIDG9pveZd8D.

127 *state Senate:* "North Carolina 2023 State Senate Map—Enacted Oct 2023," Gerrymandering Project, accessed April 19, 2024, https: //gerrymander.princeton.edu/redistricting-report-card/?planId =recG7heSxt0nJRlWC.

127 *and state House maps:* "North Carolina 2023 Bill 756 Congressional Map," Gerrymandering Project, accessed April 19, 2024, https: //gerrymander.princeton.edu/redistricting-report-card/?planId =recOeyIDG9pveZd8D.

129 *Republicans are purging:* Zachary Roth, "GOP Backs Voting by Mail, Yet Turns to Courts to Restrict It in Battleground States," Stateline, February 22, 2024, April 18, 2024, https://stateline.org

/2024/02/22/gop-backs-voting-by-mail-yet-turns-to-courts-to
-restrict-it-in-battleground-states/.

129 *We even have at least one state:* Michael Bartiromo and Nexstar Media
Wire, "Is It Illegal to Hand Out Water or Food Outside Your Polling
Place?," *The Hill*, November 1, 2022, accessed April 18, 2024, https:
//thehill.com/homenews/nexstar_media_wire/3709676-is-it-illegal
-to-hand-out-water-or-food-outside-your-polling-place/.

130 *As Barton Gellman . . . wrote:* Barton Gellman, "Trump's Next Coup
Has Already Begun," *The Atlantic*, December 6, 2021, accessed April 18,
2024, https://www.theatlantic.com/magazine/archive/2022/01
/january-6-insurrection-trump-coup-2024-election/620843/.

130 *Marc Elias has been sounding the alarm for years, claiming:* Marc
Elias, "Using the Law to Protect the Law: A Conversation with
Democratic Super Lawyer Marc Elias," October 17, 2023, in
PoliticsGirl, produced by Meidas Media Network, podcast,
https://podcasts.apple.com/at/podcast/using-the-law-to
-protect-the-law-a/id1595408601?i=1000631572222.

131 *The Republicans argue:* "John Lewis Voting Rights Advancement
Act," Human Rights Campaign, accessed April 18, 2024, https:
//www.hrc.org/resources/voting-rights-advancement-act.

131 *The bill included making Election Day a public holiday:* "The
Freedom to Vote Act," Brennan Center for Justice, accessed April
21, 2024, https://www.brennancenter.org/freedom-vote-act.

132 *Even after the Trump campaign lost every court case:* Jacob Shamsian
and Sonam Sheth, "Trump and His Allies Filed More than 40
Lawsuits Challenging the 2020 Election Results. All of Them
Failed," *Business Insider*, February 22, 2021, accessed April 18, 2024,
https://www.businessinsider.com/trump-campaign-lawsuits-election
-results-2020-11.

133 *According to the election integrity experts:* Mac Brower, "The
Republican Party Keeps Suing Over Poll Workers," Democracy
Docket, November 7, 2022, accessed April 18, 2024, https://www
.democracydocket.com/analysis/the-republican-party-keeps-suing-over
-poll-workers/.

133 *limit the ability of county officials:* Marc Elias, "Republican Anti-
Voting Lawsuits Pile Up in 2022," Democracy Docket, September

21, 2022, accessed April 18, 2024, https://www.democracydocket
.com/opinion/republican-anti-voting-lawsuits-pile-up-in-2022/.

135 *More eligible voters didn't vote:* Domenico Montanaro, "Poll:
Despite Record Turnout, 80 Million Americans Didn't Vote. Here's
Why," NPR, December 15, 2020, April 18, 2024, https://www
.npr.org/2020/12/15/945031391/poll-despite-record-turnout-80
-million-americans-didnt-vote-heres-why.

135 *much like had been done in ancient Rome:* Josep M. Colomer, "The
Electoral College is a Medieval Relic. Only the US Still Has One,"
Washington Post, December 11, 2016, accessed April 18, 2024,
https://www.washingtonpost.com/news/monkey-cage/wp/2016
/12/11/the-electoral-college-is-a-medieval-relic-only-the-u-s-still
-has-one/.

135 *a "body of wise men":* Darrell M. West, "It's Time to Abolish the
Electoral College," Brookings, October 15, 2019, accessed April 18,
2024, https://www.brookings.edu/articles/its-time-to-abolish-the
-electoral-college/.

137 *Electors are chosen by political parties:* "About the Electors," National
Archives, accessed April 18, 2024, https://www.archives.gov/electoral
-college/electors.

141 *The Twelfth Amendment was ratified in 1804:* Dave Roos, "What
Happens If There's a Tie in a US Presidential Election?," History,
November 4, 2020, accessed April 18, 2024, https://www.history
.com/news/presidential-elections-tie-electoral-college.

144 *More than thirty states (and DC):* Russell Wheeler, "Can the Electoral
College Be Subverted by 'Faithless Electors'?," Brookings, October 21,
2020, accessed April 18, 2024, https://www.brookings.edu/articles
/can-the-electoral-college-be-subverted-by-faithless-electors/.

144 *This didn't used to be something parties worried about:* Tom
Goldstein, "The Supreme Court, Faithless Electors, and Trump's
Final, Futile Fight," SCOTUS Blog, November 28, 2020, accessed
April 18, 2024, https://www.scotusblog.com/2020/11/the
-supreme-court-faithless-electors-and-trumps-final-futile-fight/.

146 *In 1979 a vote to establish a direct popular vote failed:* Warren
Weaver Jr., "Senate Rejects Proposal to End Electoral College," *New
York Times,* July 11, 1979, https://www.nytimes.com/1979/07/11

/archives/senate-rejects-proposal-to-end-electoral-college-house
-action.html.

146　*In 2000, while the Bush/Gore election:* West, "It's Time to Abolish
the Electoral College."

148　*The 2020 election had the highest voter turnout:* "2020 Presidential
Election Voting and Registration Tables Now Available," United
States Census Bureau, April 29, 2021, accessed April 18, 2024,
https://www.census.gov/newsroom/press-releases/2021/2020
-presidential-election-voting-and-registration-tables-now-available
.html.

148　*There are approximately nine million American voters abroad:*
Haley Ott et al., "Millions of Americans Overseas Can Vote—
But Few Do. Here's How to Vote as an American Living
Abroad," CBS News, March 7, 2024, accessed April 18, 2024,
https://www.cbsnews.com/news/americans-overseas-how-to
-vote-abroad/.

149　*Texas came out at around 66 percent for the 2020 election:* Shannon
Najmabadi and Mandi Cai, "Democrats Hoped High Turnout
Would Usher in a Blue Wave Across Texas. It Didn't," *Texas Tribune*,
November 4, 2020, accessed April 18, 2024, https://www
.texastribune.org/2020/11/04/texas-voter-turnout-democrats/.

150　*Stein received just over 1 percent of the vote:* Tara Golshan, "Did
Jill Stein Voters Deliver Donald Trump the Presidency?," *Vox*,
November 11, 2016, accessed April 18, 2024, https://www.vox.com
/policy-and-politics/2016/11/11/13576798/jill-stein-third-party
-donald-trump-win.

152　*As philosopher Bernard-Henri Lévy argues:* Bernard-Henri Lévy et
al., "Western Democracy Is Threatening Suicide," Open to Debate,
October 3, 2017, https://opentodebate.org/debate/western
-democracy-threatening-suicide/.

153　*We didn't always fill out the census:* Andy Kroll et al., "We Don't
Talk About Leonard: The Man Behind the Right's Supreme Court
Supermajority," ProPublica, October 11, 2023, accessed April 19,
2024, https://www.propublica.org/article/we-dont-talk-about
-leonard-leo-supreme-court-supermajority.

Principle 4: Representatives Should Represent the People Who Voted for Them

155 *Capitalism has become:* Bernard-Henri Lévi et al., "Western Democracy Is Threatening Suicide," Open to Debate, October 3, 2017, April 30, 2024, https://opentodebate.org/debate/western -democracy-threatening-suicide/.

156 *How can 85 percent of the country:* Lew Blank, "$7.25 Isn't Cutting It in This Economy. Voters Support Raising the Minimum Wage to $20 per Hour," Data for Progress, May 24, 2023, accessed April 18, 2024, https://www.dataforprogress.org/blog/2023/5/24/725-isnt-cutting -it-in-this-economy-voters-support-raising-the-minimum-wage-to -20-per-hour.

156 *Or how can a vast majority of the country:* Ivana Saric, "Fox News Poll Finds Voters Overwhelmingly Want Restrictions on Guns," Axios, April 29, 2023, accessed April 19, 2024, https://www.axios .com/2023/04/28/fox-news-poll-voters-want-gun-control.

157 *We had fewer than 100 million people:* "Historical Population Change Data (1910–2020)," United States Census Bureau, April 26, 2021, accessed April 18, 2024, https://www.census.gov /data/tables/time-series/dec/popchange-data-text.html.

157 *That means a single congressmember:* Dante Chinni, "The Country's Population Is Growing—but Congress Is Standing Still," NBC News, September 3, 2023, accessed April 18, 2024, https://www .nbcnews.com/meet-the-press/data-download/nations-population -growing-congress-standing-still-rcna103142.

158 *However, because of how representatives are allotted:* Governor's Office, "Montana Regains Second Congressional Seat with 2020 Census," Montana.gov, April 26, 2021, accessed April 18, 2024, https://news.mt.gov/Governors-Office/montana-regains-second -congressional-seat-with-2020-census.

158 *In 2020 Minnesota kept:* David A. Lieb and Steve Karnowski, "Minnesota Avoids Losing House Seat to New York by 89 People," Associated Press, April 26, 2021, accessed April 18, 2024, https: //apnews.com/article/census-2020-minnesota-government-and -politics-7cc6973f4a275aafcab3b1285845454a.

159 *This would dramatically impact how many constituents:* Dante Chinni, "The Country's Population Is Growing—but Congress Is Standing Still."

161 *The filibuster is an old-school parliamentary procedure:* Scott Bomboy, "Is Aaron Burr Really the Father of the Filibuster?," National Constitution Center, April 5, 2023, accessed April 19, 2024, https://constitutioncenter.org/blog/is-aaron-burr-really-the -father-of-the-filibuster.

162 *To be sure something they said during "purely legislative activities":* John R. Vile, "Speech and Debate Clause," Free Speech Center, February 18, 2024, accessed April 19, 2024, https://firstamendment .mtsu.edu/article/speech-and-debate-clause/.

163 *This process of overtalking bills so no one could vote:* "About Filibusters and Cloture | Historical Overview," United States Senate, accessed April 19, 2024, https://www.senate.gov/about/powers-procedures /filibusters-cloture/overview.htm.

163 *Today you don't even need to speak:* Lisa Desjardins, "How Does the Filibuster Work?," PBS, January 27, 2021, accessed April 19, 2024, https://www.pbs.org/newshour/politics/how-does-the-filibuster -work.

164 *Alexander Hamilton wrote against the idea:* "The Federalist No. 22," *The Federalist,* December 14, 1787, https://founders.archives.gov /documents/Hamilton/01-04-02-0179.

166 *Despite the fact that the Congressional Budget Office (CBO):* Lauren Fox et al., "Senate Parliamentarian Rules against Including Minimum Wage in Covid Relief Bill," CNN, February 25, 2021, accessed April 19, 2024, https://www.cnn.com/2021/02/25 /politics/minimum-wage-covid-relief-senate-parliamentarian /index.html.

167 *The Trump administration used budget reconciliation:* Richard Kogan, "Introduction to Budget 'Reconciliation,'" Center on Budget and Policy Priorities, May 6, 2022, accessed April 19, 2024, https://www.cbpp.org/research/introduction-to-budget -reconciliation.

167 *Provided the majority party has its people in line:* Paul LeBlanc, "Here's What a 'Vote-a-Rama' Is (and What It Means for Democrats' Energy and Health Care Bill)," CNN, August 4, 2022,

accessed April 20, 2024, https://www.cnn.com/2022/08/04 /politics/what-is-vote-a-rama/index.html.

170 *While the Senate has very little recourse:* "Legislative Process 101— Discharge Petitions," Indivisible, accessed April 19, 2024, https: //indivisible.org/resource/legislative-process-101-discharge-petitions.

173 *It's why they didn't put forward an official party platform:* Hilary McQuilkin and Meghna Chakrabarti, "The GOP Won't Introduce a New Party Platform for 2020. So What Does It Stand For?" WBUR, August 25, 2020, accessed April 19, 2024, https://www.wbur.org/onpoint/2020/08/25/gop-no-platform -2020-trump.

176 *Following* Buckley: "First National Bank of Boston v. Bellotti, 435 U.S. 765 (1978)," Justia, accessed April 19, 2024, https://supreme .justia.com/cases/federal/us/435/765/.

176 *The* Citizens United *decision:* Tim Lau, "Citizens United Explained," Brennan Center for Justice, December 12, 2019, accessed April 19, 2024, https://www.brennancenter.org/our-work /research-reports/citizens-united-explained.

176 *was a travesty:* Ibid.

176 *"In a time of historic wealth inequality":* Ibid.

177 *In 2014, 71 percent of outside spending:* Ian Vandewalker, "Election Spending 2014: Outside Spending in Senate Races Since 'Citizens United,'" Brennan Center for Justice, December 1, 2015, accessed April 19, 2024, https://www.brennancenter.org/our-work/research -reports/election-spending-2014-outside-spending-senate-races -citizens-united.

177 *In the 2018 midterms:* Anu Narayanswamy et al., "Meet the Wealthy Donors Pouring Millions into the 2018 Elections," *Washington Post*, October 26, 2018, accessed April 19, 2024, https://www .washingtonpost.com/graphics/2018/politics/superpac-donors -2018/.

179 *In Canada the election period:* Danielle Kurtzleben, "Why Are U.S. Elections So Much Longer Than Other Countries?," NPR, October 21, 2015, accessed April 20, 2024, https://www.npr.org/sections /itsallpolitics/2015/10/21/450238156/canadas-11-week-campaign -reminds-us-that-american-elections-are-much-longer.

181 *The Republicans of the 118th Congress*: Joe LoCascio et al., "118th
     Congress on Track to Become One of the Least Productive in US
     History," ABC News, January 10, 2024, accessed April 19, 2024,
     https://abcnews.go.com/Politics/118th-congress-track-become
     -productive-us-history/story?id=106254012.

Principle 5: The Law Applies to All of Us

184 *Not to mention the US is one of only fifty-five countries:* "How Many
     Countries Still Have the Death Penalty, and How Many People
     Are Executed?," BBC, January 25, 2024, accessed April 19, 2024,
     https://www.bbc.com/news/world-45835584/.

186 *As Kanefield points out:* Teri Kanefield, "Why Republicans Break
     Laws," Teri Kanefield, March 21, 2022, accessed April 20, 2024,
     https://terikanefield.com/833-2/.

189 *According to the White House:* "The Judicial Branch," White House,
     accessed April 19, 2024, https://www.whitehouse.gov/about-the
     -white-house/our-government/the-judicial-branch/.

189 *The Constitution gives the president:* "ArtII.S2.C1.3.1 Overview of
     Pardon Power," Constitution Annotated, accessed April 19, 2024,
     https://constitution.congress.gov/browse/essay/artII-S2-C1-3-1
     /ALDE_00013316/.

192 *The bigger part of its job:* "The Judicial Branch," The White House,
     accessed June 27, 2024, https://www.whitehouse.gov/about-the
     -white-house/our-government/the-judicial-branch.

193 *The court actually gave itself the power:* "Marbury v. Madison
     (1803)," National Archives, accessed April 19, 2024, https://www
     .archives.gov/milestone-documents/marbury-v-madison.

193 *President Andrew Jackson completely ignored:* "President Andrew
     Jackson's Veto Message Regarding Bank of the United States,
     July 10, 1832," The Avalon Project, accessed June 27, 2024, https://
     avalon.law.yale.edu/19th_century/ajveto01.asp.

193 *President Jefferson was furious:* Thomas Jefferson to Spencer Roane,
     September 6, 1819, Founders' Constitution 3, Article 1, Section 8,
     Clause 18, University of Chicago, https://press-pubs.uchicago.edu
     /founders/documents/a1_8_18s16.html.

193 *As Alexander Hamilton wrote:* Alexander Hamilton, "Federalist:

No. 78," *The Federalist Papers*, https://guides.loc.gov/federalist
-papers/text-71-80#s-lg-box-wrapper-25493470.

194 *In that same paper, Hamilton wrote that judicial independence:*
Richard W. Garnett and David A. Strauss, "Article III, Section
One," National Constitution Center, accessed April 20, 2020, https:
//constitutioncenter.org/the-constitution/articles/article-iii/clauses
/45#:~:text=78%2C%20judicial%20independence%20%E2%80%9
Cis%20the,impartial%20administration%20of%20the%20laws
.%E2%80%9D.

195 *Chevron deference:* Anthony Zurcher, Nada Tawfik, Lisa Lambert, and
Kayla Epstein, "The Chevron Deference, and Why It Mattered," BBC,
June 29, 2024, https://www.bbc.com/news/articles/c51ywwrq45qo.

195 *"makes a mockery":* Perry Stein, "Justice Sotomayor Dissent:
'The President Is Now a King Above the Law,'" *The Washington
Post*, July 1, 2024, https://www.washingtonpost.com/national
-security/2024/07/01/sotomayor-jackson-trump-immunity-dissent.

195 *Much like Justice Sotomayor wrote:* Roxanne Szal and Oliver C.
Haug, "*Dobbs v. Jackson* Recap: Seven Times Justice Sotomayor
Stood Up for Abortion Rights," *Ms.*, December 1, 2021, accessed
April 20, 2024, https://msmagazine.com/2021/12/01/dobbs-v
-jackson-supreme-court-justice-sonia-sotomayor-abortion/.

197 *According to Federal Communications Commission:* Caitlin Oprysko,
"Leo's Concord Fund Registers to Lobby," *Politico*, October 19, 2023,
accessed April 19, 2024, https://www.politico.com/newsletters
/politico-influence/2023/10/19/leos-concord-fund-registers-to
-lobby-00122598.

197 *Donors were giving $15, $17, $48 million at a time:* Sheldon
Whitehouse, "In the Federal Court Wars, the Right Has Jumped
Through a Dark-Money Looking Glass," *Washington Post*,
February 17, 2022, accessed April 19, 2024, https://www
.washingtonpost.com/opinions/2022/02/17/federalist-society
-dark-money-breyer-supreme-court-seat/.

199 *Rulings in favor of religion have increased:* Ian Prasad Philbrick, "A
Pro-Religion Court," *New York Times*, June 22, 2022, accessed
April 19, 2024, https://www.nytimes.com/2022/06/22/briefing
/supreme-court-religion.html.

200 *in 2020, after a series of court victories:* Margaret Talbot, "Amy Coney Barrett's Long Game," *New Yorker*, February 7, 2022, accessed April 19, 2024, https://www.newyorker.com/magazine /2022/02/14/amy-coney-barretts-long-game.

201 *Justice Barrett gave a speech:* Barbara Sprunt, "Amy Coney Barrett Confirmed to Supreme Court, Takes Constitutional Oath," NPR, October 26, 2020, accessed April 19, 2024, https://www.npr.org /2020/10/26/927640619/senate-confirms-amy-coney-barrett-to -the-supreme-court.

202 *"no basis in law":* Stein, "Justice Sotomayor Dissent."

203 *As . . . Thom Hartmann suggested:* Thom Hartmann, "Are SCOTUS Republicans in on a Plot to End Democratic Presidencies Forever?," Raw Story, October 20, 2022, accessed April 19, 2024, https:// www.rawstory.com/are-scotus-republicans-in-on-a-plot-to-end -democratic-presidencies-forever/.

205 *FDR proposed moving all justices:* Todd N. Tucker, "In Defense of Court-Packing," *Jacobin,* June 28, 2018, accessed April 19, 2024, https://jacobin.com/2018/06/supreme-court-packing-fdr-justices -appointments.

207 *As of June 2024, the House has initiated impeachment:* "How Federal Impeachment Works," USA Gov, February 2, 2024, accessed April 19, 2024, https://www.usa.gov/impeachment.

207 *there have been twenty-two impeachments:* Annie Grayer and Priscilla Alvarez, "House Sends Mayorkas Impeachment Articles to the Senate," CNN, April 16, 2024, accessed April 20, 2024, https: //www.cnn.com/2024/04/16/politics/house-mayorkas -impeachment-articles-senate/index.html.

207 *State legislators can file articles of impeachment:* "Gubernatorial Impeachment Procedures," Ballotpedia, accessed April 19, 2024, https://ballotpedia.org/Gubernatorial_impeachment _procedures.

208 *We only have a nine-member court:* "Significance of U.S. Circuit Courts of Appeals," United States Courts, accessed April 19, 2024, https://www.uscourts.gov/about-federal-courts/court-role-and -structure/about-us-courts-appeals.

210 *This court doesn't speak for us:* Hamilton, "Federalist: No. 78."

Principle 6: Government Should Be a Force for Good

212 *Ronald Reagan inflicted a great wound on the country:* Ronald Reagan, "I'm Here to Help," news conference, August 12, 1986, https://www .reaganfoundation.org/ronald-reagan/reagan-quotes-speeches/news -conference-1/.

213 *As John F. Kennedy said:* John F. Kennedy, September 14, 1960, acceptance address of Liberal Party nomination for president, https://www.jfklibrary.org/archives/other-resources/john-f -kennedy-speeches/liberal-party-nomination-nyc-19600914.

216 *In* Common Sense, *Thomas Paine described government:* Thomas Paine, *Common Sense* (Canada: Broadview Press, 2004).

217 *As historian Thomas Zimmer says:* Thomas Zimmer, "Who Is Democracy For?," June 7, 2022, in PoliticsGirl, produced by Meidas Media Network, podcast, https://open.spotify.com /episode/?si=wWemwl34SWChwVf1eF6h-A.

217 *We've got . . . pregnant women being left to go septic:* Sydney Persing, "Prosper Woman Who Says She Went into Sepsis Before She Could Receive Lifesaving Abortion Care Sues over Texas Abortion Ban," WFAA ABC, December 14, 2023, accessed April 21, 2024, https:// www.wfaa.com/article/news/local/prosper-woman-says-went-into -sepsis-before-she-could-get-lifesaving-abortion-care-in-texas/287 -26bf012b-bfb9-441e-b68d-a5296bcf7f02.

217 *border patrol allowing refugees to drown:* Dan Katz, "Mother and Two Children Drown in Rio Grande Near Eagle Pass Where Texas Is Blocking Access to Border Patrol," Texas Public Radio, January 13, 2024, accessed April 19, 2024, https://www.tpr.org/border -immigration/2024-01-13/three-drown-in-rio-grande-after-texas -blocks-border-patrol-from-rescue.

220 *the stated purpose of the law:* Rebekah Barber, "How the Civil Rights Movement Opened the Door to Immigrants of Color," Facing South, February 3, 2017, accessed April 21, 2024, https: //www.facingsouth.org/2017/02/how-civil-rights-movement -opened-door-immigrants-color.

220 *Before Tucker was fired:* Nicholas Confessore and Karen Yourish, "A Fringe Conspiracy Theory, Fostered Online, Is Refashioned by the G.O.P.," *New York Times*, May 15, 2022, accessed April 21, 2024.

222 *If you call yourself the party of "small government":* Tori Otten, "Florida Passes Bill Allowing Trans Kids to Be Taken from Their Families," *New Republic*, May 4, 2023, accessed April 21, 2024, https://newrepublic.com/post/172444/florida-passes-bill-allowing-trans-kids-taken-families.

224 *We don't need 544 bills denying trans people their rights:* "2024 Anti-trans Bills Tracker," Trans Legislation Tracker, accessed April 19, 2024, https://translegislation.com/.

229 *former Republican speaker of the House Kevin McCarthy:* Phillip Bump, "Kevin McCarthy Was Once Envious That Democrats 'Look Like America,'" *Washington Post*, November 30, 2023, accessed April 19, 2024, https://www.washingtonpost.com/politics/2023/11/30/mccarthy-republicans-diversity/.

230 *Kori Schake argues that while democracy:* Kori Schake, "Can the US Make the World Safe for Democracy," American Enterprise Institute, September 26, 2023, accessed April 19, 2024, https://www.aei.org/articles/can-the-us-make-the-world-safe-for-democracy/.

232 *To quote Barack Obama:* "READ: Obama Statement Marking Jan. 6," *U.S. News & World Report*, January 6, 2022, accessed April 19, 2024, https://www.usnews.com/news/politics/articles/2022-01-06/read-barack-obamas-statement-on-jan-6-anniversary.

INDEX

★ ★ ★